The New
Ford Treasury of
FAVORITE
RECIPES
from Famous Restaurants

REVISED EDITION

Recipes compiled and tested by

NANCY KENNEDY

Women's Editor, Ford Times

Art Directors, Edward Diehl and John Weigel

GOLDEN PRESS • NEW YORK

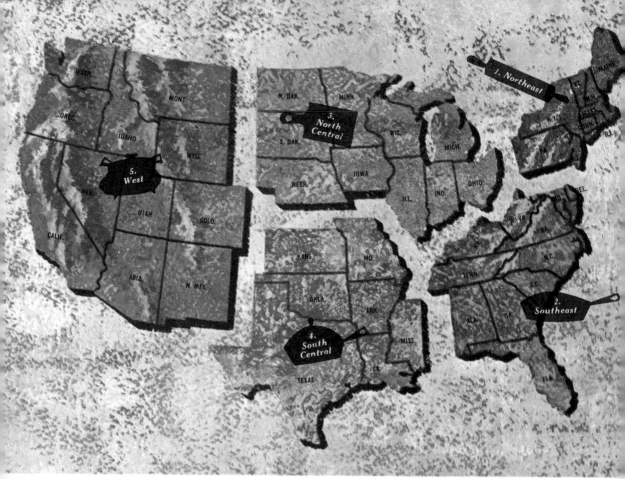

Traveler's Key to Regional Divisions of This Book

*Dedicated to
the Ford and Lincoln-Mercury dealers
of the United States
whose interest and suggestions
have made this book possible.*

1st Printing, 1963
2nd Printing, 1963
3rd Printing, Revised, 1964
4th Printing, 1966

FOREWORD

Of all the pages in FORD TIMES, none are more eagerly read each month than those in the "Favorite Recipes of Famous Restaurants" section. Both men and women find these pages, which feature leading restaurants and their selected recipes, of great interest—first as a source of fine recipes, and again as an authoritative restaurant guide when traveling.

Restaurants nominated for inclusion in our "Favorite Recipes" section are carefully selected by our Women's Editor for pleasant atmosphere and good service as well as for enjoyable food. And, since occasionally establishments do change management, our editors regularly seek local confirmation of the continued high standards of those restaurants we have featured.

Thus when we came to compile this new and greatly expanded edition, we were able to draw upon hundreds of restaurants whose recipes have appeared in FORD TIMES' pages in the past decade. Many of these were featured in "Favorite Recipes," Volumes 1, 2 and 3—books which are now collectors' items by virtue of popular demand. Over 450,000 copies of Volume 1, long out of print, were sold; similarly, the supply of successive editions has been completely exhausted.

So it is with pleasure that we are able to offer you this new collection. It is a larger book, with more complete indexing, more regional information. Once again its colorful pages will very likely be used—as were those from the previous volumes —in art classes as well as in the kitchen. This would please the artists who have delineated the restaurants and the chefs who have kindly cooperated in supplying their finest recipes.

We hope that this book and its information contribute to your pleasure when traveling as well as provide an adventure in good eating in your home.

FORD MOTOR COMPANY
C. H. Dykeman, Publications Manager

PAINTING BY RICHARD WAGNER

1

NORTHEAST

A pot of steaming Boston baked beans or a kettle of spicy clam chowder is reminiscent of this region wherever served. Scores of recipes faithfully handed down from Colonial times have resulted in more regional dishes here than anywhere else in the country. The plain, hearty fare is a heritage of a countryside rich in food resources and people to whom simplicity is a Yankee tradition. Look for seafood, maple syrup, cranberry, squash, and corn dishes.

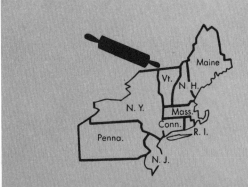

Werner's

Just an hour's drive from New York City, Werner's is located in a lovely 200-year-old home at 36 Elm Street in Westport, Connecticut. Leave the New England Thruway at Exit 17 and go to the town of Westport. Lunch every day except Sunday, and dinner served nightly. Reservations advisable on the weekend and during the summer months. Edward A. Dacher is the owner and manager.

Waverly Inn

The Waverly Inn in Cheshire is within 25 miles of Connecticut's three largest cities: Hartford, New Haven and Bridgeport. Famous since 1896, it is still a mecca for diners after Yale football games. Take Exit 61 from Wilbur Cross Parkway and go north on State Highway 10 (College Highway) to Cheshire. Lunch and dinner are served every day except Monday. Reservations suggested.

COCOANUT CREAM TORTE WITH APRICOT

Crust: Beat together 1 egg, ¼ pound soft butter and ½ cup of sugar until foamy. Add to it 1 teaspoonful of grated lemon peel and a pinch of salt. Then sift in 2 cups pastry flour, slowly mixing the batter. When thoroughly blended, place in refrigerator for 1 hour. Roll into crust and bake in a 9- or 10-inch spring form pan in a 350° oven for 25 minutes.

Filling: Spread baked crust with a generous layer of apricot marmalade, then lay on a thin layer of pound cake or other white cake and moisten this cake with sufficient rum or rum flavoring to give the pastry a rich aroma and full flavor. Make a package of prepared vanilla pudding, then cool it. Whip 1 cup whipping cream and fold into cool pudding. Spread this pudding dome-like over the layers and sprinkle with ground cocoanut which has been lightly browned in butter. Serve cold. Makes 6-8 portions.

PANCAKE STUFFED WITH CHICKEN

Pancakes: Combine: 3 eggs, 1½ cups sifted flour, 2 tablespoons sugar, 2 cups of milk and dash of salt. Beat together lightly. Add 2 more cups of milk or light cream to thin consistency. Cook in individual frying pan with sweet butter. Pancakes should be about 6 inches in diameter.

Stuffing: Melt 3 tablespoons butter, slowly add 3 tablespoons flour, salt and pepper, to taste, and a dash of curry. Make a smooth paste. Add 1½ cups milk gradually, stirring constantly, until the sauce is the desired consistency. Add 2 cups cooked chicken, diced; ½ cup mushrooms, sliced; and 1 cup sherry wine. Add more seasoning, if needed. Roll stuffing in pancakes. Cover with 2 cups Mornay Sauce (rich cheese sauce), sprinkle with grated Parmesan cheese and bake in 375° oven until golden brown. Serves 6.

TOSSED GREEN GORGONZOLA SALAD

1 average head crisp lettuce, chopped
1 green pepper, chopped
1 tomato, peeled and chopped
2 tablespoons celery, chopped
1 small onion, chopped
    Freshly ground pepper, to taste
4 tablespoons cider vinegar
4 tablespoons salad oil
    Grated Gorgonzola cheese

Rub wooden salad bowl with strong garlic. Add lettuce, green pepper, tomato, celery, onion and pepper. Mix vinegar and oil well, then sprinkle on salad. Completely cover top of salad with grated Gorgonzola. Toss gently with two forks and serve at table from bowl. Serves 4.

PAINTING BY REVINGTON ARTHUR

Manero's

Seventeen tons of beef are consumed in an average week by customers of this steak house owned by Nicholas Manero. Diners select their own cuts of perfectly aged beef, and it is cooked as ordered. You can also buy meats for home cooking. Dinner served daily, noon to 10:30 p.m. From the New England Thruway, take Exit 3 to Greenwich, Connecticut, and 559 Steamboat Road.

PAINTING BY GEORGE SHELLHASE

AUGUSTA HOUSE APPLE PIE

Line a 9-inch pie plate with a flaky pie crust. Fill crust half full with about 2 cups sliced apples. Mix together 1½ cups sugar, 5 level tablespoons flour, pinch of salt and ½ teaspoon cinnamon. Pour half of this mixture over apples. Finish filling pie with 2 additional cups sliced apples. Add remaining sugar mixture. Cover with top crust, brush crust with cream. Slit top crust and bake in 385° oven for 1 hour. Should be baked slowly for best results. Serves 6.

Augusta House

This historic hotel was built in 1831 to house members of the first Maine legislature to meet in Augusta, Maine. It is located at 170 State Street, at the intersection of the main U.S. highways which go through the city. Breakfast, lunch and dinner are served daily. Overnight accommodations and vacation facilities available. Richard L. Schenk is the manager.

The Mount Kineo

On a peninsula in Moosehead Lake this luxury hotel is built on the site of the first Kineo House, opened in 1844. Complete vacation facilities. Open June 20 to Labor Day. Breakfast, lunch and dinner served daily. Reservations. Take Maine State Highway 15 north from Greenville to Rockwood, Maine. Leave your car at the Rockwood Garage and take the boat one mile to Kineo.

PINEAPPLE PUDDING

- 5 ounces butter
- 2 cups sugar
- 3 eggs
- 3 cups crushed pineapple, drained
- ¼ teaspoon vanilla
- ½ pound graham crackers, finely crushed
- Whipped cream, for garnish

Cream butter and sugar, add eggs one at a time and beat until creamy. Fold in pineapple and vanilla. Line a 10x14-inch pan with half the graham cracker crumbs; spread pineapple mixture evenly over them. Cover filling with remaining crumbs. Chill in refrigerator for at least 8 hours. Serve very cold, topped with a dash of whipped cream. Makes 8 portions.

Bar Harbor Motor Inn

Guests at this Maine hotel on the waterfront of Bar Harbor enjoy a magnificent view of Frenchman Bay and the islands. Breakfast, lunch and dinner served from June 15 through September 15. Overnight accommodations and complete vacation facilities, including beach and pool. Located on Newport Drive, off Route 3 in the center of town. Edward J. Springer is the manager.

ONE-POT FISH CHOWDER

- 3 pounds haddock
- ½ cup salt pork, diced fine
- ⅓ cup onions, diced
- 1½ cups water
- 2 cups potatoes, diced
- 1½ teaspoons salt
- ⅛ teaspoon pepper
- 2 tablespoons butter
- 4 cups milk

Remove skin and bones from haddock and cut into bite-size pieces. Cook salt pork in heavy kettle over low heat. Add onions and sauté for 5 minutes, or until soft but not brown. Add water, potatoes and seasoning; cook about 10 minutes. Then add uncooked fish and cook 5 minutes longer over high heat. Slowly stir in milk and heat just below the boiling point. Serve immediately with crackers. Makes 4-6 portions.

RICH LEMON PIE

6 ounces sweet butter
1 cup sugar
2 lemons, juice and grated rind
3 egg yolks (save whites)
1 whole egg
1 or 2 slices white bread
6 tablespoons sugar
8-inch pie shell, baked

Melt butter over very low heat; stir in sugar and lemon rind and juice. Beat yolks and whole egg together and add to mixture when sugar is dissolved. When thickened, remove from heat. Don't allow to boil! Remove crusts from bread and cut or tear gently into large crumbs and scatter over bottom of pie shell. Make a stiff meringue of the egg whites sweetened with 6 tablespoons sugar. While lemon mixture is still hot, spoon it over bread crumbs and cover with meringue. Seal meringue to edges of pie shell. Brown in 350° oven. Cool and serve at room temperature.

BUTTERSCOTCH PEANUT CHIFFON PIE

¼ cup cold water
1 tablespoon gelatin
¾ cup brown sugar
1 cup milk
2 tablespoons butter
¼ teaspoon salt
1 teaspoon vanilla
4 eggs, separated
¼ cup roasted peanuts, chopped
¼ cup white sugar
1 cup whipping cream, whipped
8-inch pie shell, baked

Combine cold water and gelatin and let stand. Stir together in a double boiler: brown sugar, milk, butter, salt, vanilla and beaten egg yolks. Cook until mixture is consistency of custard. Remove from fire, stir in gelatin and chill. Add roasted peanuts to chilled mixture. Whip room temperature egg whites until stiff, beating in white sugar. Fold in chilled ingredients and pour into baked pie shell. Decorate with whipped cream squeezed from a pastry bag.

PAINTING BY FRANCIS MERRITT

The Yardarm

A magnificent view of Penobscot Bay and Camden Hills can be seen from the dining-room windows of Gray and Betty Jeffrey's restaurant, a 100-year-old house built for a sea captain. It is on U.S. 1, near Searsport, Maine. Breakfast served 7:00 a.m. to 10:00 a.m.; dinner served daily 5:00 p.m. to 8:30 p.m. Closed October 15 to May 15. Motel reservations advisable during July and August.

PAINTING BY JANE TRUMBORE

Fieldstones

New England dishes are the specialty of this excellent restaurant located in an old colonial farmhouse. Lunch and dinner served every day except Tuesday. Reservations optional but advisable. Not far from the famous Phillips Academy, the inn is at 400 South Main Street (State Highway 28) in Andover, Massachusetts. Edward A. Romeo is your host. Cocktails and gift shop.

Jack August's Restaurant

Jack August developed his popular seafood restaurant at 5 Bridge Street, on Route 9 in the center of Northampton, Massachusetts, from a small fish market. So popular are the excellent fish dishes served here that today a complete line of canned favorites is available by mail order and in fancy grocery stores across the country. Open daily 11:00 a.m. to 8:30 p.m.; closed on Monday.

BROILED FISH

Buy fresh fish from a reliable source. Wash lightly, do not soak. Cut into portions, season to taste, roll in cracker meal and place on well-buttered foil on a broiler rack, cookie sheet or pie plate. Brush with drawn butter, sprinkle lightly with paprika and place in preheated broiler at least 4 to 6 inches below the flame so that fish will get a fine golden glow and not a quick burn. Allow fish to cook 8 to 12 minutes, depending on the thickness of the cuts. Do not turn as the fish will cook from the underside through the heat of the pan. Fish with skin on should be cooked skin down.

Durgin Park

A Boston institution, this restaurant has been famous for over a hundred years for such Yankee specialties as New England boiled dinners, Boston baked beans and baked Indian pudding. It is housed in a century-old building at 30 North Market Street, opposite sprawling Faneuil Hall Market. Open 10:30 a.m. to 8:30 p.m. Monday through Saturday. Closed Sunday and major holidays.

BOSTON BAKED BEANS

    2 pounds pea beans
    1 teaspoon soda
    1 pound salt pork
    1 medium-size onion
    ⅔ cup molasses
    2 teaspoons dry mustard
    4 teaspoons salt
    ½ teaspoon pepper

Soak beans overnight. In morning parboil for 10 minutes with soda. Run cold water through the beans in a colander. Dice rind of salt pork in 1-inch squares, cut each in half. Place half of pork on bottom of 2-quart bean pot with whole onion. Pour beans into pot and top with the rest of the pork. Mix other seasonings with hot water. Pour over beans. Bake in 300° oven for 6 hours. Add water as necessary to keep beans moist. Makes 10 portions.

DATE AND PINEAPPLE BREAD

Combine ⅓ cup milk, 1 well-beaten egg, ⅓ cup melted shortening, 1 cup chopped dates, a 9-ounce can crushed pineapple and 1 cup chopped walnuts. Sift together 3 cups sifted flour, ¾ cup sugar, 3 teaspoons baking powder, ¼ teaspoon soda and ¾ teaspoon salt. Add to first mixture and blend only to moisten. Bake in a greased 1-pound loaf pan at 350° 50-55 minutes.

BEEF BOURGUIGNONNE

2½ pounds beef rump
    Beef suet
1 pint beef stock or canned consommé
2 yellow onions, chopped fine
½ pound mushrooms, sliced
    Bouquet garni (celery tops, garlic clove, bay leaf, parsley and leaf thyme tied together in cheesecloth)
2 teaspoons glacé de viande (or commercial meat glaze)
1½ cups Burgundy or California red wine
½ teaspoon Ac'cent
18 small white onions
2 ounces brandy

Heat beef suet until it is rendered. Cut meat into 1½-inch squares and dredge in flour seasoned with salt, pepper and paprika. Sauté meat quickly in beef fat; meat should be browned until it is almost black. Remove meat from skillet and add to beef stock in cooking pot. Sauté yellow onions until they are golden, then pour over meat cubes. Sauté mushrooms and add to meat. Add bouquet garni, meat glaze and half of red wine. Season with salt, pepper and Ac'cent. Cover pot and cook over slow fire for two or three hours, adding remainder of wine during that time. During last hour of cooking add small white onions. Before serving add brandy. It is delicious served with parsley potatoes and small young carrots. The flavor is improved when dish is warmed up the following day. Makes 6 portions.

PAINTING BY C. ROBERT PERRIN

The Overlook Hotel

Situated on a hillside on famous Nantucket Island, Massachusetts, this delightful inn is located at Three Step Lane. Each guest room bears an authentic Nantucket Indian name and most have an excellent view of the harbor. Breakfast only, served 8:00 to 11:00 a.m. every day; after Labor Day, dinner served to hotel guests only. Overnight accommodations. Open May 14 to November 1.

PAINTING BY GEORGE YATER

The Opera House

Theatrical posters and playbills from the nineteenth century adorn the walls of this restaurant owned by Harold and Gwen Gaillard. It is open daily from June 25 to October 15. Dinner served from 5:30 p.m. to 10:30 p.m. Reservations advisable. Entertainment nightly. This charming eating place is located at 4 South Water Street, Nantucket Island, Massachusetts.

BAKED STUFFED SHRIMP

Peel, split and devein 16 raw jumbo shrimp leaving on tails. Cut pocket through center backs. Combine 1½ cups bread crumbs and 4 ounces ground cooked lobster, crabmeat or scallops. Stir in 4 ounces melted butter. Season with salt, pepper, 1 teaspoon paprika and dash of cayenne. Add enough dry sherry to hold together (about ½ cup). Stuff shrimp; place in shallow pan, backs up. Bake at 450° about 4 minutes. Serve with melted butter, lemon wedges. 4 portions.

Grey Gull Inn

Colorful Liberty Street, just off the square in Nantucket, Massachusetts (on Nantucket Island), is the location of this delightful summer restaurant owned by Carl and Helga Stig. Fresh seafood is a specialty—often a 200-pound swordfish hooked at four in the morning will be on the restaurant's dinner menu the same day. Open 8:00 a.m. to 9:00 p.m. from June 25 to just past Labor Day.

BAKED WHITE ROCK CHICKEN
"Farmer Style"

 3 broiler chickens, halved
   Lemon juice
   Olive oil for cooking
 4 shallots, finely diced
 1 pound fresh mushrooms, cubed
 1 cup whole ripe olives
 1 cup whole stuffed olives
   Rosemary, thyme, oregano
 1 cup Burgundy wine
 6 cups thin brown sauce (veal stock base)
 1 cup canned tiny white onions

Dry chickens with towel. Brush with fresh lemon juice, dip in flour and sauté to a golden brown in hot olive oil. Add shallots. Drain excess oil and add mushrooms, olives and season with a sprig of rosemary, thyme and oregano, to taste. Add wine, let simmer until chicken is tender, about 30 minutes. While simmering add 6 cups thin brown sauce. This will thicken by its own reduction. Add onions. Serves 6.

Schine Inn

Hailed as a prototype of the motor inn of the future, this inn has facilities for everything from a family vacation to a convention, including a 40-lane bowling center, an ice skating rink, swimming pool, putting greens, and seven restaurants. Built on 12 acres fronting on Massachusetts Turnpike at Chicopee (Springfield Exit 6). Breakfast, lunch, dinner daily; supper until 1:00 a.m.

PROVINCETOWN INN
CLAM CHOWDER

¼ pound salt pork
1 medium onion, chopped fine
3 tablespoons flour
1 pint sea clams
¼ cup flour
2 cups milk
   Salt, white pepper and Ac'cent,
    to taste

Fry out salt pork. Cook onion in pork until tender. Mix with flour and take from fire. Grind clams; combine with 2 cups water and boil 5 minutes. Combine clams with onions. Make a smooth paste with ½ cup water and ¼ cup flour and simmer a few minutes before adding to clam mixture. Stir in milk; season. Serve hot. Makes 4-6 portions.

PAINTING BY GEORGE YATER

Provincetown Inn and Motel

This famous inn stands on the tip of Cape Cod in the exact spot where the Pilgrims first set foot on America in 1620. The dining room is open daily from 7:30 a.m. to 9:30 p.m. Overnight accommodations and excellent recreation facilities. Closed November 1 to March 31. The Inn's address is 1 Commercial Street, Provincetown, Massachusetts. Chester G. Peck, Jr., is the owner-manager.

CLAMS CASINO

2 dozen clams
¼ cup butter
1 teaspoon anchovy paste
   Lemon juice
¼ cup minced pepper
¼ cup onion, chopped
2 teaspoons pimento, finely chopped
   Salt and pepper
3 slices bacon

Open clams, remove from the half shell and drain juice from shells. Blend butter and anchovy paste thoroughly. Spoon a small amount of the mixture into each shell. Cover with the clams. Sprinkle each clam with a few drops of lemon juice. Combine green pepper, onion and pimento and spoon over clams. Season with salt and pepper. Cut bacon slices into small pieces and top each clam with a few bits of bacon. Place shells in a 15½ x 10½ x 1-inch pan filled ¼-inch deep with coarse salt, pushing each shell firmly down into the salt. Bake at 450° for 15-20 minutes, or until bacon is thoroughly cooked. Makes 4-6 servings.

PAINTING BY ROBERT J. LEE

The Christopher Ryder House

This historic inn, built about 1790 as a sea captain's residence, overlooks Ryder Cove on Route 28, Chathamport, Massachusetts, on the "elbow" of Cape Cod. Dinner is served every evening in a setting of candlelight, old pine panels and beamed ceilings. Guests may see a Broadway revue-type show at the inn's "Opera House" at 9:15 and 11:15 p.m. Closed October 1 through June 15.

Wequassett Inn

Overlooking Pleasant Bay, this inn is housed in a beautiful colonial mansion built over 200 years ago by a sea captain. Breakfast, lunch and dinner served daily. Reservations preferred. Overnight accommodations and vacation facilities. Open June through September. Edwin and Jeannette Dybing own and manage the Inn, which is on State Highway 28, East Harwich, Cape Cod, Massachusetts.

RICH FRUIT CUPCAKES

½ cup butter
1⅓ cups sugar
3 eggs, separated
⅓ cup milk
¼ teaspoon mace
2¼ cups flour
¼ teaspoon salt
3 teaspoons baking powder
¼ cup each: currants, raisins, citron, candied pineapple and candied cherries

Cream butter, add sugar and egg yolks. Sift dry ingredients together and combine with finely chopped fruit. Stir alternately into first mixture with the milk. Beat thoroughly. Beat egg whites and fold into mixture. Drop batter into small greased cupcake pans. Dust top with granulated sugar and bake in 350-375° oven about 25 minutes. Do not ice. Serves 6.

The Eating House

On Cranmore Mountain in North Conway, New Hampshire, this restaurant is located on the Cranmore Mountain Road, off State Highway 16. Its diamond-shaped windows look out onto the Skimobile, a unique mountain-climbing tramway. May 30 to October 15, meals are served daily from 8:00 a.m. to 9:00 p.m. December 23 to April 15, the cafeteria closes at 5:00 p.m.

CORN MUFFINS

Sift together: 1½ cups sifted flour, 3 teaspoons baking powder, 1 teaspoon salt and 3 tablespoons sugar. Add ¾ cup corn meal. Blend together: 1 well-beaten egg, 1 cup milk and ¼ cup melted shortening; then stir into dry ingredients. Add 1 teaspoon chopped onion, 1 tablespoon chopped green pepper and ½ cup grated sharp cheese. Pour into greased muffin tins and bake 25-30 minutes in 400° oven.

RUTH LESLIE'S PECAN PIE

Beat the following ingredients together with a rotary beater: 3 eggs; ⅔ cup sugar; ⅓ teaspoon salt; ⅓ cup butter, melted; and 1 cup dark corn syrup. Mix in 1 cup pecan halves. Pour into a 9-inch unbaked pie shell and bake in 350° oven until set and browned. Cool. Delicious served with a small scoop of vanilla ice cream.

WALNUT PIE

6 eggs, slightly beaten
1 cup white sugar
½ teaspoon salt
1 pint dark Karo syrup
1½ teaspoons vanilla
2 cups walnut meats, chopped
   10-inch pie shell, unbaked

Add ingredients in order listed and combine with whisk, but do not beat hard. Pour into pie shell and bake at 360° for about 1 hour, or until reasonably firm. Cool and serve with whipped cream or ice cream. Serves 10.

BAKED STUFFED LOBSTER

1 2-pound lobster
1½ cups coarse bread crumbs, dry
1 tablespoon thick steak sauce
½ teaspoon prepared mustard
½ teaspoon horse-radish
2½ ounces lobster, bite size
   Melted butter
   Lemon

Lay lobster on back and cut entire length of body. Clean lobster, removing and saving tomalley. Bake lobster in shell in 500° oven for 15 minutes. Combine tomalley and remaining ingredients, blending with enough melted butter to form a ball. It should not be soggy. Stuff body with this mixture and bake in 500° oven for 5 minutes. Garnish with lemon and drawn butter. Serves 1.

COTTAGE CHEESE SPREAD

Whip following ingredients in electric mixer: 1 pound cottage cheese; 1 tablespoon green pepper, finely chopped; 1 tablespoon carrot, finely chopped; 1 teaspoon onion, finely chopped; and garlic salt, to taste. Spread on crackers or Melba toast.

PAINTING BY DAVID C. BAKER

Eastern Slope Inn

Situated in the heart of New Hampshire's White Mountains, the Inn is open the year round with vacation facilities for each season. Breakfast, lunch and dinner served daily; overnight accommodations. Reservations advisable in summer. It is located on Main Street in North Conway, New Hampshire. Charles Pinkham is the manager of this delightful New England inn.

PAINTING BY THOMAS BAKER

Ye Cocke and Kettle Inn

Now managed by Anthony Bersacola, the Inn has been famous for outstanding food since it was founded in 1928. Breakfast, lunch and dinner served daily the year round. Overnight motel accommodations and swimming pool. Reservations necessary in vacation season. In Seabrook, New Hampshire, the restaurant and motel are on Lafayette Road (U.S. 1) near Interstate Highway 95.

The Inn at Steele Hill

A spectacular panoramic view of the mountains sets off the Inn, a year-round family resort with excellent skiing and skating; overnight accommodations and complete recreation facilities. Lunch and dinner served daily, and smorgasbord on Saturday night. Reservations necessary. The Inn is about five miles west of Winnisquam, off U.S. 3, at Sanbornton, New Hampshire.

Franklin Arms Tea Room

The homestead which houses this restaurant was built by Thomas Davis in 1670 and occupied by his descendants until 1903. Carl and Marie Demmert now own and manage this establishment, which serves lunch and dinner every day except Monday. Closed the last two weeks of August. Two blocks west of Garden State Parkway, it is located at 409 Franklin Street, Bloomfield, New Jersey.

SAVORY BAKED VEAL

8 pounds rump of veal, boned and rolled
1 clove garlic
Salt and pepper, to taste
1 pound butter
1 large onion, grated
¾ cup parsley, minced
1 can beef consommé

Place veal on a breadboard, cut off and discard string. Rub unrolled meat thoroughly with cut clove of garlic and sprinkle with salt and pepper. Cream butter with a wooden spoon, then work in grated onion and minced parsley. Spread unrolled meat generously with seasoned butter. Roll meat up carefully, tying with soft white twine in several places. Rub outside of roast with garlic and season with salt and pepper. Cover with a good coating of butter. Place on a rack in an uncovered roasting pan with the veal bones set around the sides. Brown in preheated oven of 450° for 15 minutes, then add consommé and equal amount of water to pan. Cook for 10 minutes, then turn heat down to 325° and continue cooking for about 2 hours, or until tender. A gravy may be made with pan drippings; add a small amount of red wine for flavoring. Makes 8-10 portions. Serve with potatoes roasted in with meat.

LEMON PIE

Blend together 4 tablespoons cornstarch, 1½ cups sugar, ¼ teaspoon salt and slowly add to 1½ cups boiling water, 3 slightly beaten egg yolks and 2 teaspoons butter. Cook over medium heat stirring constantly for about 6 minutes, or until mixture is thickened. Remove from heat and add juice of 2 lemons and grated rind of 1 lemon. Beat 3 egg whites and slowly add 6 teaspoons sugar and.pinch of cream of tarter until stiff and peaked. Pour lemon mixture into a 9-inch baked pie shell and top with meringue. Brown meringue in hot oven.

LAMBERTVILLE HOUSE
HOT BREAD

½ cake yeast
1½ cups milk
½ cup water
1 tablespoon sugar
1 tablespoon salt
2 tablespoons vegetable shortening
2 pounds flour

Crumble yeast into lukewarm milk and water. Add sugar, salt and shortening. Stir in enough flour to make dough workable on board; add flour in small quantities and knead until mix becomes elastic. Place in bowl in a warm, draft-free place; cover with a towel and let rise until double in bulk. Cut into five equal portions and shape into loaves and place in greased loaf pans. Cover again and let rise in warm place until double in bulk. Bake for about 30 minutes at 375°, until golden brown. This recipe will make five 8-ounce loaves.

PAINTING BY JOSEPH CSATARI

Lambertville House

Established in 1812, this noted hostelry has been in continuous operation ever since. Two blocks from Route 29, the address is 32 Bridge Street (U.S. Highway 202) in Lambertville, New Jersey. Near the New Hope Bridge, it is 15 miles from Trenton. Breakfast, lunch and dinner served daily. Overnight accommodations and vacation facilities. Reservations advised during the summer.

APRICOT STRUDEL

Crust: Combine 1 cup flour and ½ cup butter with fork or knife. Add 4 ounces water, stirring gently with fork. Flour board and roll out dough. It should be about 12 inches long, 4 inches wide and about ⅛ inch thick.

Filling: Reduce syrup from 1 No. 2½ can apricots. Mix 2 teaspoons cornstarch with a little cold water, then blend this mixture into syrup. Pour apricot halves into thickened syrup. Pour filling over crust. Roll the sheet like a jelly roll or roll over edges. Brush pastry crust with beaten egg yolk. Bake in 350° oven 20-25 minutes. Serves 6-8.

PAINTING BY EDWARD C. GRESSLEY

The Newarker

Although this restaurant is located in the new administration building at Newark Airport, Newark, New Jersey, the majority of its patrons are local residents who enjoy superior food and service. The spacious air-conditioned dining room overlooks the flight deck, offering diners a panoramic view of the busy 2,200-acre airfield. Lunch and dinner are served daily.

PAINTING BY CLARA GEE KASTNER

Tony Yonadi's Homestead Restaurant and Golf Club

On a former potato farm stands this elegant restaurant and adjoining golf course. Lunch and dinner served daily until 1 a.m. Closed Mondays, except holidays and during the winter. Take Exit 96 from Garden State Parkway to Spring Lake, New Jersey. Located on Allaire Road.

PAINTING BY GRANT REYNARD

Clinton Inn

Located at 6 East Clinton Avenue, the Inn has been a landmark of Tenafly, New Jersey, for over sixty years. Today it boasts one of the most modern and scientifically planned kitchens in the country, but the atmosphere to the overnight guest or diner still retains the homeyness of an Early American hostelry. Open for lunch and dinner, noon to 1 a.m. Overnight accommodations.

LOBSTER FRA DIAVOLO

4 1½-pound live lobsters
3 large cloves garlic
1 large onion
   Olive oil, to cover pan bottom
2 No. 2 cans tomatoes
1 small can tomato paste
2 cups white wine
   Pinch of leaf oregano
   Pinch of dry basil leaves
3 ounces salt
2 ounces sugar
   Dash of Tabasco sauce
   Pinch of hot pepper seeds
2 ounces Strega (Italian cordial)

Split live lobsters from head to tail. Detach claws and cut into 4 pieces. Cut the rest of the lobster across in 2-inch pieces. Save juice. Chop garlic and onion very fine and sauté in olive oil. Add tomatoes, paste and remaining ingredients, except lobster and Strega. Cook 15 minutes over brisk fire. Add lobster pieces and juice and cook over medium heat for 25 minutes. When done, pour into serving dish and pour Strega over top; serve either plain or flaming. Makes 4 portions.

SALAD DRESSING

6 ounces sugar
3 cloves garlic, finely chopped
1 small onion, finely chopped
1 teaspoon paprika
1 pint white vinegar
   Pinch of black pepper
¼ teaspoon dry mustard
1 teaspoon salt
1 pint salad oil

Thoroughly mix all ingredients, adding the salad oil last. Shake well before using. Makes a little more than a quart and may be kept in the refrigerator.

MAPLE SPONGE CAKE WITH MAPLE ICING

Make your favorite sponge cake, substituting maple syrup for the flavoring and part of the liquid, if your recipe calls for any.

Maple Icing: Boil ¾ cup maple syrup with 1 tablespoon light corn syrup to the stage where a teaspoonful of it forms a soft ball in water. Add a few grains salt to 1 egg white and beat until stiff but not dry. Pour syrup in a thin stream onto egg whites, beating constantly. Continue beating until icing reaches spreading consistency. This is enough to frost one 9-inch tube cake. The subtlety of the maple taste, which is easily lost in cooking, comes through exceptionally well in this recipe. Also, if made one day and kept covered until the next, icing stays moist and soft.

PAINTING BY FRED ZIMMER

Deer's Head Inn

Built in 1800, this is the oldest hostelry in the Adirondacks, and one of the few that stay open year around. The owner, Eugene Bastian, was pastry-chef at the Gotham, Plaza and Roosevelt Hotels in New York City for twenty years before buying this hotel on U.S. 9 and 9N in Elizabethtown, New York. Breakfast, lunch and dinner served daily; overnight accommodations.

LAND'S END DUCK 'N' SAUCE

Cover 4 medium-size cleaned Long Island ducklings with a heavy coat of salt and sprinkle lightly with garlic powder and place in roasting pan. Roast at 400° for 2½ hours. Pour off fat after first hour. Remove from roasting pan and allow to cool and chill. After chilling, split duck in half; remove rib bones and thigh bones and cut into quarter portions. Reheat 15 minutes, remove from oven and add Duck Sauce *(below)*.

Duck Sauce:
  1 cup consommé
  ½ cup currant jelly
  2 cups brown gravy
  1 orange peel

Bring consommé to a boil, add jelly. Cook and stir slowly for 5 minutes. Add brown gravy to bring to the right consistency. Cut orange peel in narrow strips and add to sauce. Simmer for 10 minutes before ladling over hot roast duckling. Serves 8.

PAINTING BY GEORGE SHELLHASE

Land's End

Ellen Burke and Mary Hayes manage this resort, formerly a beautiful private waterfront estate. Lunch and dinner served daily until 2 a.m. Closed Monday during the winter. Overnight accommodations and vacation facilities. Reservations recommended. Turn off Route 27 into Sayville (Long Island), New York. Take Foster Avenue to bay front, left to 80 Brown's River Road.

Hereford House—Hotel Gramatan

The Hereford House dining room is located on the street level of the Hotel Gramatan, only a short drive from anywhere in New York's Westchester County. Dinner is served daily from 5:00 p.m. to 10:00 p.m. Closed Mondays. Reservations suggested. Overnight accommodations at the hotel. Situated two blocks from the Bronx River Parkway in downtown Bronxville, New York.

Lüchow's Restaurant

Located at 110 East 14th Street in New York City, it is still one of the most famous restaurants in the country. Founded in 1882, Lüchow's has retained the delightful old-fashioned dark-paneled dining rooms, hearty German fare and music of its early days. Christmas dinner here is a lifelong tradition for many. Open daily except Monday from 11:30 a.m. (noon on Sunday) to midnight.

ONION SOUP

2 quarts beef or chicken broth
3 pounds fresh onions, sliced
3 ounces butter
2 tablespoons Worcestershire sauce
½ clove garlic (optional)
  Salt and pepper, to taste
  Small lemon twist
6 slices stale French bread or rolls
  Parmesan cheese

Sauté onions in butter, don't brown. Add broth. Cook over moderate heat for 45 minutes. Check taste. Add Worcestershire sauce, seasonings, and lemon twist. Boil for 5 minutes. Toast stale French bread or sliced rolls. Top with cheese and melted butter and toast lightly again. Serve one of these slices on top of each bowl of onion soup. Extra Parmesan cheese may also be served separately. Makes 6 portions.

ROAST WATERTOWN GOOSE WITH STEWED APPLES

Have a 12-pound fat young goose cleaned and drawn. Chop off wings, neck, head and feet. Wash goose inside and out, drain. Cover with cold water and let soak 15 minutes. Drain; pat dry. Rub with salt inside and out. Place in baking pan. Add 4 cups water, ½ onion, sliced, and 6 peppercorns. Roast in 325° oven. When water has boiled down, baste frequently with ¼ pound melted and browned butter. A young goose should be cooked 15-20 minutes a pound. Remove goose to warm platter. Place pan on top of range and sift 2 tablespoons flour into juice. Stir, then add 2 cups water. Let boil 2-3 minutes, stirring constantly. Serve gravy with goose. Makes 6 portions.

STEWED APPLES

Wash, peel and core 2 pounds of apples. Cut in thick slices. Sauté in 2 tablespoons butter for 2-3 minutes. Sprinkle with ½ cup sugar. Add ½ cup water, ½ cup white wine, small piece of lemon peel and 1 tablespoon lemon juice. Cover, cook slowly until apples are tender. Serves 6.

CHICKEN AND HAM

½ small Bermuda onion, minced
¼ cup butter
½ cup mushrooms, sliced
1 teaspoon paprika
1 teaspoon salt
¼ teaspoon nutmeg
6 slices white meat of chicken
6 slices boiled ham
1¾ cups hot cream
3-4 tablespoons Parmesan cheese,
  grated

Sauté onion in butter in a 1½-quart casserole until tender. Add mushrooms and seasonings, then cook for 5 minutes. Arrange chicken and ham slices in alternate layers in the casserole; add enough hot cream to cover. Place in 400° oven for 10 minutes. Cover with grated cheese and return to oven to brown. Serve when bubbly. Makes 6 portions.

ROCK CORNISH GAME HEN FLAMBÉ AU COGNAC

6 1-pound Rock Cornish game hens
  Melted butter
  Salt, pepper and paprika
½ ounce brandy

Fill game hens with Dressing *(below)* and brush with melted butter. Sprinkle each lightly with salt, pepper and paprika. Roast in 300° oven for about 1½ hours. Serve in chafing dish — pour Cherry Sauce *(also below)* over hens just before serving. Pour brandy over sauce; light with match. Makes 6 servings.

Dressing: Cook ¼ pound sausage, chopped, in a large skillet. Add 4 tablespoons water, 1 medium onion, chopped fine, and 3 mushrooms, sliced thin. Sauté until meat is well done. Add 1 cup cooked wild rice and season to taste with salt, pepper, poultry seasoning and 1 tablespoon brandy. Add ¼ cup bread crumbs and mix ingredients thoroughly.

Cherry Sauce: Combine 1 cup water, ¼ cup burgundy wine, ¼ cup sugar add ¼ teaspoon salt. Bring to a boil and thicken slightly with cornstarch. Add 1 No. 2½ can black Bing cherries.

PAINTING BY RICHARD WAGNER

The Homestead Inn

Overlooking Mirror Lake, the Inn offers a full program of winter sports. Breakfast, lunch and dinner served every day. Reservations requested. Overnight accommodations. Mrs. M. A. Roland is the owner of this resort in the heart of the Adirondack Mountains. It is at 16 Main Street (State Highway 86) in Lake Placid, New York, an outstanding winter and summer resort area.

PAINTING BY MILT GROTH

The Treasure Chest

Built in 1741, this picturesque restaurant is linked with its historic past by an antique shop on the premises. Mel and Doris Cohen are the owners. Lunch is served from noon to 2:00 p.m.; dinner, 5:30 p.m. to 9:30 p.m. Closed on Tuesday. Three and a half miles south of Poughkeepsie, New York, the address is 568 South Road (U.S. 9). Reservations advisable on weekends.

PAINTING BY ALOIS FABRY

CLAM CHOWDER

½ pound salt pork, cubed
5 carrots, diced
4 onions, diced
4 green peppers, diced
12 cups water
2½ dozen clams
4 potatoes, diced
Salt and pepper, to taste
½ teaspoon thyme
1 teaspoon Ac'cent

Fry salt pork until brown. Add carrots, onions and green peppers and sauté slowly. Add water and boil until vegetables are done, about 30 minutes. Open clams and add to soup with potatoes and cook until potatoes are done. Taste, then add seasonings. Makes 8 hearty servings.

Perkins Inn

Dorothy Draper did the interior design of the Hunt Room at this delightful Long Island country inn on Main Street in Riverhead. The history of the area has been woven into the decor with antique guns, powder pouches and bugles from Revolutionary days. Open for breakfast, lunch and dinner daily. Overnight accommodations and vacation facilities. Reservations necessary.

PAINTING BY REVINGTON ARTHUR

The White Inn

The two magnificent maple trees that flank the Inn's entrance were planted in 1821 when it was still a private estate. Located at 52 East Main Street (U.S. 20) in Fredonia, New York, the Inn is only three miles from Lake Erie. The dining room is open for breakfast (except Sunday), lunch and dinner the year round. Overnight accommodations and vacation facilities.

WHITE INN
ROQUEFORT DRESSING

2 eggs
1½ teaspoons salt
½ teaspoon dry mustard
¼ teaspoon white pepper
2 cups salad oil
1 lemon, juice
1 tablespoon vinegar
1 teaspoon onion juice
1 cup Roquefort cheese

Beat eggs with salt, mustard and pepper. When thick, add salad oil very slowly, beating continuously. Slowly add lemon juice, vinegar and onion juice. Stir in crumbled cheese. Store in refrigerator. Yields about 1 quart.

POPOVERS À LA VIRGINIAN

1 quart fresh milk
4 cups bread flour
8 whole eggs
1 tablespoon melted butter
1 teaspoon salt

Combine milk and flour. Add eggs one at a time while beating batter. Add butter and salt and beat for 5 minutes. Pour into well-greased *hot* muffin tins. Bake 10 minutes at 400°, then at 350° for 15 minutes. Makes 24 popovers.

PAINTING BY ALOIS FABRY

The Virginian

Specializing in Southern food, this fine restaurant is located at 72 Palmer Avenue, Bronxville, New York. Lunch, tea and dinner served daily. Closed on Tuesday. Traffic on the Bronx River Parkway should take the exit for Palmer Avenue. Lessie Bowers and William Guion are the owners and managers. Popovers and chocolate cream pie are favorites here.

BEEKMAN FRUIT MUFFINS

2¼ cups flour
¾ cup sugar
1 tablespoon baking powder
1 teaspoon salt
1 scant teaspoon cinnamon
3 ounces butter
2 eggs, beaten
¾ cup milk
¾ cup apples, finely chopped
¾ cup fruit glacé mix

Sift dry ingredients together. Melt butter and combine with eggs and milk. Blend in apples and fruit glacé and stir all into dry mix. Scoop into muffin tins lined with paper muffin cups. Bake at 400° to 425° for 30 to 35 minutes, or until done. Makes about 2 dozen muffins.

PAINTING BY FRED ENG

The Beekman Arms

Established in 1700, this country hotel is said to be the oldest American hotel in continuous operation. In early days the hotel provided bed and board for the old Albany Post Road travelers and later George Washington lived here. Located at State Highway 308 and U.S. Highway 9 in Rhinebeck, New York, the inn is open for lunch and dinner daily, and offers overnight accommodations.

McCarthy's

Twenty-six years ago, Ruth and Herb McCarthy started a restaurant at Bowden Square in the fashionable resort village of Southampton, Long Island. Since then it has been popular with celebrities, socialites and everyone who enjoys fine food served in a gay holiday atmosphere. Lunch, dinner and late supper daily. Reservations are necessary for dining room and overnight accommodations.

The Black Bass Hotel

Charming and picturesque, the hotel was built on the Delaware River around 1745. The favorite drink then was a brew of hot ale, apple pulp and spices served in steaming mugs. In Bucks County, Pennsylvania, at Lumberville, on Route 32, the old hotel is open for lunch and dinner every day except Christmas. Overnight accommodations. Reservations necessary on Saturday.

FRIED PECONIC BAY SCALLOPS

1 quart scallops
1 tablespoon olive oil
2 tablespoons lemon juice
½ teaspoon parsley, finely chopped
1 teaspoon chives, finely chopped
Salt and pepper, to taste
2 eggs, beaten
½ cup flour
½ cup cream
Deep fat for frying

Drain (don't wash) scallops and let stand in a mixture of olive oil, lemon juice, parsley, chives, salt and pepper. Drain scallops well and dip in combination of beaten eggs, flour and cream. Place in wire basket and fry in deep fat at 375° until light brown. Place in 300° oven for a few minutes. Serve with tartar sauce and lemon wedges. Serves 6.

TURKEY CREOLE

4 slices of cooked turkey
1 banana
2 cups rice, cooked and drained
Turkey gravy
4 tablespoons sauterne
Blanched almonds, sliced

Cut banana in quarters, sauté until brown. On each plate place a mound of the hot rice. Top with banana quarter. Over this place a generous slice of turkey. Heat turkey gravy and add sauterne. Pour gravy over turkey and sprinkle each serving with almonds. Place under broiler until almonds are brown. Makes 4 servings.

CURRY SOUP

Sauté 6 sliced apples and 3 chopped onions in butter until soft, then add 1 tablespoon curry powder. Add 1 quart turkey stock and 1 quart tomato juice seasoned with ½ teaspoon of salt. Simmer for 20 minutes. Strain, forcing apples and onions through sieve or food mill. Serve hot or cold. 4 servings.

HOT DROP BISCUITS

2 cups flour
2 heaping teaspoons baking powder
1 teaspoon salt
1 teaspoon sugar
½ cup powdered milk
½ cup shortening
Water to moisten

Sift dry ingredients; work in shortening thoroughly with a fork. Moisten with 1¼ cups cold water, mixing as little as possible. Drop batter by teaspoonfuls on oiled cookie sheet. Bake at 400° about 15 minutes, until brown. Yields about 4 dozen small or 3 dozen large biscuits.

WINTER JELLY

Mix 2 cups apple juice, 2 cups orange juice, 2 cups crushed pineapple and 8 cloves (or 4 pieces dried ginger). Stir in 1 package Sure Jell and bring to boil. Add 7 cups sugar and stir constantly. Season to taste with 2-5 teaspoons concentrated lemon juice. Boil to jelly stage, about 5 minutes. Skim and pour into 10 jelly glasses. Seal with hot wax.

SHRIMP JAMBALAYA

2 cups cooked shrimp, cut in pieces
3 slices bacon, diced
3 tablespoons chopped onion
2 tablespoons chopped celery
2 tablespoons chopped parsley
3 tablespoons green pepper
1 tablespoon flour
4 cups tomatoes
1 teaspoon salt
1 teaspoon chili powder
3 cups cooked rice
1 cup buttered bread crumbs
Pinch of gumbo filé powder

Fry bacon, then add onion, celery, parsley and pepper. Cook until onions are yellow, then blend in flour. Add tomatoes, salt and chili powder. Simmer in an uncovered pan until mixture is thick. Add rice, shrimp and filé powder. Pour into casserole; just before serving, top with buttered bread crumbs. Brown under broiler. Makes 6 portions.

PAINTING BY RICHARD BROUGH

The Briar Patch

The original pine walls and beams distinguish this country inn, once a Dutch farmhouse. It is three miles from the Somerset Interchange of the Pennsylvania Turnpike on Route 2 off U.S. Highway 219 North. Lunch served 11:00 a.m. to 2:00 p.m.; dinner, 5:00 p.m. to 10:00 p.m. daily from June 15 to October 15. Overnight accommodations and vacation facilities. Reservations preferred.

PAINTING BY RANULPH BYE

The Homestead Restaurant of Lavender Hall

The original fireplace and carved beams can be seen in the oldest portion of this house built in 1707. Lunch and dinner served daily except Mondays and Christmas; buffet style on Wednesday, Thursday and Saturday. On State Highway 532, north of Newtown, Pennsylvania.

Green Gables

In addition to operating a fine dining room, owners Edith and James Stoughton maintain the Mountain Playhouse, the pioneer theater of the Allegheny Mountains, and the Jenner Art Gallery on their property. Lunch and dinner served every day. Reservations advisable on summer weekends. It's a quarter of a mile north of U.S. 30 on U.S. 219 at Jennerstown, Pennsylvania.

The Penn-Wells Hotel

Built in 1925 by the people of Wellsboro, Pennsylvania, the hotel is still operated by them for the thousands of annual visitors to this spectacular mountain area. The official Pennsylvania State Laurel Festival is held here each June. Breakfast, lunch and dinner served daily. Overnight accommodations; vacation facilities. It is a block south of U.S. 6 at 62 Main Street (Route 287).

OYSTER PIE

2 9-inch pie crusts
12 ounces oysters and juice
6 ounces butter
   Freshly ground black pepper, to taste
1 cup half-and-half (milk and cream)

Line a pie pan with a rather thick bottom crust. Pour oysters into shell. Cut butter into six pieces and place on oysters. Season with pepper. Cover with top pie crust and cut a 1-inch hole in the center. Place in 400° oven and fill pie to brim with cream. Bake for 30 minutes. Makes 6 portions. This recipe has been handed down in the Stoughton family from colonial times.

SALMON AND TOMATO PIE

2 tablespoons onion, chopped
2 tablespoons green peppers, chopped
1 ounce shortening
½ ounce flour
1¼ cups canned tomatoes
¼ teaspoon salt
   Dash of pepper
½ tablespoon sugar
8 ounces canned salmon, drained
1 ounce American cheese, grated
6½ ounces rich biscuit dough

Sauté onions and green pepper in shortening until tender, but not browned. Add flour. Combine tomatoes, seasonings and sugar; add to flour mixture. Bring to a boil, stirring constantly. Arrange layer of salmon in shallow casserole, cover with tomato mixture and sprinkle with grated cheese. Roll biscuit dough to ⅜-inch thickness; cut to fit top of casserole. Place on top of salmon mixture. Make openings in crust to permit escape of steam. Bake in 400° oven 20-25 minutes, or until crust is done. Serves 4.

SNAPPER SOUP

1 small snapping turtle or ¾ pound
    boiled turtle meat
3 ounces butter
3 ounces flour
½ scant teaspoon each: mace, thyme,
    allspice, cloves and dry
    mustard
    Salt and pepper, to taste
2 cups turtle stock
2 hard-boiled eggs, chopped fine
3 ounces sherry

Boil turtle until meat falls off bones.
Separate meat from broth. Make a
smooth paste of butter and flour and
cook until dry, then add seasonings. Stir
this mixture into turtle stock and simmer for 1½ hours. Add turtle meat in
small pieces, eggs and sherry. Simmer
for ½ hour. Serve hot. Makes 1 quart.

The Stock Yard Inn

Nationally known for half a century, this restaurant is
in Lancaster, Pennsylvania, at 1147 Lititz Avenue (U.S.
222 and State Highway 501), "just over the fence" from
the largest stockyards east of Chicago. Meals served
daily from 6:00 a.m. to midnight; on Sunday, noon to
8:30 p.m. Closed Christmas. Fine food is a tradition and
specialities are prime beef and fresh seafood in season.

CREAMED MUSHROOMS

1 pound fresh mushrooms
6 tablespoons butter
3 tablespoons flour
¾ teaspoon salt
1 cup milk
1 cup light cream
½ cup mushroom stock
2 tablespoons sherry
4-6 toast slices or toast cups
    Parsley, chopped for garnish

Wash, stem, and slice mushrooms. Boil
stems in ¾ cup water for 8-10 minutes
for mushroom stock. Sauté the sliced
mushroom caps in 3 tablespoons butter.
Melt remaining 3 tablespoons butter and
blend in flour and salt. Slowly stir in
milk, cream and mushroom stock. Boil
until thick, stirring constantly. Add
sautéed mushrooms and sherry. Serve
on toast and sprinkle with chopped
parsley. Serves 4-6.

Red Rose Inn

This fine eating place is located in a charming brick
building, one wing of which was built in 1740 and another in 1828. Ray and Janis Clanton own and manage
the Inn. Overnight accommodations. Breakfast, lunch
and dinner served daily except Tuesday. The location is
Jennersville, near West Grove on U.S. 1 in the southeastern corner of Pennsylvania. U.S. 30 and 40 are close by.

The Bull Tavern

Situated in the beautiful Schuylkill Valley, two miles from Washington's headquarters at Valley Forge Park, this historic restaurant has been receiving guests since its establishment in 1734. It is owned by A. C. and P. J. Valerio and is open daily for lunch through dinner. Reservations necessary. In Phoenixville, Pennsylvania, it is located on Route 23 West.

Gautreau's

Rhode Island lobster, Rock Cornish game hens and Rhode Island johnny cake are specialties of this fine country restaurant, located on Putnam Pike (U.S. 44), Chepachet, fifteen miles from Providence, Rhode Island. Lunch and dinner served daily from 12:00 noon until 8:30 p.m. Closed on Mondays. Reservations suggested for this popular eating place.

RUM PUDDING

1 pint heavy whipping cream
3 eggs, separated
8 tablespoons sugar
4 tablespoons rum
1 teaspoon vanilla
1 teaspoon nutmeg

Beat cream until stiff, set aside. Beat egg yolks until foamy. Add 4 tablespoons sugar, rum, vanilla, and nutmeg to beaten yolks. Beat egg whites stiff, forming peaks. Add 4 tablespoons sugar. Lightly blend the egg yolk mixture and whipped cream into beaten egg whites. Pour into individual large soufflé cups and freeze. Serve frozen.

ROCK CORNISH GAME HENS

Place 3 stuffed (see stuffing recipe below) 21-ounce Cornish game hens in a roasting pan on a rack. Rub with melted butter, salt, pepper and Alamo (John Sexton Co.) seasoning. Roast in open pan in 325° oven, basting frequently for 1½ hours or until done. Before serving, pour 1 ounce of cognac over birds. Serve flaming.

Rice Pilaf Stuffing:

1⅓ cups Minute Rice
1¾ cups boiling chicken broth
½ teaspoon salt
½ teaspoon Ac'cent
¼ pound mushrooms, chopped
2 tablespoons butter
1 ounce cognac or brandy

Prepare rice as usual but use chicken broth instead of water, adding salt and Ac'cent. Use just enough so the rice will come out fluffy. Then sauté chopped mushrooms in butter until done, add rice. Pour in cognac and mix. Bake 15-20 minutes in 1-quart shallow greased pan at 375°. Cool, then stuff game birds.

OLD-FASHIONED PEA SOUP

½ pound whole green peas
½ pound split green peas
1 smoked ham shank, uncooked
1 medium onion, chopped
　Salt and pepper, to taste

Soak whole green peas overnight in a four-quart kettle filled with water. In the morning add split peas and remaining ingredients. Boil slowly for about 4 hours. Remove ham shank and serve soup without straining. Makes about 12 hearty portions.

PEPPER RELISH

6 green peppers
6 sweet red peppers
6 onions
1 cup sugar
2 tablespoons salt
1 pint cider vinegar

Grind peppers and onions in a meat grinder, then cover with hot water and let stand five minutes. Drain and add sugar, salt and vinegar. Boil 20 minutes. Put into small jars and seal while hot. Serve with meats. Makes about 1 quart.

PUMPKIN-MINCE PIE

1 cup canned pumpkin
½ cup brown sugar
1 teaspoon pumpkin pie spice
½ teaspoon salt
2 eggs, slightly beaten
14½ ounces evaporated milk
2½ cups mincemeat
　9-inch unbaked pie shell

Combine pumpkin, sugar, spice, salt, eggs and milk and beat until smooth. Spread mincemeat evenly over pie shell. Ladle pumpkin mixture carefully over mincemeat. Bake at 450° for 10 minutes, then at 350° about 45 minutes, until filling is firm in center.

PAINTING BY DWIGHT SHEPLER

The Clement's Tavern

Just a few miles from some of Vermont's most famous ski areas is this century-old inn owned by Mrs. Clara Clement and her son, John. Breakfast, lunch and dinner served every day. Closed Tuesday evenings. Overnight accommodations. Reservations desired. The address is 64 South Main Street, Waterbury, Vermont. The inn is in the center of town, on U.S. 2 and State 100.

PAINTING BY ALICE PAULINE SCHAFER

Colburn House

A four-season resort, this inn has been in constant operation since it was built in 1872. Breakfast, lunch and dinner served daily. Reservations necessary Saturday nights and Sundays in summer. Overnight accommodations and vacation facilities. It is located at the junction of U.S. Highway 7 and State Highways 11 and 30 in Manchester Center, Vermont.

The Waybury Inn

Furnished with antiques, this delightful country inn owned by R. C. Kingsley and H. M. Curtiss was built in 1810. Dinner served in the evening and Sunday noon to other than houseguests. Overnight accommodations; vacation facilities. Reservations advisable. Closed Tuesdays November 1 to June 1. It is a mile east of U.S. 7 on State Highway 125 in East Middlebury, Vermont.

The Lodge

At the foot of Mt. Mansfield, in one of the superb ski areas of the East, The Lodge is within walking distance of the ski school and chair lift. Overnight accommodations and vacation facilities. Meal reservations necessary for non-guests. Closed April 15 to May 20 and October 28 to December 15. Located at Smuggler's Notch, Vermont, six miles north of Stowe on Route 108.

KIDNEY BEAN RELISH

Chop together 1 small onion, 3 stalks celery, and 1 or 2 hard-boiled eggs. Add 2 cups drained kidney beans. Mix in 1 tablespoon mayonnaise, 2 teaspoons mustard relish, 1 teaspoon curry powder, ¼ teaspoon white pepper and ½ teaspoon salt. Serve cool and keep under refrigeration. Makes 6 portions.

WAYBURY HOT FRUIT COMPOTE

Combine ½ cup each: prunes, pears, peaches and pineapple with 1½ cups applesauce and arrange in casserole. Then add 1 teaspoon cinnamon and ½ teaspoon each ginger and nutmeg. Add the juice of ½ lemon and its rind, chopped. Mix the fruits and place covered in a 250° oven for at least 1 hour before serving. The longer it bakes the better it is. Other fruits can be substituted and either fresh or canned may be used. Serve hot with meat or fowl.

SAUTÉED TENDERLOIN PEPPER STEAK WITH WILD RICE

    2 cups wild rice
    7 tablespoons butter
    ½ beef tenderloin (about 3 pounds)
    3 green peppers
    1½ medium-size onions

Add 2 cups of boiling water to wild rice. Let steep about 12 hours. Then put rice and same water into a stew pan, adding about ¼ cup more water and 3 tablespoons butter. Cover pot well and boil until rice is tender, about 22 minutes. Cut beef tenderloin into quarter-inch slices. Cut the larger slices in half. Cut green peppers into coarse strips and blanch them by boiling for one minute. Drain. Cut onions into thin half-slices. Heat 4 tablespoons butter in a large frying pan, add onions and let sizzle for a minute. Then add tenderloin and peppers and sauté on a very brisk fire until brown. Serve over wild rice in 6 individual casseroles. Sprinkle a few drops of Worcestershire sauce on tenderloin.

BLACKIE'S
BEEF VEGETABLE SOUP

Place a 4-pound meaty soup bone in large pot. Add 1 large chopped onion, ½ bunch chopped celery and cover with water. Cook slowly for four hours. Skim off top of beef stock occasionally. Sauté in ¼ pound butter: 2 large chopped onions, ½ bunch chopped celery, 3 large sliced carrots and 3 green peppers. Add 2 cups stewed tomatoes, 4 ounces tomato purée and 3 large diced potatoes. Cook 30 minutes over medium heat. Add beef stock, 4 teaspoons salt and ½ teaspoon pepper. Remove meat from beef bone, chop in small pieces and add to soup. Then add ¼ pound frozen green peas, ¼ pound frozen baby Lima beans and 4 drops of Tabasco. Cook 30 minutes over low heat. Makes 10-12 hearty main-dish portions.

PAINTING BY A. JOHN OAKLEY

Blackie's House of Beef

Although it is located in the center of Washington, D.C., this restaurant with antlers over the bar, checkered tablecloths and Western etchings on the pine-paneled walls has a frontier atmosphere and specializes in Western roast beef. Lunch and dinner served every day except Sunday. Reservations advisable. Owner is Ulysses Auger, and the address is 1217 22nd at M Street N.W.

CHEF MACEROLLO'S
PLUM PUDDING

Beat 5 eggs until fluffy, add ⅔ cup brown sugar. Stir in ½ cup of molasses and mix thoroughly. Add 1⅓ cups Sultana raisins; 1⅓ cups currants; 1⅓ cups dark raisins; ¾ cup citron, chopped; ¾ cup candied orange peel, chopped; ⅔ cup candied lemon peel, chopped; 1 cup suet, chopped; ½ cup bread crumbs; 1⅓ pounds apples, peeled and chopped; pinch of salt; 1 tablespoon cinnamon; ½ tablespoon nutmeg; 1 tablespoon ginger; 1 tablespoon allspice; 1 tablespoon caramel; ½ tablespoon orange extract; ½ tablespoon lemon extract; 3 ounces beer; 2½ ounces vermouth and ¾ ounce liquor (brandy, bourbon, rum or triple sec). Mix thoroughly. Place mixture in 3 greased quart molds with covers, or tie on wax paper. Place in pan of water. Steam for approximately 2-2½ hours in 325° oven. After cooling pudding to room temperature, seal over tops with melted paraffin wax and age for at least 2 weeks. Serve resteamed with warm brandy sauce.

PAINTING BY LOIS JONES

Mayflower Hotel

Just six blocks from the White House at Connecticut Avenue and De Sales Street N.W., this hotel entertains some of the most famous people in the world, including presidents and kings. A traditional Thanksgiving feast is served every year in the Presidential Room. Meals served daily from 7:00 a.m. to 1:00 a.m. Overnight accommodations; sight-seeing. Reservations advised.

PAINTING BY GEORGE CRESS

SOUTHEAST

Bountiful meals are a
tradition in the Southeast,
dating back to plantation days
when meals were sumptuous
and elaborate. Southern
fried chicken, pecan pie,
hot breads and biscuits, crab,
shrimp, and ham and yams
cooked a score of ways are
at home in this region.
Seasoning reaches its peak
here with wines, brandies,
and herbs incorporated into
everyday cooking. Nowhere
is there a greater variety
of soups and broths, a legacy
of the European settlers.

PAINTING BY RICHARD BROUGH

The Coffee Pot

A handy motorists' stop—for in addition to a dining room there is quick curb service and an adjoining motel. Meals are served from 6:00 a.m. to 10:00 p.m. every day except Christmas. It is a mile south of Luverne, Alabama, on U.S. Highways 29 and 331. Owners are Mr. and Mrs. Carl Tacker, who also manage The Coffee Pot. Chocolate pie is their specialty.

CHOCOLATE PIE

3 egg yolks
1 cup sugar
2 squares bittersweet chocolate, melted
1 pint milk
2 tablespoons cornstarch
2 tablespoons butter
9-inch pie shell, baked

Combine above ingredients except crust and cook in double boiler until mixture thickens. Cool and pour into pie shell.

Meringue: Beat 3 egg whites (room temperature) until stiff. Slowly add 3 tablespoons sugar, pinch of salt and teaspoon of vanilla. Pour over chocolate filling and bake in 225° oven until golden brown, about 10-15 minutes.

PAINTING BY DALE NICHOLS

Grand Hotel

On the shores of Mobile Bay, this resort hotel has excellent facilities for a complete vacation for the entire family. In addition to golf, swimming and sight-seeing, guests have their choice of fresh- or salt-water fishing. Breakfast, lunch and dinner served every day. Reservations suggested. The hotel is 25 miles southeast of Mobile on U. S. Highway 98 at Point Clear, Alabama.

PORK CHOPS À LA CREOLE

8 6-ounce pork chops, baked
4 cups brown sauce
4 cups cooked rice, moistened with 2 cups brown sauce
8 slices fresh tomato, broiled
8 slices American cheese
8 pats butter
Parsley and paprika, to garnish
16 small candied yams

Salt and pepper chops to taste. Place ½ cup of moistened rice on top of each baked pork chop. Place broiled tomato slices on rice, followed by cheese slices. Pour remaining brown sauce into casserole around chops and heat in 375° oven just long enough to melt cheese. Remove and garnish with parsley and paprika. Arrange candied yams around chops and place under broiler for 3 minutes just before serving. Serve uncovered and piping hot. Makes 8 portions.

BEEF ESTOUFFADE

2 pounds boneless beef
½ cup cooking oil
3 pounds small onions
1 pound onions, diced
2 tablespoons vinegar
½ cup claret wine
5 cloves garlic
1 cup tomato juice
3 bay leaves
1 teaspoon pickling spices, tied
    in cheesecloth
    Salt and pepper, to taste

Cut meat in small pieces, the size of walnuts, and brown slightly in oil. Peel small onions and add with diced onions to meat in a Dutch oven. Add remaining ingredients and cover oven. Cook in a 350° oven for 2 hours, or until meat and onions are done. Remove bay leaves and pickling spices immediately and serve. Makes 5-7 portions.

PAINTING BY DALE NICHOLS

Constantine's

For more than 28 years this fine restaurant in Mobile, Alabama, has maintained an enviable reputation for delicious food and excellent service. It is open 24 hours a day, every day of the year. Take U. S. Highway 90, leading from the Bankhead Tunnel, and go three blocks to 9-11 North Royal Street. Constantine N. Panayiotou is the host as well as the owner.

CRAB GUMBO

6 tablespoons flour
4 tablespoons bacon fat
1 green pepper
4 medium onions
1 stalk celery
2 pounds okra
1 No. 2 can tomatoes
2 small cans tomato paste
9 cups chicken stock
12 fresh crabs (or 2 pounds crab
    meat or 2 pounds shrimp)
2 bay leaves
    Salt and pepper, to taste
6 cups boiled rice.

Brown flour in bacon fat. Cut pepper, onions, celery and okra into small pieces and add to fat. Stir constantly and cook for 20 minutes. Add tomatoes and paste, then combine mixture with stock. Simmer for 1 hour. Add cleaned crabs or shrimp with bay leaves and simmer for 30 minutes more. Season to taste. Serve with boiled rice. Makes 20 portions. For main course, add more seafood.

PAINTING BY ADOLPH KRONENGOLD

The Colonial Inn

A rare combination of sea breezes and the scent of pine surrounds the Inn, situated on a pine-covered bluff overlooking Mobile Bay. The address is 201 South Mobile Avenue on U.S. 98 in Fairhope, Alabama. The Inn is a popular vacation spot, and the dining room is open for breakfast, lunch and dinner daily. Reservations requested for overnight accommodations and meals.

The Ranch Restaurant

Owned and managed by Henry McCown, the Ranch is famous for its unusual and delicious food. Southwest of downtown Montgomery, Alabama, it's at 3118 Mobile Road, within the city limits (U. S. Highway 80W and Alternate U. S. Highways 82 and 31.) The restaurant is open daily from 6:00 a.m. to 11:00 p.m. Closed on Christmas Day.

The Town Club

Owner Margaret Brown converted a fifteen-room mansion into this delightful tea room at 612 North Wood Avenue in Florence, Alabama, four blocks north of U.S. 43 and U.S. 72. Lunch and dinner served; reservations necessary. Closed on Sunday. Specialties include a broiled boned half chicken, in the Southern "home-cooked" style, and spoon bread.

CHICKEN COUNTRY CAPTAIN

    1 2-pound frying chicken
    1 cup flour
    ½ cup butter
    1 onion, finely chopped
      Pinch of sage
    1 green pepper, chopped
    2 fresh tomatoes or 1 cup canned
    ½ cup unsalted pecans
    ½ cup seedless raisins or currants
    2 cups water
      Salt and pepper, to taste
    4 ounces peach brandy (optional)
    2 cups hot buttered rice

Disjoint chicken and cut into 8 pieces. Roll in flour and fry lightly in butter until browned. Remove chicken from pan; add onion, sage, green pepper, tomatoes, pecans, raisins and 1 cup water. Bring mixture to a boil, then replace chicken, cover and simmer for 45 minutes. About 5 minutes before chicken is done season and add brandy, if desired. Serve over rice. Makes 4 portions. (This is an old-fashioned Southern dish.)

SOUTHERN SPOON BREAD

    ½ teaspoon soda
    ½ teaspoon baking powder
    1 cup buttermilk
    2 eggs
    1 heaping tablespoon corn meal
    ½ teaspoon salt
    1½ ounces butter or margarine,
        melted

Add soda and baking powder to buttermilk. Beat eggs lightly and combine with milk. Then add meal, salt, melted butter and mix well. Pour into casserole and bake 20 minutes at 325°, or 25 minutes at 350°. It is done when firm and brown. Yields 6 portions.

CRÈME OF TOMATO SOUP WITH ALMONDS

2 cups milk
1 cup light cream
1 medium can tomato paste, or 1
  No. 2 can tomato purée
1 tablespoon sugar
1 teaspoon salt
2 tablespoons Parmesan cheese
2 ounces butter
2 tablespoons flour
1 cup whipping cream
2 dozen almonds, toasted and sliced

Bring milk and light cream to a boil, then add tomato paste or purée and stir briskly. Stir in sugar, salt and cheese. Melt butter and blend in flour to make a smooth paste, then add to the soup and beat until it is smooth and thick as heavy cream. Whip the whipping cream and top each bowl of soup with a generous tablespoon of it. Sprinkle with almonds and serve. Serves 6.

PAINTING BY ALBERT GOLD

Holiday Inn

Located about 10 miles north of the Delaware Memorial Bridge, this restaurant is at 1843 Marsh Road in Wilmington, Delaware. Open for lunch and dinner every day of the year; closed Christmas Day. The Holiday Inn also has a cocktail lounge. Reservations necessary on weekends. Many guests choose to start off their meals with crème of tomato soup with almonds, a taste-tempting specialty.

BROOK TROUT POLONAISE

4 12- to 14-ounce brook trout,
  cleaned and boned
1 shallot, chopped
1 clove garlic, chopped
1 cup fresh mushrooms, chopped
¼ pound butter
½ cup flour
4 ounces sauterne
1 pound crabmeat
  Water cress, for garnish

Sauté trout in butter until browned on both sides. Remove. Sauté shallot, garlic and mushrooms in butter. Add flour and stir. Bring mixture to a boil. Blend in wine to make a thick sauce. Then stir crabmeat into sauce. Chill and stuff trout with the crab mixture. Bake in 350° oven for 20 minutes. Garnish with water cress. Makes 4 portions.

PAINTING BY JEROME KAPLAN

The Surrey

Located at 1101 Philadelphia Pike (Route 13 going south) and Holly Hill Road in Wilmington, Delaware, this fine restaurant is owned and operated by Jimmy Stromberg, and has an unusual collection of old picture frames. Lunch and dinner served every day. The Surrey is only four miles from Longwood Gardens, one of the most famous botanical exhibits in the world.

The Grill

Owned and managed by Fred Anthony, this restaurant specializes in ocean-fresh seafood. Open daily 5:00 a.m. to 10:00 p.m. Closed Christmas. It is located on U.S. 98 in downtown Apalachicola on the northwest Gulf coast of Florida at the mouth of the Apalachicola River. Nearby tourist attractions include the Gorrie Museum, named for the inventor of the artificial ice process.

Chesler's

Celebrated for its fine food, this restaurant is also noted for its beauty—magnificently paneled walls of walnut, oak, cypress and mahogany. Open for lunch and dinner during the season; entertainment in the evening. Reservations advisable. Closed May 1 to October 1. The address of the restaurant is 235 Worth Avenue, Palm Beach, Florida. Hylan Chesler is the owner.

CRABMEAT PERFECTION

1 medium onion, minced
1 medium green pepper, chopped fine
½ cup mushrooms
1 cup medium white sauce
1 pound crabmeat
2 hard-boiled eggs
  Paprika and Worcestershire sauce, to taste
  Salt and pepper, to taste
1 cup American cheese, grated

Mix ingredients, except cheese, together thoroughly. Place in greased 8x10-inch casserole and sprinkle cheese on top. Bake in 325° oven for 15 minutes. Makes 6-8 portions.

HUSH PUPPIES

Combine 1 medium onion, grated; 1½ cups corn meal; 1 cup flour; 1 egg; 1 tablespoon baking powder; ½ teaspoon salt; 1 teaspoon sugar and 1 cup milk. Mix well. Drop dough by tablespoonfuls into 350° deep fat and fry until brown. Serves 6.

SIRLOIN STEAK WINE MERCHANT

2 1-pound prime sirloin steaks
2 soup spoons black pepper, freshly crushed

Cover sirloin steak with black pepper and place it in a red hot skillet for 30 seconds on each side. Broil steak to desired degree and serve with sauce (below). Makes 4 portions.

Sauce:
¼ pound butter
1 teaspoon shallot or onion, diced
1 teaspoon parsley, chopped
2 cups red wine
  Salt, to taste

Melt butter and sauté shallot or onion and parsley over low fire. Add wine and cook over medium fire until sauce reduces in volume.

MOLASSES SQUARES

½ cup sugar
¾ cup molasses
5½-ounce package Rice Krispies

Boil sugar and molasses until it forms a soft ball in a glass of water. Butter a 12x18-inch rectangular pan and line with cereal. Pour syrup over it, stir fast and pat down with wet hand. Serve with vanilla ice cream.

CREAM CHEESE MOLDED SALAD

2 packages lemon Jello
  Juice from pineapple
3 small packages cream cheese
1 tablespoon cream
½ teaspoon mustard
1 can crushed pineapple, drained
1 small can pimento, chopped fine
½ cup cream, whipped

Prepare Jello with 2 cups boiling water and juice from pineapple. Combine soft cream cheese, cream, mustard, pineapple and pimento. Whip cream and fold into cheese mixture. When Jello begins to thicken add to cheese mixture and mold. Makes 25 three-ounce molds.

BAKED PORK CHOPS A LA BORDEAUX

4 heavy-cut loin pork chops
  Salt and pepper, to taste
⅛ teaspoon nutmeg
⅛ teaspoon clove, ground
1 tablespoon brown sugar
1 cup Bordeaux wine
  Spiced apples, for garnish

Wipe chops dry and sprinkle with salt and pepper. Broil chops golden brown on both sides. Remove from broiler and drain excess fat. Sprinkle chops with nutmeg and clove. Add brown sugar and wine to pan and bake covered in a 350° oven for 10 minutes. Remove cover and bake an additional 10 minutes. Serve on hot platter garnished with spiced apples and topped with a glass dome. Makes 4 portions.

PAINTING BY SETON SHANLEY

Siple's Garden Seat

Located at 1234 West Druid Road in Clearwater, Florida, the restaurant is set on the bay amidst century-old oak trees. Turn west from U. S. Alt. 19 at Jeffords Street. Lunch and dinner served daily, with cocktails and supper in "The Pub" until 11:30 p.m. every day except Sunday and Monday. Entertainment. R. B. Siple is the manager of this colorful dining spot.

PAINTING BY ROBERT CHASE

Zinn's

Mrs. William Zinn and her son Billie own and manage this well-known eating place which specializes in fine roast beef and charcoal-broiled steaks and chops. A new dining room has been added, featuring a large waterfall. The restaurant is located at 6101 North Tamiami Trail (U.S. 41) between Sarasota and Bradenton. Dinner is served 5:00 p.m. to 10:30 p.m. Open at noon on Sunday.

Fred Abood's Steer Room

Started in 1946 as a lunch counter for farmers in the Jacksonville produce market, Abood's has grown into a nationally famous steak house where beef is king. Open for breakfast, lunch and dinner every weekday; closed Sunday. Located at 1780 West Beaver Street, at the foot of the viaduct, it is a quarter-mile from the Beaver or Stockton Street exits of the Jacksonville Expressway.

Creighton's—Johnston's Coffee Shop

"The World's Best Apple Pie" is the motto of this excellent restaurant in Daytona Beach, Florida. Meals are served in three dining rooms from 11:30 a.m. to 9:00 p.m. daily the year round. It is located at 200 Magnolia at Palmetta, east of U.S. 1 and south of U.S. 92.

KIBBIE

Meat Mixture: Grind together ¾ pound of beef, ¾ pound lamb, ½ small onion and ½ small bell pepper. Season with 1½ teaspoons salt, 1 teaspoon each cinnamon and allspice, and pepper to taste. Soak 1 cup crushed wheat germ in water until soft, then squeeze dry and blend with meat mixture.

Filling: Sauté 1½ large chopped onions in lamb fat. Add ½ cup pine nuts or pecans. Season with salt, pepper and allspice as in meat mixture.

Spread meat mixture *(above)* ½-inch thick on bottom of baking pan. Spread generous portion of filling over it. Put another ½ inch of meat mixture on top of filling and press down and smooth. Cut squares through meat, checkerboard style. Top with 2 ounces of flaked butter. Bake at 400° for 45 minutes. Makes 12 portions of this Oriental dish.

PICNIC CHICKEN

  2 3-pound chickens, cut in pieces
  1 cup flour
2½ teaspoons salt
½ teaspoon onion salt
  1 cup shortening
  1 cup hot water

Mix flour, salt and onion salt. Coat each piece of chicken with seasoned flour. Heat shortening, then add chicken, filling pan without crowding sides. Fry slowly, turning often until chicken is brown on all sides, about 35-40 minutes. Add hot water, cover pan loosely and cook over low heat until water has evaporated, about 15 minutes. Chicken may be wrapped in heavy brown paper and it will keep hot for a short time for picnics. Makes 6-8 portions.

SPANISH BEAN SOUP

½ pound of garbanzos
    (Spanish beans)
1 beef bone or 1 ham bone
2 ounces lard
1 onion, chopped fine
4 ounces white bacon
1 pound potatoes
1 pinch saffron
1 tablespoon salt
1 chorizo (Spanish sausage)

Soak garbanzos overnight with a table-spoon salt in sufficient water to cover beans. When ready to cook, drain the salted water from beans and put garban-zos and beef bone or ham bone in two quarts of water with lard. Cook for 45 minutes on slow fire. Fry bacon and onion; place these in pot, adding pota-toes, saffron and salt. When potatoes are done, remove from fire, add chorizo cut in thin slices. Serves 4.

PAINTING BY ROBERT CHASE

Spanish Park Restaurant

A favorite gathering place for major league baseball play-ers during spring training, this bustling restaurant is popular year around with people who enjoy good Spanish food. Located on East Broadway at 36th Street in Tampa, Florida, it is open every day for breakfast, lunch and dinner. The Spanish Park Restaurant is owned and man-aged by Joe and Tony Valdes.

REDFISH
À LA ROD AND GUN CLUB

Sprinkle six individual filets of redfish with salt and pepper, then lightly dust with flour. Melt ¼ cup butter in large frying pan and sauté fish lightly on both sides. Melt ¼ pound butter in saucepan and sauté ½ cup blanched and sliced almonds. Remove from fire and add 1 teaspoon diced pimentos; 2 teaspoons sweet relish, chopped; ½ lemon, juice; 2 teaspoons Lea and Perrin sauce; salt and pepper, to taste. Pour this over the cooked fish and broil for five minutes. Serves 6.

PAINTING BY MARTIN DIBNER

The Rod and Gun Club

One of the famous specialties here is the redfish. A por-tion of the building was once a Seminole Indian trading post. Breakfast, lunch and dinner served daily. Air-con-ditioned overnight accommodations and vacation facili-ties. Closed June 1 to October 31. Located midway be-tween Miami and Fort Myers on State Road 29, just south of U.S. 41 in Everglades, Florida.

Aunt Fanny's Cabin

Located at 375 Campbell Road in Smyrna, Georgia (about sixteen miles northwest of Atlanta), is this simple restaurant on an old plantation. Meals are served family style. Open for dinner every day from 6:00 p.m. to 9:30 p.m.; lunch and dinner on Sunday from 1:00 p.m. to 9:00 p.m. Closed Christmas Eve and Christmas Day. Harvey Hester and Marjorie Bowman are the owners.

Davis Brothers Suburban Restaurant

An open charcoal pit in the center of the dining room where meat is broiled is one of the unusual features of this fine family eating place in Albany, Georgia. Meals are served from 7:00 a.m. to 11:00 p.m. daily. It is on U. S. Highways 19 and 82 at 101 North Slappey.

AUNT FANNY'S BAKED SQUASH

3 pounds small yellow squash
(about 6 cups when cooked)
¼ cup butter
Salt and pepper, to taste
1½ cups onion, chopped
½ cup milk
2 large eggs
Melted butter
½ cup cracker crumbs

Wash — don't peel — squash; cut into small pieces and cook in salted water until tender. Don't overcook. Drain and pour squash into baking dish, immediately add butter, then salt, pepper and onions. Combine milk and eggs and mix well with squash. Top with a little melted butter and cracker crumbs. Bake for 20 minutes, or until brown, in a 450° oven. Serves 8 to 10.

COUNTRY BAKED HAM

Soak a 10- to 12-pound ham for 12 hours; then boil, cooking very slowly for 4-5 hours until tender. Cool in cooking water. When cold, remove skin and make crisscross gashes in the top of the ham with a sharp knife. Sprinkle top of ham with 2 tablespoons cracker crumbs, 2 tablespoons brown sugar and a light sprinkling of pepper. Stick the ham with 2 cloves. Sprinkle a wine glass of sherry over the top to improve flavor. Bake in 450° oven for 30 minutes, or until brown.

GEORGIA PECAN PIE

2 tablespoons butter
1 cup sugar
1 cup dark Karo syrup
2 eggs
1 cup unbroken pecan meats
1 teaspoon vanilla
9-inch pie shell, unbaked

Cream butter and sugar; add syrup, the unbeaten eggs and vanilla. Beat together well. Line pie shell with pecans and pour in filling; bake in 275° oven 30 minutes. Top with whipped cream.

PORK BALINESE

1 pound pork, sliced in
    1-inch squares
2 teaspoons salad oil
¼ pound celery, chopped
¼ pound onions, chopped
¼ pound water chestnuts, sliced
¼ pound bamboo shoots, sliced
    1-inch long
¼ pound mushrooms, sliced
1 pound bean sprouts, washed
    and drained
1 teaspoon salt
1 cup chicken broth
2 teaspoons cornstarch

Sauté pork slices in oil, then add vegetables, salt and chicken broth and cook about 5 minutes over medium fire. Mix cornstarch with water and blend into sauce to thicken gravy. Serves 4.

PAINTING BY LOGAN BLECKLEY, III

Luau Restaurant

Each of the five dining rooms features the décor and mood of one of the most beautiful Pacific Islands—Tahiti, Fiji, Samoa, Oahu and Hawaii. The chefs have been assembled from the islands and are masters of the art of Polynesian cuisine. Lunch, 11:30 a.m. to 2:30 p.m.; dinner, 5:30 p.m. to 10:30 p.m. Closed Sunday. Just twelve minutes from downtown Atlanta, Georgia, at 1999 Peachtree Road.

HOT EGG BREAD

2 cups "Pine Mountain" water-
    ground white corn meal
¼ teaspoon soda
2 teaspoons baking powder
1 teaspoon salt
2 eggs, beaten
2 cups sour milk or buttermilk
2 tablespoons melted fat or oil

Sift dry ingredients together. Add eggs and milk into dry ingredients, then fat. Pour into greased 8-inch square pan and bake in 425° oven 20-30 minutes. Serve hot. Makes 8 portions. Here it is served with the inn's own muscadine sauce or jelly, available from Gardens Country Store, Pine Mountain, Georgia.

PAINTING BY M. K. SCHAUER

Callaway Gardens Clubhouse

This inn is located in the unique, nonprofit Callaway Gardens, a 2,500-acre natural beauty spot on the shoulder of Pine Mountain. Here visitors may explore wildflower or bird trails, picnic, fish or swim. The Clubhouse is open for breakfast, lunch and dinner. Overnight accommodations; vacation facilities. On U.S. 27 near Pine Mountain, Georgia, 30 miles north of Columbus.

The Pirates' House

Preserving the atmosphere of the romantic days of "wooden ships and iron men," the Pirates' House Restaurant is in the newly restored Trustees' Garden Village at 20 East Broad Street in Savannah, Georgia. Just a short block from the Savannah River, it was once a sailors' rendezvous. Meals served from noon until 9:45 p.m. daily except Christmas; 10:45 p.m. on Saturday.

Village Inn Restaurant

Located on the largest man-made lake in the country, this restaurant is on U. S. 641 and 62 in Kentucky Dam State Park near Gilbertsville, Kentucky. Breakfast, lunch and dinner served daily; open to 8:30 p.m. Overnight accommodations and excellent vacation facilities, including an eighteen-hole golf course, tennis courts, and fishing, are readily available.

DATE AND NUT PUDDING

1 egg
1 cup sugar
1 teaspoon baking powder
1 teaspoon vanilla
1 cup dates, chopped
1 cup nuts, chopped
   Whipped cream

Beat egg; add sugar, baking powder and vanilla. Stir in nuts and dates. Put into greased 8x8-inch pan. Bake in a pan of water about 25 minutes in a 350° oven. A crust will form on top. Serve hot or cold with whipped cream. Makes 6-8 portions.

ANGEL PIE

4½ tablespoons cornstarch
 ¾ cup sugar
1½ cups boiling water
 ⅜ teaspoon salt
 3 eggs (whites only)
 3 tablespoons sugar
1½ teaspoons vanilla
 1 cup whipping cream
 1 square bitter chocolate, grated
   9-inch pie crust, baked

Mix cornstarch and sugar in top of double boiler. Add boiling water, stirring constantly. Cook until thick and clear, about 10-12 minutes. Add salt to egg whites and beat until stiff. Add 3 tablespoons sugar and vanilla, beating until eggs are creamy. Pour hot cornstarch mixture slowly over the egg whites beating continuously. Cool slightly, then pour into pie shell. Top with whipped cream and sprinkle grated chocolate over pie. Chill for at least 2 hours before serving.

KENTUCKY BOURBON YAMS

Open 4 No. 2½ cans of yams. Heat potatoes and juice, mash well, then add 2 cups sugar, 4 tablespoons butter, 4 tablespoons milk and 8 ounces of Bourbon. Beat mixture until light and fluffy. Pour out into 1-quart casserole and top with marshmallows. Bake in 350° oven about 15 minutes. Serves 8.

SUPREME OF PHEASANT GRAND VENEUR

Remove the breast of a pheasant (one makes 2 servings), leave skin on. Marinate for 24 hours in a mixture of: 2 ounces olive oil; 2 ounces brandy; 2 ounces sherry wine; 1 bay leaf; 2 whole cloves; a few parsley sprigs; ¼ stalk celery, diced; salt and pepper, to taste; ½ cup onion, diced; 4 shallots, diced, and a pinch of 4 spices (select your own favorites). After 24 hours remove pheasant from marinade and dry in clean towel. Cook in a hot thick skillet with clarified butter. Place in 350° oven for 25-30 minutes, until done and golden brown. Remove fat from pan, then add 6 ounces fresh mushrooms, diced; 2 ounces shallots, chopped; and 3 ounces sherry. Let simmer covered in oven for five minutes.

Set pheasant breasts on toast squares covered with ham slice; arrange on serving dish. Keep covered and hot while finishing sauce. Add 3 ounces coffee cream to simmering sauce and boil together until it thickens. Put in 1 ounce game meat glacé, 2 ounces sweet butter, juice of ½ lemon and 1 tablespoon freshly chopped parsley. Pour a little sauce over pheasant and serve rest from a separate dish. Garnish platter with gondolas of sweet potatoes, filled candied fruit, topped with marshmallow glaze and glazed pineapple rings with kumquats. Serve hot wild rice separately. If, even in reading, all this work tires you, better plan to visit the Campbell House Hotel where this dish is elegantly served with no effort on your part.

PAINTING BY MAURICE METZGER

Indiana Cafe

For twenty-four years Erma Bullock has owned and operated this popular restaurant on U. S. Highway 41 in Crofton, Kentucky. The dining room is open daily from 9:30 a.m. to 10:30 p.m. In addition to the regular tasty menu there is a special one for children, and a smorgasbord with an outstanding array of dishes is served on Sunday, noon to 8:30 p.m.

PAINTING BY ROBERT WATHEN

Campbell House Hotel

This year-round resort in the famed Bluegrass section of Kentucky is on U.S. 68 South (the Old Harrodsburg Road) about a quarter-mile south of the city limits of Lexington. Winners Circle dining room is open daily 6:30 a.m. to 11:30 p.m. Golf and swimming in all seasons. Overnight accommodations and vacation facilities. Len B. Shouse, III, is the manager.

Wilbur Hotel

The Barnhill family owns and operates this friendly hotel on U.S. 25 W (corner of Laurel and Center Streets) in downtown Corbin, Kentucky. Surrounded by the beauty of the Cumberland National Forest recreation area, the dining room is popular with tourists the year around. Breakfast, lunch and dinner served every day; dining room closed Sunday evening from October to June.

The Butlers' Canvasback Motor Inn

Midway between Baltimore and Wilmington on U. S. Highways 40 and 222, this fine inn is in Perryville, Maryland. Meals served daily 7:45 a.m. to 10:00 p.m. Overnight accommodations and vacation facilities. Owned and managed by Mr. and Mrs. Richard S. Butler.

FROSTED LIME WALNUT SALAD

1 package lime Jello
1 cup boiling water
1 No. 2 can crushed pineapple (do not drain)
1 cup cottage cheese
½ cup celery, chopped
½ cup walnuts, chopped
8 ounces cream cheese
1 tablespoon mayonnaise
1 teaspoon lemon juice

Combine Jello with boiling water. When dissolved add crushed pineapple, cottage cheese, chopped celery and chopped walnuts. Pour into a 8 x 4-inch loaf pan or mold. Refrigerate. Combine cream cheese with mayonnaise and lemon juice, and when gelatin is firm and has been removed from pan, spread this mixture on top. Slice into 6-8 portions and serve on crisp lettuce.

COLE SLAW

1 head cabbage, shredded
1 small carrot, shredded
1 tablespoon celery seed
1 cup crushed pineapple, drained
1 cup salad dressing
Salt, to taste

Mix ingredients thoroughly. Chill overnight before serving. Makes 6-8 portions.

SALAD DRESSING

2 tablespoons sugar
½ teaspoon dry mustard
1 heaping tablespoon flour
1 teaspoon salt
3 generous dashes of Tabasco
1 tablespoon butter
½ cup vinegar
½ cup water
2 whole eggs
½-1 cup salad oil

Mix dry ingredients with butter, vinegar and water. Place in double boiler and cook until smooth. Add well-beaten eggs. Stir constantly until thickened. Remove from heat and cool. Beat in oil until dressing has absorbed as much as it will hold. Dressing should not be oily or greasy. Makes 1 quart.

PECAN PIE

Slowly beat ¾ cup sugar into 3 lightly beaten eggs. Add 1 cup dark corn syrup and ¼ pound melted butter. Pour this mixture into a 9-inch unbaked pie shell and bake in 300° oven for about 40 minutes. Then completely cover pie with 1 cup pecan halves and return to 350° oven for 10-15 minutes. Serve cold, topped with whipped cream.

PAINTING BY HOWARD FRECH

Francis Scott Key Hotel

Located at West Patrick and North Court streets in Frederick, Maryland, the hotel is forty-two miles northwest of Washington, D. C. Meals are served every day from 7:00 a.m. to 10:00 p.m.; light snacks, 11:30 a.m. to midnight. Overnight accommodations. W. J. Casey is the manager. Nearby tourist attractions include Barbara Frietchie's home and the grave of Francis Scott Key.

CRAB SOUP, SHORE STYLE

1½ cups celery, chopped
1 cup carrots, chopped
1 cup onion, chopped
2 quarts hot water
1 cup whole-kernel corn
1 small green pepper, chopped
¾ teaspoon mixed pickling spices
⅜ teaspoon red pepper
⅜ teaspoon white pepper
1 tablespoon Worcestershire sauce
2¼ teaspoons salt
3 jumbo-size hard crabs, steamed and chopped into large pieces
1 cup raw potatoes, diced
1½ cups tomato
⅜ pound crab clawmeat
2 cups additional water

Place celery, carrots and onion in a large saucepan containing 2 quarts hot water. Cook until half tender. Add corn, green pepper, pickling spices, red and white pepper, Worcestershire sauce and salt. Cook 1 hour. In the meantime steam crabs, preferably just long enough to kill them. Remove back shell, "devil" and face of crab. Add remainder of crabs, shell and all, which have been chopped into large pieces. Stir in potatoes, tomato, clawmeat and 2 cups water. Simmer 1 hour. Makes 1 gallon. Serves 10-12.

PAINTING BY EVERETT C. ROSE

Chesapeake Restaurant

Located at 1707 North Charles Street in downtown Baltimore, Maryland, this fine restaurant is open noon to 2 a.m. every day except Monday. Closed two weeks in July. The Friedman family owns and manages this popular eating place. It has been remodeled and enlarged recently to include three adjoining buildings. Reservations advisable.

Fergus' Ark

This unusual floating restaurant is moored in the Cape Fear River directly across from the battleship *U.S.S. North Carolina* at Wilmington, North Carolina. It is just three blocks from U. S. Highways 17, 421, 74 and 76, at the foot of Princess Street. Open 11:30 a.m. to 10:00 p.m. every day. Closed Christmas Eve and Christmas Day. Eldridge Fergus is the owner.

Boundary Tree Motor Lodge

On U.S. Highway 441, in Cherokee, North Carolina, at the entrance to the Great Smoky Mountains National Park, this motor lodge is set against a backdrop of massive mountains and faces Oconaluftee River. Owned and operated by the Eastern Band of Cherokee Indians, it offers breakfast, lunch and dinner daily; reservations advisable for overnight accommodations and vacation facilities.

STUFFED SOUTHERN FLOUNDER

4 18- to 20-ounce whole flounder
1/2 tablespoon chopped parsley
1/2 tablespoon Worcestershire sauce
1/2 teaspoon salt
1/8 teaspoon cayenne pepper
1/4 teaspoon lemon juice
1/8 teaspoon dry mustard
3/4 tablespoon butter
1/2 tablespoon flour
1/2 cup milk
8 ounces crabmeat
1/2 cup bread crumbs
8 raw shrimp (optional)
1/2 cup water

Clean flounder, removing head and trimming tail. Make a split 4 to 5 inches long down the center of each and form into a pocket by separating the meat from the bone. Mix together in a bowl: parsley, Worcestershire, salt, cayenne, lemon juice and mustard. Set aside. Then melt butter, stir in flour and add to milk. Cook to boiling point but do not boil. Add first mixture and mix well. Fold in crabmeat and blend in bread crumbs thoroughly. Divide into 4 portions and stuff pockets of flounder. Top each with two raw shrimp (optional). Broil for 10 minutes. Then steam in closed pan with 1/2 cup water for 20 minutes at 350°. If each flounder is cooked in individual pan, use 4 tablespoons water per fish. Serves 4 to 6.

CHERRY COBBLER

Combine 3 tablespoons cornstarch with 3/4 cup of sugar; gradually add 1 cup cherry juice. Heat to boiling point over direct heat and boil gently for 3 minutes, stirring constantly. Add 1 tablespoon butter, 1 tablespoon lemon juice, 1/4 teaspoon almond extract and 4 cups pitted cherries, drained. Pour into deep baking dish. Place 1 1/2-inch wide strips of pastry *(below)* on top of cherries and bake 15 minutes at 425°.

Pastry: Mix 2 cups flour with 1 teaspoon salt. Cut in 1 cup shortening or lard. Mix in 1/4 cup cold milk.

OUTER BANKS
CLAM CHOWDER

¼ pound salt pork or bacon,
    diced fine
1 cup onion, diced
2 cups clams, chopped or ground
    (save juice)
4 cups water
2 cups white potatoes, finely diced

Brown pork or bacon in a heavy iron or aluminum pot. Sauté onion in fat. Add clams and simmer mixture for 15 minutes. Add 4 cups water and simmer 1 hour. Add potatoes and 3 to 4 cups additional water depending on how thick a chowder is desired. Simmer covered for 2 hours. This will serve 6. If kept in refrigerator it may be reheated and served again.

PAINTING BY JULIA BRISTOW

The Carolinian

On U. S. Highway 158, eighty-six miles southeast of Norfolk, Virginia, at Nags Head, North Carolina (on the Outer Banks), this resort hotel faces the Atlantic Ocean. Breakfast, lunch and dinner served every day. Guest rooms in the hotel or in detached cottages. Complete recreation facilities. The clam chowder is a typical dish of the region. Manager is Julian Oneto.

CHOCOLATE
UPSIDE-DOWN CAKE

¾ cup white sugar
3 tablespoons cocoa
1½ tablespoons butter
½ cup milk
¾ cup sifted flour
1½ level teaspoons baking powder
⅛ teaspoon salt
¾ teaspoon vanilla
¾ cup black walnuts

Combine sugar and cocoa, add to melted butter. Then add milk and dry ingredients. Add vanilla and nuts to batter and pour into a 5x7-inch greased pan. Then pour sauce *(below)* over batter and bake in 300° oven for approximately 45 minutes. Leave in pan; turn each piece upside down onto plate. Serve cold with whipped cream. Makes 10 portions.

Sauce: Combine ½ cup white sugar and ½ cup brown sugar with 3 tablespoons cocoa. Add mixture to 1⅓ cups boiling water. Pour over cake batter.

PAINTING BY CORYDON BELL

The Towne House

The dining room was added on to an old home which was built in the 1870's. Southern dishes are a specialty and all of the breads and desserts are prepared in the restaurant's own kitchen. Lunch served noon to 2:00 p.m. and dinner 5:30 p.m. to 8:00 p.m. every day. In Waynesville, North Carolina, the address is 460 Main Street (U.S. Highways 19A and 23), near the business district.

PAINTING BY WILLIAM HALSEY

Jack Tar Francis Marion Hotel

One of the most popular dining areas in this Charleston, South Carolina, hotel is the Swamp Fox and Trophy Room with its décor reminiscent of a delightful old Southern courtyard. Lunch and dinner served in this room every weekday until midnight. Closed on Sunday. Overnight accommodations and vacation facilities. Entertainment nightly. Joe R. Woods is the manager.

PAINTING BY WILLIAM HALSEY

La Brasca's Spaghetti House

When La Brasca's was opened in 1943, it had a seating capacity of 44. The latest addition to this family-run restaurant is now complete, and there is room for 194. Located a half-mile west of U.S. 17 at 975 King Street in Charleston, South Carolina. Lunch and dinner served daily. Reservations not necessary. Effie and George La Brasca, Jr., are the managers.

CHICKEN COUNTRY CAPTAIN

2 frying chickens, disjointed
¾ cup parsley, chopped
4 green peppers, chopped
4 large onions, chopped
2 tablespoons cooking oil
4 cups whole tomatoes
1 teaspoon mace
2 teaspoons curry powder
  Salt and pepper, to taste
1 clove garlic, chopped fine
1½ cups flour, seasoned with salt,
  pepper and paprika
1 cup currants
4 cups cooked rice
½ pound toasted almonds

Sauté parsley, peppers and onions in oil until tender. Pour into roaster adding tomatoes, spices, salt and pepper. Cook for 15 minutes. Add garlic. Dredge chicken in seasoned flour and fry in oil until brown. Lay chicken pieces in sauce and bake covered at 275° for 1½ hours. Add currants 20 minutes before serving. Arrange chicken pieces on top of rice, top with sauce. Sprinkle with toasted almonds. Serves 8-10.

SPARERIBS BARBECUE

4 pounds spareribs
⅓ cup catsup
¾ cup vinegar
2 teaspoons sugar
1 ounce butter
2 teaspoons hot pepper sauce
1 teaspoon salt
1½ teaspoons Worcestershire sauce

Cook spareribs in water in a 6-quart pan for 1 hour. Remove and cut in serving pieces. Place in pan. Combine remaining ingredients and bring to a boil. Pour over ribs and bake in 375° oven for 30 minutes. Remove and serve hot with sauce. Makes 6 portions.

PEDRO'S BARBECUED PHEASANT

2 pheasants (1½-2 pounds)
1 cup light brown sugar
½ cup table salt
¼ cup black pepper
¼ cup Spanish paprika
½ cup port wine

Mix sugar, salt, pepper and paprika together. Rub this mixture into cleaned pheasants, inside and out. Place pheasants on foil, then sprinkle with wine before wrapping tightly. Marinate overnight in refrigerator. Roast in foil in 350° oven 1½-2 hours. Serve with Wild Rice *(below)* and Wine Sauce *(also below)*.

Wild Rice: Rinse 1 cup wild rice thoroughly in sieve. Bring 5 cups water to a boil and add rice. Boil until rice becomes light and fluffy. Drain in sieve. Do not stir.

Wine Sauce: Melt ½ cup butter in pan. Sauté 1 shallot or 1 teaspoon onion in butter, do not brown. Dissolve 1½ teaspoons cornstarch in 1 cup bouillon or stock. Blend slowly into butter, stirring constantly. Add 3 ounces sauterne wine and bring to a boil. Simmer for 15 minutes or until mixture thickens, stirring occasionally. Remove from heat and add 1 tablespoon sour cream and a dash of lemon juice. Serve sauce over wild rice.

COCONUT CREAM PIE

Mix 2 cups milk and 1 cup sugar in double boiler and bring water to boil. Blend 3 beaten egg yolks and 2 heaping tablespoons cornstarch; add to mixture in double boiler. Boil until thick, about 3-4 minutes, stirring to prevent lumping. Remove from heat; add 4 tablespoons butter, ¼ teaspoon salt, 1 teaspoon vanilla and 1 cup coconut. Cool. Pour into a 9-inch baked pie shell. Top with 1 cup sweetened whipping cream and garnish with coconut. Refrigerate.

PAINTING BY WILLIAM HALSEY

South of the Border

A convenient stop for motorists, this establishment rambles over 40 acres which include a restaurant, motel, swimming pool, gift shop and a well-equipped service station. The dining room is open 'round the clock and serves light snacks as well as gourmet dishes. Located on U.S. 301N and U.S. 501, just six miles north of Dillon, South Carolina, at the North Carolina line.

PAINTING BY CORYDON BELL

Mountain View Hotel

Surrounded by thirty acres of grounds, this fine resort hotel is located in the center of Gatlinburg, Tennessee, a small mountain village on the north central boundary of the Great Smoky Mountains National Park. Breakfast served 7:00 to 9:30 a.m.; lunch, noon to 2:00 p.m.; and dinner, 6:00 to 8:00 p.m. Overnight accommodations. The area offers limitless family recreation facilities.

J & R Grill *(formerly Todd's)*

In an area of lush tobacco fields and horse-breeding farms, the restaurant is located on the Public Square on U.S. 31 in Franklin, Tennessee. Opens for breakfast every day at 6:30 a.m.; closes at 8:00 p.m. Closed the first week in June. Specialties are homemade rolls and biscuits, and Tennessee country ham. Mr. and Mrs. Jesse Jones are the owners.

ROLLED ROAST WITH MUSHROOMS

1 6-pound rib roast of beef
1 No. 303 can mushrooms
1 large can pimentos, well drained
1 green pepper
2 hard-boiled eggs
　Salt and pepper, to taste
¾ cup each onion and celery,
　chopped

Have ribs removed from beef. Chop combined mushrooms, pimentos, green pepper and eggs. Season. Spread on meat, roll tightly and tie securely. Place in 450° oven for 45 minutes. Reduce heat to 350° and roast for 60 minutes. Baste with water and a little bacon fat while roasting. When meat is finished add onion and celery to the pan broth. Boil and add light thickening and simmer. Serve gravy over meat slices. Makes 12 portions.

Blackberry Farm

High on a spur of Chilhowee Mountain in the Great Smokies, this picturesque inn lies in the midst of a 750-acre estate. Breakfast, lunch and dinner served daily to non-guests, except Monday. Overnight accommodations and recreation facilities. Open March 15 to November 15. Take State Highway 73 out of Maryville to Walland, Tennessee; turn west on Millers Cove Road to the Farm.

JEFFERSON DAVIS PIE

½ cup butter
2 cups light brown sugar
4 eggs, separated
2 tablespoons flour
1 teaspoon cinnamon
1 teaspoon freshly grated nutmeg
½ teaspoon allspice
1 cup cream
½ cup pecans, chopped
½ cup raisins
½ cup dates, chopped
　10-inch pie shell

Cream butter and sugar together, then beat in egg yolks. Sift flour, cinnamon, nutmeg and allspice into mixture. Add cream, pecans, raisins and dates. Brown empty crust in 450° oven for 5 minutes; add filling. Bake in 300° oven until set, about 40 minutes. When cool, top with meringue made of egg whites. Brown meringue in 300° oven 15-20 minutes.

BLACK BOTTOM PIE

1¼ cups milk
2 eggs, well beaten
½ cup sugar
3⅔ tablespoons cornstarch
1 ounce Baker's bitter chocolate, melted
1 teaspoon vanilla
1 tablespoon light rum
¾ cup whipping cream
½ ounce bitter chocolate, tiny chips
9-inch gingersnap crust

Scald milk in double boiler, then slowly add beaten eggs and blend well. Mix sugar and cornstarch and stir into egg mixture. Cook 15-20 minutes in double boiler, stirring occasionally. When cooked custard generously coats spoon it is done. Take ⅓ of hot custard and mix slowly with melted chocolate until cool. Add vanilla to chocolate custard. Stir balance of custard slowly until cool to avoid lumping. When cool add rum and blend. Whip cream until it peaks. Add chocolate filling to cooled gingersnap crust, completely covering crust. Add rum custard and level across pie. Top with whipped cream and sprinkle with chips of chocolate.

Gingersnap Crust: Roll 14 crisp gingersnaps out fine and then add 5 tablespoons melted butter. Pat evenly into 9-inch pie tin and bake 10 minutes at 300°. Cool.

PELL'S BREAD

Heat 2¼ cups homogenized milk to 180°; cool to 110-112°. Dissolve 1 ounce dry yeast, 1 ounce salt, 1½ tablespoons honey or sugar, 2 well-beaten eggs and ¼ cup melted shortening into cooled milk. Mix into 2 pounds hard wheat flour with electric mixer at low speed 5-8 minutes. Knead dough, then let rise at room temperature until double in size. Shape into 2 loaves and place on a greased baking sheet, allowing to rise a second time until double in size. Bake at 340° for 30 minutes, remove and brush loaves with butter. Slice an inch thick or more and serve very hot. Yields two 27-ounce loaves.

PAINTING BY HAM EMBREE

Dobbs House Luau

A pool of water from which a flame erupts and a twenty-five-foot Easter Island idol are a few of the spectacular decorative features of this Polynesian-style restaurant. In addition to the exotic menu, it serves many old Southern favorites. Lunch and dinner served daily. It is five miles east of downtown Memphis, Tennessee, at 3135 Poplar Avenue (U. S. Highway 72). Open the year round.

PAINTING BY CORYDON BELL

Newport Motor Court and Restaurant

At the city limits of Newport, Tennessee, on West Broadway (U. S. Highways 70, 25W and E, and 411) this restaurant is only 12 miles from the Great Smoky Mountains National Park. Open 6:00 a.m. to 10:00 p.m. Closed Christmas. Overnight accommodations.

Dixie Hotel Dining Room

On the Public Square in Shelbyville, Tennessee, 1 block off U.S. Highway 231 at 316 North Main Street, this hotel is famous for serving the old-fashioned Southern dishes which have made the region's home cooking famous. Furnished with interesting antiques, the dining room is open for breakfast, lunch and dinner. Closed on Saturday and Sunday nights. Overnight accommodations.

Christiana Campbell's Tavern

This quaint restaurant is part of the Williamsburg Restoration in Virginia. In the summer, diners may eat on the porch overlooking the reconstructed colonial garden. Lunch served noon to 2:30 p.m.; dinner, 6:00 p.m. to 8:30 p.m. every day. Reservations necessary for dinner. Overnight accommodations available at other facilities in the Williamsburg Restoration.

DIXIE FRIED CHICKEN WITH GRAVY

    1 2-pound chicken, cut to fry
    1 cup cooking oil
    1 egg
  ½ cup sweet milk
    1 cup all-purpose flour
    1 teaspoon salt
  ¼ teaspoon black pepper

Heat oil in heavy cast-iron skillet. Beat egg and combine with milk. Sift together flour, salt and pepper. Dip chicken, piece by piece, in milk and egg mixture and then in flour. Drop gently in hot oil and brown, turning as necessary. Reduce heat and cook until done, about 30 minutes.

Gravy: Remove chicken from skillet and pour off excess fat. Lightly brown 2 tablespoons flour in the remaining 2-3 tablespoons oil and add a mixture of 1 cup water, 1 cup milk, ½ teaspoon salt and ¼ teaspoon black pepper. Stir constantly over high heat until desired thickness is reached. This gravy is not completely smooth as it includes the scrapings from the bottom of the skillet. Makes 3 servings.

RUM CREAM PIE

    5 egg yolks
  ¾ cup sugar
    1 envelope gelatin
  ½ cup cold water
  ¾ cup whipping cream
1½ ounces dark rum
       9-inch crumb pie shell

Beat egg yolks until light and add sugar. Soak gelatin in cold water; put over low fire and bring to a boil and pour it over sugar-egg mixture, stirring briskly. Whip cream until stiff, fold it into the egg mixture and flavor with rum. Cool until mixture begins to set and pour into pie shell. Chill until firm. Sprinkle top of pie with shaved chocolate, and garnish with whipped cream if desired. Serve cold.

ICE BOX CHEESE CAKE

Beat 3 eggs; add ⅓ cup milk and 1 pound cottage cheese sieved through a ricer. Combine 7 tablespoons sugar, ⅓ teaspoon salt, 3 tablespoons flour and ¾ teaspoon lemon rind. Add to cheese mixture and cook in top of double boiler until thick, about 15 minutes over medium heat, stirring. Remove from heat, add 1 teaspoon lemon juice and cool. Whip 1 cup whipping cream and fold into cooled mixture. Roll ½ pound graham crackers fine; add ⅓ teaspoon cinnamon, pinch of salt and 3 tablespoons melted butter. Line a 4x10-inch loaf pan with waxed paper and cover with ⅓ of the crumb mixture. Pour in half of cheese mixture, add another ⅓ of crumb mixture, and finally the remaining cheese topped with crumbs. Let stand in refrigerator about 5 hours. Turn out and slice. Keeps for a week in refrigerator. Makes 8 portions.

PAINTING BY HORACE DAY

Dorothy's Inn

On one of the seven bends in the Shenandoah River, this delightful country hotel is two miles south of Woodstock, Virginia, on U.S. 11. Meals are served continuously from 6:00 a.m. to 9:00 p.m. daily. Overnight accommodations. Mr. and Mrs. R. T. Satchell are the owners and managers of Dorothy's Inn and all of the food is prepared by Mrs. Satchell.

HUGUENOT TORTE

  4 eggs
  3 cups sugar
  2 cups bread flour
  5 teaspoons baking powder
½ teaspoon salt
  2 cups tart cooking apples
  2 cups chopped pecans or walnuts
  1 teaspoon vanilla
    Whipped cream

Beat whole eggs in electric mixer or with rotary beater until very frothy and fluffy. Fold remaining ingredients in gently except whipped cream. Pour into two *well-buttered* baking pans about 8 by 12 inches. Bake in 325° oven about 45 minutes or until crusty and brown. Cool to serve, scoop up with pancake turner in 4-inch squares (keeping crusty part on top). Put on dessert plate and cover with sweetened whipped cream and a sprinkling of chopped nuts. Makes 12 servings. This dessert is very moist and chewy and will keep for a week.

PAINTING BY JULIA BRISTOW

Evans Farm Inn

The gracious atmosphere of life in the Old Dominion is recaptured in this unique Virginia inn. Located five miles from Washington, D.C., at 5743 Chain Bridge Road (Route 123), McLean, Virginia, the Inn features early American cookery amid early American decor. Buffet lunch served noon to 2:30 p.m.; dinners served from 5:00 until 9:00 p.m. Closed on Christmas Day.

Thomas Jefferson Inn

One of the finest motor hotels in America, this establishment was opened in 1951. The dining room is famous for its excellent food. Breakfast is served 7:00 to 9:30 a.m.; lunch, noon to 2:00 p.m.; dinner, 6:00 to 8:30 p.m. Overnight accommodations and recreation facilities. Located on U.S. 29 north of Charlottesville, Virginia, near the U.S. 250 by-pass.

GLAZED STRAWBERRY PIE

    1 quart ripe, firm strawberries
    1 cup whipped cream
      10-inch pie shell, baked

Brush a thin coating of hot glaze over the bottom of the pie shell. Arrange strawberries in the shell and brush only enough glaze on berries to cover their exposed surface. When the pie is cool border or strip with whipped cream.

Transparent glaze: Bring the following ingredients to a boil: 1 cup sugar, ⅔ cup water, 2⅔ teaspoons glucose or white corn syrup, and red food coloring. Hold out enough water to dissolve 2⅔ tablespoons tapioca flour. When sugar mixture has come to full boil add the dissolved flour, stirring constantly until thick. Let this mixture return to a full boil. It is best to use the glaze while hot.

Seawell's Ordinary

In the early 1730's, the first horse race in Virginia was held on this property, and in 1757, this was an established eating place. On U.S. 17 in Gloucester, Virginia, the restaurant is a few miles northeast of Williamsburg. Open for breakfast, lunch and dinner seven days a week the year round. Southern bread pudding is a specialty. Maggie Emerson is the owner.

SOUTHERN BREAD PUDDING

     6 eggs
    ½ cup sugar
     2 quarts milk
     1 tablespoon vanilla
    12 slices bread, cut in ½-inch cubes
    ¼ pound butter
    ½ cup raisins

Beat eggs and sugar well; add milk and vanilla; fold in bread cubes. Melt butter in 10x12x2-inch pan and pour in mixture. Sprinkle raisins on top. Cook at 350° for 45 minutes. Remove from oven and let cool. Serve with sauce *(below)*. Yields 20 servings.

Sauce: Beat 1 egg; add 2 tablespoons sugar, 1 pint milk. Cook in double boiler until thick. Remove from heat and add 2 tablespoons sherry; cool. Serve warm or cold on bread pudding.

JELLIED CRANBERRY SALAD

½ pound cherry-flavored gelatin
3 cups raw cranberries, ground
¾ cup pecans, chopped
2 cups celery, chopped
2 cups apples, chopped
2½ tablespoons vinegar
1 teaspoon salt
1 cup sugar

Dissolve gelatin in 1 quart hot water. Add 1 quart cold water. When gelatin starts to congeal, add other ingredients and pour into molds to chill. Serve on lettuce leaf with dressing. 18 portions.

ALMOND COOKIES

Beat ¾ cup egg whites until stiff and combine with 1 pound almond paste to form a stiff paste. Add 1 cup flour, 1 teaspoon baking powder, ½ cup sugar and ½ teaspoon salt. Drop onto greased cooky sheet. Bake in 350° oven for 10 minutes. Makes 25 cookies.

CORN PUDDING

Mix 1 No. 303 can cream-style corn, ½ cup milk, ¼ pound melted butter, 1 beaten egg and dash of salt. Combine 1 tablespoon flour and 1 tablespoon sugar, then fold into corn mixture. Pour into a greased 1-quart casserole and bake in a 300° oven for 45 minutes, or until mixture is browned on top. Serves 4.

ASPARAGUS CASSEROLE

Arrange 2 10½-ounce cans green asparagus tips on bottom of greased baking dish. Season 2 10½-ounce cans mushroom soup with salt and pepper to taste and pour over vegetable. Grate ½ pound sharp cheese over top and sprinkle with 1½ cups cornflake crumbs. Bake at 300° for about 25 minutes. Makes 6 portions.

PAINTING BY FRED D. MESSERSMITH

Chancellor Hotel

At Seventh and Market streets, on Routes 50 and 21A in Parkersburg, West Virginia, this hotel is noted for its well-prepared food and pleasant hotel accommodations. Food service from 6:00 a.m. until midnight. There are three dining areas for guests offering breakfast, lunch and dinner daily except Saturday. Reservations advisable. William Turley is the manager.

PAINTING BY CHARLES L. RIPPER

El Rancho Restaurant and Motel

At 2843 McCorkle Avenue (U.S. Highway 60) in St. Albans, West Virginia, this restaurant is only ten miles west of Charleston. Dining area and motel rooms designed with Western décor. Dining room is open 7:00 a.m. to 9:30 p.m. daily. Closed December 24 and 25.

PAINTING BY GEORGE YATER

NORTH CENTRAL

Seasonings are sophisticated
in this region, the legacy
of good European cooks of
bygone generations who
flocked to the New World and
settled here. Look for a
liberal sprinkling of Old World
dishes—such as sauerbraten,
obst kuchen (fruit cake), and
braccioline (veal rolls).
Orchards are far-flung and
farmlands rich. Fresh-water
fish from the Great Lakes
and the inland lakes and
streams of Michigan, Wisconsin
and Minnesota are a specialty
of the area.

PAINTING BY BERNARD H. BRADLEY

The Milk Pail

Country-style luncheons, game and trout dinners are specialties of this fine restaurant located at Fin'n Feather Farm on Highway 25, Dundee, Illinois (one mile north of Northwest Tollway). The country shops feature their own homemade sausage, smoked hams, bacon, turkey and pheasants. Open daily, 11 a.m. to 9 p.m. except Mondays. Closed December 22 to January 2. Reservations advisable.

SOUR CREAM PANCAKES

2½ cups all-purpose flour
1 tablespoon baking powde:
1 teaspoon salt
1 tablespoon sugar
2 teaspoons baking soda
3 eggs
2 cups buttermilk
2 tablespoons melted butter
1 cup sour cream

Sift dry ingredients together. Beat eggs. Blend liquid and flour mixture alternately. Beat gently until smooth and then fold in melted butter. Cook on hot grill. Serve with melted butter and maple syrup. Makes 18 large pancakes.

PAINTING BY GERALD HARDY

Azuma Sukiyaki Restaurant

Unusual food and the exotic atmosphere of old Japan are combined in this fine restaurant at 5116-20 N. Broadway, Chicago, Illinois. Dishes such as sukiyaki, tempura and teriyaki are prepared at your table by kimono-clad hostesses while you sit on low cushions. Open at 5:00 p.m. daily; on Sunday from 1:00 to 9:00 p.m.; closed Monday and Christmas week.

CHICKEN OR STEAK TERIYAKI

2 broiler chickens, cut in serving pieces, or 5 individual steaks

Using charcoal broiler (charcoal preferable) broil steak or chicken to desired degree of doneness. Just before removing from broiler, baste chicken or steak with sauce on both sides. Turn over several times, exposing the basted side to the heat until a slight glaze is formed. Remove and serve.

Sauce: Heat 1 cup shoyu (Japanese soy sauce) on high fire, then add ⅓ cup Japanese sweet rice wine (Mirin sake) or 3-4 tablespoons sugar, according to taste. Mix well and remove from flame just as sauce comes to a boil. Add 1 tablespoon Japanese rice wine (sake) or any other sweet wine. If desired, add either pinch of garlic, red pepper or ginger. Stir well.

HAM LOAF WITH MUSTARD SAUCE

Grind together 2 pounds lean smoked ham, 1 pound lean beef and ½ pound pork sausage. Mix together thoroughly but lightly with: 1½ cups tomato juice, 2 cups soft bread crumbs, ½ cup finely chopped celery, 2 eggs and 1 level teaspoon freshly ground pepper. Pack into a greased 9¼ x 5¼ x 2¾-inch bread pan. Stand pan in water and bake at 350° for 1½ hours. Makes 8 portions. Serve hot with Mustard Sauce *(below)*.

Mustard Sauce: Fold 1 cup mayonnaise and ¼ cup prepared mustard into 1 cup heavy cream which has been whipped. Add salt to taste.

HAZELNUT PIE

Beat 3 eggs slightly. Add the following ingredients and stir well: ½ cup sugar, ¼ teaspoon salt, 1 cup dark corn syrup, ½ teaspoon vanilla and 1 cup hazelnuts, toasted and chopped. Pour mixture into 9-inch unbaked pie shell and bake in 300° oven for 45 minutes or until set. Serve cold with whipped cream.

GINGER PIE

¼ pound butter
¾ cup confectioners' sugar
2 tablespoons coffee cream
¼ cup preserved ginger, grated
2 tablespoons syrup of ginger
2 cups whipping cream
1 10-inch layer of cake,
  ¼-inch thick
1 tablespoon semisweet chocolate, melted

Cream butter and sugar together. Thin slightly with coffee cream and mix thoroughly. Add ginger and syrup in which ginger is preserved. Whip cream and fold into mixture. Place cake layer in 9-inch pan so that it forms side "crust" for pie. Pile filling onto cake and smooth top surface. Drizzle melted chocolate over top in lacelike pattern. Refrigerate for at least 3 hours. Serves 8-10.

PAINTING BY JIM FISHER

Plentywood Farm

For 32 years the Howell family has run this log cabin restaurant in the same location at 130 South Church Road in Bensenville, Illinois. It is just 20 miles west of Chicago's loop. Lunch served 11:30 a.m. to 2:30 p.m.; dinner, 5:00 p.m. to 9:00 p.m. daily. Sunday and holiday hours are noon to 7:00 p.m. Closed on Monday. A new building adjoins the log cabin.

PAINTING BY WILLADINE NICHOLAS

The Country Squire

This was once a country estate before **Martin** and **Edna Giesel** converted it into a gracious country restaurant. It is north of Chicago, just off U.S. 45, on State Highway 120 in Grayslake, Illinois. Meals are served every day, except Monday, noon to midnight. Reservations are advisable at this popular dining spot. The Giesels' ginger pie is a treat you won't forget.

PAINTING BY GEORGE YATER

Clifty Inn

This inn is at the entrance of Clifty Falls State Park, a 617-acre preserve of wild and rugged beauty near Madison, Indiana. Breakfast, lunch and dinner served daily; overnight accommodations and vacation facilities, including horseback riding, square dancing and trail hikes. The entrance to the Park is on State Highways 56 and 62 or State Highway 107.

PAINTING BY NANENE ENGLE

Smitty's Holiday Inn Restaurant (formerly Hillie's)

At 1241 North Main Street, Evansville, Indiana, this restaurant is just a mile west of U.S. 41. Meals served daily except Sunday, 11:00 a.m. to midnight. Five dining rooms feature smorgasbord every Wednesday night. Owners are Edna K. and Harold Smith.

WHIPPED CREAM TOPPING

½ pound dried apricots
1 teaspoon plain gelatin
1½ cups granulated sugar
1 pint whipping cream
1 angel food cake
2 ounces sliced almonds, toasted

Cover apricots with water and cook until tender. Strain while still hot. Add gelatin which has been dissolved in ⅛ cup cold water. Add sugar and chill. Whip cream and fold in apricot mixture. Pour over cake wedges and sprinkle with nuts.

APPLE DIVINITY

8 apples
1 cup sugar
1½ teaspoons nutmeg
½ pint whipping cream

Line the bottom of an 8x10-inch pan with combined apples, sugar and nutmeg. Put dough over top (below); bake in 350° oven for 25 minutes. Cool; serve with whipped cream. 8 portions.

Dough: Combine 2 eggs, 1 cup sugar, 1 cup flour, 2 tablespoons butter, 1 tablespoon baking powder, and ½ teaspoon salt.

BROILED TROUT

Butter pan. Place 6 cleaned and buttered trout seasoned with salt, pepper and paprika next to each other in the pan. Place pan four inches below broiler and broil until done without turning, about 8 minutes. A good test is to split one of the trout along the backbone; the meat will be juicy and white if the trout is done. Serve hot with parsley, water cress or chive butter (below).

Parsley, Water Cress or Chive Butter: Melt ¼ cup butter and combine with ½ teaspoon salt, ⅛ teaspoon pepper, ¾ teaspoon lemon juice and 2 tablespoons either parsley, water cress or chopped chives over low heat.

CHEESE SPREAD

Grate ½ pound American cheese and let soften. Chop 12 large stuffed olives and crumble ¼-inch wedge Roquefort cheese. Combine ingredients with ⅛ teaspoon garlic extract. Add mayonnaise to spreading consistency. Spread on crackers, bread, toast or potato chips. Garnish with sliced stuffed olives, sweet pickle chips, hard-boiled egg slices or anchovy filets.

PAINTING BY STUART HODGE

The Lark Restaurant

Dale Dahnke is the owner and manager of this Tiffin, Iowa, establishment. Dinner is served every day except Sunday. Closed December 22 to January 3. Only individually prepared foods are served. Specialties are choice steaks, unusual salads, dressings and baked potatoes with sour cream sauce. It is on U.S. 6, about six miles west of Iowa City. No reservations necessary.

OBST KUCHEN (Fruit Cake)

1 cup milk
1½ cups sugar
1 tablespoon salt
1 cake compressed yeast
1 cup lukewarm water
6 cups sifted all-purpose flour
6 tablespoons shortening, melted
3 tablespoons butter, melted
2 cups sliced apples, rhubarb,
    pitted cherries or sliced peaches
2 tablespoons flour
1 egg, beaten
2 tablespoons cream

Scald milk, ½ cup sugar and salt together. Cool until lukewarm. Dissolve yeast in lukewarm water and add to cooled milk. Add 3 cups of flour and beat until smooth. Add melted shortening and remaining flour. Knead well. Place in greased bowl, cover and set in warm place away from drafts. Let rise until double in bulk or about three hours. This makes enough dough for five 9-inch kuchens. Store extra dough in refrigerator. Roll out ⅕ of quantity and place in greased 9-inch pie plate; make a high rim of dough around outside. Brush with butter and sprinkle with ¼ cup sugar. Let rise. Press prepared fruit into dough close together. Sprinkle remaining sugar and flour over fruit. Before baking, combine beaten egg and cream and spoon over fruit. Cover cake with pan and bake for 10 minutes at 425°, then remove pan and continue baking for about 25 minutes more.

PAINTING BY PAUL NORTON

Bill Zuber's Restaurant

This Amana Colony eating place, owned by Bill Zuber, former baseball star, offers Old World foods and hospitality. Located in historic Homestead, Iowa, just off U.S. 6 and State 149, twenty miles west of Iowa City. Open weekdays, 10:30 a.m. to 2:00 p.m., and 4:30 p.m. to 8:30 p.m. Sunday hours are 10:30 a.m. to 8:30 p.m. Closed July 4, December 24, 25 and 31, and January 1.

Lloyd's Restaurant

R. A. Peterson and M. G. Randgaard are the present owners of this famous restaurant. Ten years ago, a new dining room was built on U.S. 30 (the Lincoln Highway), four miles west of Marshalltown, Iowa. It is open 11:00 a.m. to 9:00 p.m. every day except Monday. This fine eating place is closed December 18 to March 5. No reservations necessary.

Ox Yoke Inn

In the midst of the famous Amana Colony, this restaurant is in the century-old home of one of the early settlers. Lunch and dinner served daily, family style. William and Lina Leichsenring own and manage this establishment which is two blocks east of Iowa Highway 149, in Amana, Iowa (20 miles west of Iowa City). Hickory-smoked meats may be ordered by mail.

THANKSGIVING SALAD MOLD

> 2 cups juice of any fruit *except* lemon or grapefruit
> 1 package lemon gelatin
> 1 cup whole cranberry sauce
> 1 cup fresh apple, diced
> 1 cup celery, diced
> ½ cup pecans, chopped
> ½ cup Tokay grapes, halved
> Tiny marshmallows (optional)

Heat fruit juice over low fire and add gelatin, stir until it dissolves. Add remaining ingredients and pour into 12 individual molds. Refrigerate.

BUTTER RUM SAUCE

Heat in double boiler 1 cup orange juice, 1 cup water, ¾ cup sugar and 4 tablespoons butter. Add enough moistened cornstarch to thicken. When mixture is smooth and thick add salt, to taste, 2 tablespoons rum flavor and 1 teaspoon vanilla. Serve warm over mincemeat pie. Makes 8-10 servings.

OX YOKE SAUERBRATEN

Combine: 3 cups vinegar; 3 cups water; 1 onion, sliced; 3 bay leaves; 3 cloves; 1 teaspoon salt; 2 whole peppers and ½ lemon, sliced. Marinate 3 pounds beef, sirloin or chuck, in combined spices and liquids for 3 days. Turn meat once a day. Save vinegar broth. Brown meat in hot fat on third day. Remove meat from fat and brown ½ cup flour in fat. Add vinegar broth; boil mixture until it thickens. Add meat to gravy and cover. Bake in 325° oven 2½-3 hours. Turn and baste meat several times. About 30 minutes before meat is done add ¼ cup red wine, 3 gingersnaps and 1 tablespoon sugar. When meat is done remove from gravy, skim grease from gravy and strain. Serve with potato dumplings or noodles. Makes 6 portions.

CHOCOLATE CAKE

½ cup butter
2 cups sugar
2 eggs, well beaten
2 cups cake flour
2 teaspoons baking powder
½ teaspoon salt
4 squares chocolate, melted
1½ cups milk
1 teaspoon vanilla
1 cup nut meats, chopped

Cream butter and sugar together; add eggs and mix well. Sift flour, baking powder and salt together. Add chocolate to batter and alternate adding dry ingredients with milk and vanilla (about three parts of each). Add nut meats. Bake in three 9-inch tins at 350° about 30 minutes or until done.

Frosting: Cream together ½ cup butter and 1½ cups confectioners' sugar. Add 1 well-beaten egg, blend well. Stir in 2 squares melted chocolate, ½ teaspoon salt, 1 teaspoon vanilla, 1 teaspoon lemon juice and 1 cup chopped nut meats. Blend and frost cooled cake.

ALMOND RUM CREAM PIE

⅔ cup fine granulated sugar
⅓ cup cake flour
Generous dash of salt
2 large eggs, slightly beaten
8 tablespoons rum
1½ cups scalded milk
½ cup almonds, blanched and toasted
1 cup whipping cream, whipped
½ cup unsweetened chocolate, shaved
9-inch crumb pie shell, chilled

Sift sugar, flour and salt into top of double boiler. Stir in eggs with 3 tablespoons of rum. When thoroughly blended, stir in scalded milk with 5 tablespoons rum very gradually, almost drop by drop. Cook over hot water, stirring constantly, until the mixture thickens. Cool. Sprinkle pie shell with almonds and pour in rum cream filling. Cover with whipped cream and garnish with shaved chocolate.

PAINTING BY CHARLES CULVER

Indian River Inn

A fine year-round resort in northern Michigan, the Inn is distinguished by its excellent food, charming décor and the Southern hospitality of its hosts, Mr. and Mrs. Jerry DeVore. Breakfast, lunch and dinner served daily 7:00 a.m. to 10:00 p.m. Overnight accommodations and vacation facilities. Located on State Highway 27 in Indian River, south of the Mackinac Bridge.

PAINTING BY DON GOOCH

Weber's Supper Club

Located two miles west of Ann Arbor, Michigan, at 3050 Jackson Road (U.S. Highway I-94, off ramp at Ann Arbor), this restaurant is open daily noon to midnight. Closed all legal holidays. Owner Herman Weber also operates the Holiday House Motel, open the year around. The restaurant's almond rum cream pie is a favorite.

Chimney Corner

Walls papered with menus from all over the world lend a decorative touch to this excellent restaurant located in the center of one of Michigan's booming winter sports areas at Petoskey. Conveniently situated at the intersection of U.S. Highway 31 and State Highway 131-North, it is open the year around for lunch and dinner. Their famous shrimp batter has made fried shrimp a favorite.

Hillside Inn

The Stemich family owns and manages this delightful Colonial restaurant at 41661 Plymouth Road, east of Plymouth, Michigan (about twenty-five miles west of Detroit). The parking lot is cleverly lighted with antique gas street lights which were collected from salvage yards all over the country. Lunch and dinner served daily except Sunday. Closed holidays.

FAMOUS SHRIMP BATTER

    6 pounds raw shrimp
    2 eggs, separated
    1 teaspoon paprika
    1 tablespoon butter, melted
    ⅔ cup milk
    ¼ cup water
    ½ cup flour
    1 teaspoon salt
    1 tablespoon lemon juice
       Deep fat

Beat together egg yolks, paprika and butter. Add milk, water and flour alternately to mixture, stirring constantly. Add salt and lemon juice. Mix well. Beat egg whites until stiff and fold into batter. Clean raw shrimp and run hot water over them. Dip shrimp in batter and fry in deep fat at 375° until they are golden brown. Serve with hot sauce. Makes 8-10 servings.

CHICKEN LIVER PASTE

    2 pounds chicken livers
    1 pound fat pork
    1 medium-size onion
    ½ teaspoon sage
    ½ teaspoon allspice
    ¼ teaspoon mace
    ¼ teaspoon nutmeg
    ½ teaspoon clove
    2 teaspoons salt
    ½ teaspoon black pepper
    2 tablespoons flour
    3 tablespoons cream
    4 tablespoons brandy
    2 eggs, slightly beaten

Put meat portions through medium food chopper three times. Add remaining ingredients and put through chopper again, using fine cutter.

Rub baking pan with clove of garlic around sides before filling with mixture. Place baking pan in a larger pan filled with water to the level of meat. Bake in water pan bath at 300° for 3 hours. If crust forms at top of liver paste before 1½ hours, cover with greased paper for rest of time. Cool in baking pan until room temperature, then cover and refrigerate until serving time. Excellent for appetizers or open-face sandwiches.

SIRLOIN TIPS RAGOUT AU VIN

3 pounds sirloin tips, 1-inch cubes
3 tablespoons butter
3 ounces tomato paste
2 tablespoons wine vinegar
1 cup Burgundy
1 stick of cinnamon
2 bay leaves
2 pounds tiny whole onions, peeled
1 teaspoon salt
¼ teaspoon pepper
1 teaspoon cornstarch

Place cubes of meat in deep saucepan with butter. Simmer meat over medium heat, stirring constantly, until meat is brown and tender. Mix tomato paste, vinegar and wine with browned meat. Add remaining ingredients, except cornstarch. Simmer covered for 1 hour. Mix cornstarch with ¼ cup water and blend into sauce. Serve hot. Makes 6 portions.

BARBECUED PORK SPARERIBS

2 pounds back pork spareribs
1 cup apple juice
1 cup grapefruit juice
¼ cup chili sauce
¼ cup brown sugar
1 tablespoon soy sauce
Dash of Liquid Smoke
Dash of Worcestershire
1 clove garlic, chopped
Pinch of freshly ground pepper

Bake spareribs, seasoned with salt, in a moderate oven for 1 hour. Combine remaining ingredients and baste spareribs often with this sauce during next ½ hour of baking. Makes 4 portions.

SPECIAL SEAFOOD SAUCE

½ cup chili sauce
½ cup tomato catsup
1 teaspoon horse-radish
½ stalk celery, chopped fine
¼ small onion, grated
1 clove garlic, grated
¼ green pepper, chopped fine
Few drops of Worcestershire sauce
Salt and pepper, to taste

Combine ingredients well and chill. Serve with shrimp or other seafood.

PAINTING BY BILL MOSS

The Surf

The three dining rooms overlook Lake Michigan at this restaurant which is set amidst 250 acres of woodland. It is open until 1:00 a.m. daily, serving breakfast, lunch and dinner. Closed November 25 to April 15. The Surf is on U.S. 2 (Lake Shore Drive), just two miles east of Manistique, in Michigan's Upper Peninsula. Beach is across from the restaurant.

PAINTING BY CHARLES CULVER

Colonial Inn

Jack Davis and Fred Renker are the owners of this elegant antique-filled summer hostelry in Harbor Springs, Michigan, close to State Highway 131 and U.S. 31. The area offers golf, boating and sight-seeing. Breakfast, lunch and dinner served daily June 1 to October 1. Overnight accommodations available. Reservations advised. Mackinac Bridge is nearby.

PAINTING BY BIRNEY QUICK

The Lowell Inn

Just forty-five minutes from the Twin Cities, on State Highways 95, 212 and 36, this famous country inn is at 102 North 2nd Street in Stillwater, Minnesota. Breakfast, lunch and dinner served daily; overnight accommodations. Reservations advisable. Nelle O. Palmer has owned and managed this outstanding hostelry for thirty-two years, maintaining its excellent standards.

LOWELL INN RED CABBAGE

1 medium head red cabbage
1 medium sweet onion
2 large apples
1 heaping tablespoon bacon fat
1 teaspoon salt
½ cup sugar
1 cup vinegar
1½ cups water
1 bay leaf
2 whole allspice
2 cloves (heads removed)
6 peppercorns

Remove outer leaves from cabbage and wash the head. Core cabbage and slice. Peel onion and apples and slice. Toss cabbage, onion and apple together. Add remaining ingredients to cabbage mixture and simmer 1½ hours in a covered pan. Thicken slightly with about 2 tablespoons of cornstarch blended with cold water. This dish is especially good with wild game of any kind and is excellent reheated. Makes 6 servings.

PAINTING BY GEORGE RUNGE

Hollands

At 216 First Avenue S.W., in downtown Rochester, Minnesota, Hollands is a block from the famed Mayo Clinic. Two cafeterias and a sandwich shop are open daily except Sunday for breakfast, lunch and dinner. Newton Holland was one of the first restaurant owners to display art works; today there are three galleries. Leon Latz now owns the 54-year-old restaurant.

HOLLANDS REQUEST SALAD

½ cup dry raisins
¼ cup mayonnaise
¼ cup crushed pineapple
⅓ teaspoon salt
2 cups carrots, shredded
½ cup celery, chopped
¼ cup pineapple, diced

Soak raisins overnight. Drain. Combine mayonnaise, crushed pineapple and salt. Combine all remaining ingredients. Serve on lettuce. Makes 10 portions.

HAMBURG SOUP

In the oven brown 3 ounces ground onion and 8 ounces ground beef; season with salt and pepper and ⅓ teaspoon sugar. Add 1½ cups tomato; 2 cups tomato juice; 1 cup carrots, diced; 2 cups water and ¼ pound rice. Simmer mixture on top of stove for 1 hour. Add 1 teaspoon horse-radish, ½ teaspoon vinegar before serving. Makes 8 cups.

LEMON VELVET ICE CREAM

Mix together 2 cups whipping cream, 2 cups milk and 2 cups sugar. Milk and cream should be very cold. Then add ⅓ cup fresh lemon juice, stirring slowly. Mixture thickens as juice is added. Place in 2-quart dasher-type ice cream freezer and freeze immediately to prevent curdling. Remove dasher before ice cream is completely frozen. Pack in salt and ice and let stand for an hour or more. For best flavor use the same day. This ice cream can also be made with good results in tray of electric refrigerator. Makes about 1½ quarts.

ANGEL PUFF

  8 egg whites (room temperature)
½ teaspoon cream of tartar
  2 cups sugar
  1 teaspoon vanilla
  1 teaspoon vinegar
  1 quart fresh berries
  1 pint whipping cream, whipped

Beat egg whites until frothy, add cream of tartar and beat until almost dry. Slowly add 1 cup of sugar, vanilla and vinegar while continuing to beat. Add remaining cup of sugar slowly, beating until well blended and mixture is stiff. Pour into greased 8-inch spring form pan and bake in 250° oven for 1 hour and 15 minutes. Torte should not be baked on a humid day. Top cooled torte with berries and heap with whipped cream. Makes 8-10 portions.

CHICKEN À LA POLLY

Select one small stewing chicken, cut up into serving portions. Rub with garlic, salt, pepper and flour. Brown in butter or chicken fat. Add 1 large onion, chopped; fry a few minutes. Place in a covered casserole with 1 cup chicken broth or water. Add 1 teaspoon allspice, 1 bay leaf and 1½ cups sherry wine. Slice 1 unpeeled orange; add to chicken casserole. Cook in 300° oven until tender. Makes 3-4 portions.

PAINTING BY BIRNEY QUICK

Otis Lodge

There is a parking lot for guests arriving by car as well as a private airport and seaplane base for those coming by air. On Sissebakwet (Sugar) Lake in Grand Rapids, Minnesota, this resort is seven miles west of U.S. 169 on Highway 17. Breakfast is served from 7:30 to 9:00 a.m.; lunch, 12:00 to 1:00 p.m.; and dinner, 6:00 to 7:00 p.m. from May 15 to October 1.

PAINTING BY BIRNEY QUICK

Shorewood Terrace

This restaurant on the shores of Lake Superior is surrounded by eighteen acres of woods and gardens. Breakfast served from 7:00 a.m.; lunch, 11:30 a.m.; and dinner, 5:00 p.m. Closed Mondays and November 1 to May 15. Reservations preferred. It is on U.S. 61, sixteen miles northeast of downtown Duluth, Minnesota. Arthur B. Neeb is the owner and manager.

PAINTING BY BIRNEY QUICK

CURRIED TURKEY IN PATTIE SHELLS

½ cup onion
½ cup celery
2 tablespoons butter
1 tablespoon flour
3 cups cream sauce
¼ cup red and green peppers, chopped fine
¼ teaspoon curry powder
Salt, to taste
4 cups cooked turkey, cubed
10 rich pattie shells

Van's Cafe

For over thirty-seven years this attractive restaurant owned by C. C. Van Essen has been famous for its good food. At Sixth and Washington in Brainerd, Minnesota, it is on U.S. Highways 371 and 210, in the state's beautiful lake country. Meals are served 7:00 a.m. to 1:30 a.m. every day except Tuesday. W. E. Van Essen is the manager of Van's.

Chop onion and celery very fine and sauté in butter. Blend in flour and cook to a golden color. Then fold into cream sauce. Add peppers and seasonings, to taste. Blend in turkey and heat over low fire until hot. Pour into pattie shells and serve.

PAINTING BY BERNARD H. BRADLEY

SCOTCH OATMEAL MUFFINS

1 cup quick-cooking oatmeal
1 cup buttermilk
1 cup flour
1 teaspoon baking powder
½ teaspoon salt
½ teaspoon soda
1 egg, slightly beaten
⅓ cup brown sugar
⅓ cup liquid shortening

Timber Bay Lodge

On the shores of Birch Lake, this lodge is in Superior National Forest at Babbitt, Minnesota, which is about 18 miles south of Ely. It is open May 15 to the first of October and offers complete vacation facilities. Breakfast, lunch and dinner served daily. The dining room specializes in regional American cooking. Reservations necessary for meals and overnight accommodations.

Soak oatmeal in buttermilk for 15 minutes. Sift flour, baking powder, salt and soda together and stir into oatmeal. Add egg, brown sugar and shortening until just blended. Bake in greased muffin tins in 400° oven for 20-25 minutes. Makes 12 large muffins.

BLITZ TORTE

Cream ½ cup butter with ½ cup sugar; beat in 4 egg yolks. Add 5 tablespoons milk and 1 teaspoon vanilla. Sift 1 teaspoon baking powder with 1 cup pastry flour into batter. Pour into 2 greased 8-inch layer cake pans.

Topping: Beat 4 egg whites until stiff; add 1 cup sugar and continue beating. Put on top of torte batter; and sprinkle with ½ cup chopped almonds. Bake at 325° for 1 hour. Cool; serve ice cream between layers. Makes 8 portions.

BRACCIOLINE WITH SAUCE

Sauce:
- 1 onion, chopped
- 2 large green peppers, chopped
- 1 stalk celery, chopped
- ½ cup olive oil
- 1 clove garlic, chopped
- 1 No. 2 can whole tomatoes
- 4 6-ounce cans tomato paste
- 8 cups water
- ½ teaspoon oregano
- ½ teaspoon rosemary
- Salt and pepper, to taste
- ½ cup dry red wine

Sauté onion, peppers and celery in olive oil. Add all remaining ingredients, except wine. Simmer until sauce has thickened. Then add wine.

Veal:
- 2 pounds veal steak
- Salt and pepper
- 1 cup bread crumbs
- 1 cup Parmesan cheese, grated
- 4 hard-boiled eggs, chopped
- 1 sprig parsley, chopped
- ½ cup olive oil

Cut veal into six pieces. Pound meat to flatten and season with salt and pepper. Mix bread crumbs, cheese, chopped eggs and parsley. Spread this mixture evenly on each piece of meat, roll tightly and secure with toothpicks. Brown rolls on all sides in hot olive oil, place in hot tomato sauce and simmer until tender (about 1 hour). Serve in rolls or sliced and topped with sauce. Makes 6 portions.

PAINTING BY BIRNEY QUICK

Crystal Waters Lodge

This rustic resort on Johnson Lake in Itasca County, northern Minnesota, is fifteen miles north of Grand Rapids on State Highway 38. Guests enjoy comfortable accommodations, excellent meals, good fishing. Breakfast, lunch and dinner served daily; overnight accommodations and vacation facilities. Reservations necessary. Open May 30 to September 20.

PAINTING BY BILL J. HAMMON

Ross' Steak House

Diners may select their steaks or seafood and have them cooked to order in this handsome new restaurant which specializes in steaks and Italian cuisine. Open from 11:00 a.m. daily; closed on Sunday. Ross Lorello is the owner of this Omaha, Nebraska, establishment at 909 South 72nd Street. Its reputation for braccioline with sauce is widespread.

The Compass Room

An excellent dining room at the Municipal Airport in Lincoln, Nebraska, it attracts travelers as well as residents of the city. Meals are served from 11:30 a.m. to 2:30 p.m. and from 5:00 p.m. to midnight on weekdays; Sunday serving, noon to 10:00 p.m. The airport is located four miles west of Lincoln on U.S. 34 and State Highway 2.

Tillman's Plaza Restaurant

An interesting cave décor distinguishes one of the dining rooms in this eating place at 2110 Winthrop Road, in Lincoln, Nebraska. Dinner is served every day except Monday. Steaks and prime ribs are the specialties of the house. A "Little Dinosaur" steak is a favorite with the children, who also like the chocolate pie, another feature of the restaurant.

POTTED SWISS STEAK

1 large onion
2 cloves garlic
1 large carrot
1 large green pepper
1 small bunch celery
4 ounces mushrooms
3 tablespoons butter
   Salt and pepper, to taste
2 bay leaves
½ teaspoon oregano
2 pounds choice top round steak
1 cup milk
2 ounces rich beef stock
2 ounces sherry
   B.V. meat extract

Dice the onion, garlic cloves, carrot, green pepper, celery and mushrooms. Sauté in butter until partially done. Add salt and pepper, bay leaves and oregano. Season steaks, which have been cut into 4 portions, with salt, pepper, oregano; then pat with flour on both sides. Pan-fry or grill steaks until lightly browned. Place steaks in a roasting pan and cover with vegetables. Make a light brown gravy from drippings combined with milk, stock, wine and B.V. meat extract to make it light in color. Pour gravy over steaks and cook 30 minutes at 300°. Remove from oven, place steaks in 4 individual casseroles and serve.

FRENCH SILK CHOCOLATE PIE

½ cup butter
¾ cup sugar
1 ounce Baker's bitter chocolate, melted
1 teaspoon vanilla
2 eggs
   9-inch pie shell, baked
1 cup whipping cream, whipped
½ cup walnuts, chopped

Thoroughly cream room-temperature butter with sugar. Blend in melted chocolate and vanilla. Add eggs one at a time, beating 5 minutes after each addition. Pour into cooled pie shell and chill at least two hours before serving. Top with whipped cream, then sprinkle walnuts over the top.

BARBECUE SAUCE

2 cups vinegar
½ clove garlic, mashed
1 tablespoon Worcestershire sauce
2 teaspoons dry mustard
¼ teaspoon Tabasco
1 cup sugar
2 cups catsup
1½ tablespoons salt

Combine ingredients and simmer for 10 minutes. At the Lodge, this sauce is served with the specialty of the house, "Smokqued Ribs."

GOOSE STUFFED WITH WILD RICE DRESSING

Bring to a boil 4 cups water and ½ pound wild rice and cook slowly for 10 minutes. Melt 1¼ pounds butter in a heavy pan then add and sauté: 3 cups celery, chopped; 2 cups onion, chopped; 5 strips cooked bacon, chopped; and ½ pound hamburger, fried. Season with 3 teaspoons salt and 1 teaspoon pepper. Soak ½ loaf of broken dry bread slices in warm water and squeeze dry. Mix all ingredients well. Stuff a 10- to 12-pound goose and roast as usual.

TENDERLOIN TIPS EN BROCHETTE

5 pounds tenderloin tips, 1-inch cubes
5 cups oil
¼ cup dry Burgundy
2 tablespoons apple cider vinegar
2 teaspoons salt
1 teaspoon each: white pepper, garlic powder and onion juice
2 tablespoons Hickory Smoke

Mix marinade ingredients in stone crock or stainless-steel kettle. Add meat cubes and marinate, refrigerated, for 2 days. Place meat cubes on steel skewers and broil. Makes 10 portions. Serve broiled meat on bed of wild rice.

PAINTING BY ELMER H. HALVORSON

Riverside Lodge

This up-to-the-minute lodge is a quarter-mile southeast of Minot, North Dakota, on U.S. Highway 2, near the State Fair Grounds. Famous for steaks, seafood and barbecued dishes, the dining room of the Riverside Lodge is open from 5:00 p.m. to midnight, every day except Sunday. Motel accommodations are available. Reservations recommended.

PAINTING BY ELMER H. HALVORSON

Grand Pacific Hotel and Steakhouse

This hotel, at 205 North 4th Street in Bismarck, North Dakota, was once a stagecoach stop across the Missouri River from General Custer's cavalry post. The Steakhouse is open for dinner daily except Sunday. Overnight accommodations are also available.

Antioch Inn

This inn has been operated for over 30 years by Antioch College on its campus in Yellow Springs, Ohio. The address is North College Street, 1½ blocks from U.S. 68. Lunch and dinner served daily. Overnight accommodations and vacation facilities. Closed December 24 to January 7. Recreational facilities nearby. R. J. Faust is the manager.

Jai Lai

Between Fifth and King avenues, the cafe is at 1421 Olentangy River Road in Columbus, Ohio. Lunch, dinner and late supper served daily. Closed on Sunday and holidays except Easter and Mother's Day. This popular dining spot started in 1933 with a single small room. Today five rooms seat five hundred people. Owners are E. J. Docherty and R. D. Wright.

VICHYSSOISE

2 medium onions, thin slices
3 whole stalks celery, thin slices
3 tablespoons butter
4 medium potatoes
4 cups chicken stock
1 pint light cream
  Salt and pepper, to taste
  Chives or parsley, chopped for garnish

Cook onions and celery in covered pan with butter until transparent and tender—don't brown. Pare and dice potatoes. Add, with the broth, to onions and celery and cook until potatoes are tender. Put mixture through food mill or in electric blender. Just before serving add cream and heat until piping hot. Season to taste. Add chopped parsley or chives to each of the servings.

CHICKEN POT PIE

1 medium-size boiling hen
3 bay leaves
1½ cups flour
8 raw carrots, diced
1 stalk celery, diced
10 medium-size raw potatoes
1 pound frozen peas
  Salt and pepper, to taste
  Parsley, chopped
12 pie-crust circles, baked

Cover chicken with water, add bay leaves and simmer for three hours or until tender. Skim fat off water, remove chicken, and bone and dice it. Add a little stock to flour and make a smooth paste. Blend into rest of stock. Add vegetables, except parsley, and cook slowly. When finished, add chicken and parsley. Divide filling into individual dishes. Top each with baked crust before serving. Serves 12.

THOUSAND ISLAND DRESSING

Combine 1 cup mayonnaise; ⅓ cup sweet relish; 1 hard-boiled egg, chopped; 4 tablespoons chili sauce and 2 tablespoons pimento, chopped. Mix all ingredients thoroughly, chill and serve. Makes 4-6 servings.

LOBSTER AMERICANO

1½ to 2-pound live lobster
3 tablespoons butter
1 cup sherry wine
5 ounces celery, chopped
5 ounces carrots, chopped
3 ounces chives, chopped
1 No. 2 can tomato purée
½ lemon, juice
Salt and pepper, to taste

Take live lobster and cut through shell into pieces 1 inch in length. Sauté in butter for 5 minutes. Add 1 cup wine and simmer 10 minutes. Add vegetables, tomato purée and lemon. Season and cook for 15 minutes with lid on skillet. Serves 4.

DATE NUT PUDDING

2 cups light brown sugar
4 teaspoons butter
1 cup sifted flour
½ teaspoon salt
1 teaspoon baking powder
½ cup milk
¾ cup dates, cut up
¾ cup pecans, broken
1½ cups boiling water
½ teaspoon vanilla

Mix together 1 cup brown sugar and 2 teaspoons butter. Sift flour, salt and baking powder together and add to sugar. Stir in milk, dates and pecans. Pour into 8-inch square cake pan. Combine boiling water, 1 cup brown sugar, 2 teaspoons butter and vanilla. Pour over batter in baking pan. Bake at 350° for 40 minutes. Serves 8.

BANANA BREAD

Cream together 1 cup sugar and ½ cup butter. Add 3 ripe bananas and 2 eggs. Beat well. Sift together 2 cups sifted flour, 1 teaspoon baking soda and ¼ teaspoon salt; add to batter. Pour into loaf pan and bake at 350° for 1 hour.

PAINTING BY ROBERT O'MEARA

Grandview Inn

The address is 1127 Dublin Road (U.S. Highway 33) in Columbus, Ohio. Lunch and dinner served every day except Sunday. M. J. Flesch owns and manages the restaurant. No reservations necessary. Lobster Americano is only one of the many delicious seafood dishes served here. The Grandview Inn is also noted for its charcoal-broiled steaks.

PAINTING BY DELANO FOOTE

West Milton Inn

One of the attractions on the two acres of landscaped grounds which surround the Inn is a spring-fed stream which cascades over the thirty-foot falls. Mrs. Bessie Coate recently retired as owner and Virginia and Ray Malkin are carrying on. Closed November 1 to March 15. The address is 136 North Miami Street, intersection of State Highways 48 and 571, in West Milton, Ohio.

PAINTING BY EDITH HARPER

Grammer's

Located at 1440 Walnut Street in downtown Cincinnati, Ohio, this restaurant has been an institution in the city since it was founded by Anton Grammer in 1872. Today the restaurant faithfully maintains its Old World atmosphere and German menu. Lunch and dinner served throughout the year; open 11:00 a.m. to 1:00 a.m. Closed Sunday and holidays.

HASENPFEFFER

1 medium-sized rabbit (about 5 pounds)
   White distilled vinegar, to cover
2 medium-sized carrots
2 medium-sized onions
1 small stalk celery
1 ounce whole mixed pickling spices
2 tablespoons salt
1 tablespoon pepper
3 cloves garlic
½ pound old-fashioned gingersnaps
2 ounces imported port wine

Cut rabbit into six equal portions and place in a crock. Cover with vinegar, vegetables, spices and garlic. Marinate for 3 days. Remove rabbit and sauté to a golden brown. Place in a roasting pan, strain the vegetables from the marinade and place over rabbit. Add gingersnaps and wine. Cover and roast at 425° for 1½ hours. For a real German feast, serve with potato pancakes.

PAINTING BY STEPHEN KNAPP

Jim's Steak House

Specializing in prime steaks, the restaurant is located at 1800 Scranton Road, Cleveland, Ohio. The glass-walled dining room affords diners a magnificent view of lake freighters navigating Collision Bend on their way to steel mills and limestone docks. Lunch and dinner served weekdays throughout the year. Closed Sundays and holidays.

OUTDOOR BROILING OF STEAKS

Top-quality steaks with a minimum of marbling, cut not less than one inch thick, are best for broiling. Allow charcoal to become ash-white, then drippings will not flame and burning of meat is avoided. Salt first side after meat has begun to cook for better penetration and maximum flavor. Repeat for second side, adding pepper to individual taste.

STEAK HOUSE POTATOES

Potatoes are boiled with the jackets on and set to cool. Then they are peeled and diced, and for a distinctive flavor are cooked individually in grease rendered from the steak trimmings. Potatoes are fried on one side, then flipped as a pancake to brown the other side a golden brown. These potatoes have been served exclusively at this eating place for over 31 years.

GIBLET GRAVY

1 pound chicken gizzards and hearts
    (equal number of each)
1 medium onion, chopped
1 garlic clove, minced
2 tablespoons paprika
3 tablespoons shortening
½ cup flour
½ cup thick sour cream
    Salt and pepper, to taste

Clean and wash gizzards. Sauté onion and garlic in shortening; add giblets and 1 quart of water. Simmer until tender. Add paprika then simmer 7-10 minutes. Beat flour with 1 cup water until smooth before blending in sour cream; beat until fluffy. Stir sour cream mixture into giblets; cook over low fire for 20 minutes. Season to taste. Makes 10 servings.

PAINTING BY HAROLD ZIMMERMAN

Young's

In business for 109 years, this restaurant on Portage Lakes is now managed by the fourth generation of the founding family. It was once a popular overnight stop for Ohio Canal travelers. Meals served 11:30 a.m. to 1:00 a.m.; closed on Sunday. The address is 2744 Manchester Road (State Highway 93), about a quarter-mile south of U.S. 224 in Akron, Ohio.

BLACK STEER BARBECUED SPARERIBS

5 pounds lean pork back ribs
2 teaspoons salt
1 teaspoon pure ground black pepper
1 teaspoon barbecue spice
1 teaspoon powdered thyme
½ teaspoon oregano
2 cups barbecue sauce

Season ribs with spices evenly on both sides. Brush ribs well on both sides with barbecue sauce. Bake in 350° oven for 1½ to 2 hours. Serve with hickory smoked barbecue sauce. If desired these ribs may be put on a charcoal broiler for about 10 minutes before serving for extra flavor. Makes 6-8 portions.

PAINTING BY BILL HAMMON

The Black Steer Restaurant

The Black Steer, 3rd and Pine Street, in Yankton, South Dakota, specializes in the preparation of charcoal broiled steaks and ribs. Just four miles west on State Highway 52 are Lewis and Clark Lake and Gavins Point Dam. Dinner only, 4:30 p.m. to midnight; open seven days a week. The restaurant's own salad dressing may be purchased for home use or mailed as gifts.

State Game Lodge

Both Presidents Coolidge and Eisenhower have stayed at the Lodge in Custer State Park. In the Black Hills of South Dakota, it is 22 miles from Mount Rushmore on U.S. 16A. Breakfast, lunch and dinner served daily. Overnight accommodations. Open May 15 to the first of October. Buffalo steaks are among the specialities served at the lodge.

Capitol Cafe and Lounge

Specialties of this restaurant are its steaks, seafood and Chinese-style dishes. Breakfast, lunch and dinner are served daily. Open 7:30 a.m. to 1:30 a.m. It is one and a half blocks north of the intersection of U.S. Highways 12 and 281, at 420 South Main Street in Aberdeen, South Dakota. Closed Memorial Day, July 4, Thanksgiving, Christmas and New Year's.

BUFFALO SWISS STEAK

Take 8 rounds of buffalo round steak cut in ¾-inch slices and cut into pieces for individual servings. Dredge in flour and brown in cooking oil which has been lightly flavored with garlic. Slice 4 green peppers, 6 large white onions and 12 ounces of mushrooms. Place a layer of meat in the bottom of a flat oven pan and cover with a separate layer each of onion, green pepper and mushrooms. Over the top pour 1 No. 10 can of tomatoes. Add salt and pepper to taste and bake in 250° oven until tender. Serves about 40. (If you are going to the trouble of finding buffalo steak, you might as well invite a large group.)

DICED HAM FRIED RICE

- 4 tablespoons cooking oil
- 1 teaspoon salt
  Dash of white pepper
- 2 eggs
- 1 pound smoked ham, cut in squares
- ½ cup button mushrooms
- 4 green onions, chopped fine
- 1 cup fresh bean sprouts
- 6 cups cold boiled rice
- 1 teaspoon Ac'cent
- 2 tablespoons soy sauce

Place oil, salt and pepper in a pre-heated heavy 12-inch frying pan. Scramble eggs into oil until firm. Add ham, mushrooms, green onions and bean sprouts. Stir and fry for about 3 minutes. Blend in rice and fry 3 more minutes. Add Ac'cent mixed with soy sauce; mix thoroughly and serve. Makes 6 portions.

CHINESE BOILED RICE

Thoroughly wash 1 pound long-grain white rice, rinse 4-5 times. Drain and add 3 cups water. Boil vigorously over high heat until rice is nearly dry, about ten minutes. Cover kettle with tight-fitting cover; turn heat low and let it steam about 20 minutes. Makes 6 cups.

FRESH ORANGE CHIFFON PIE

Crust: Blend ¼ cup soft butter with ¼ cup sugar and crumbs from 16 graham crackers. Put crumb mixture in 9-inch pie pan and set an 8-inch plate on top. Bake in 375° for about 8 minutes. Cool, then add filling *(below)*.

Filling:

    1 tablespoon Knox gelatin
    ¼ cup cold water
    4 eggs, separated
    ½ cup sugar
      Pinch of salt
    1 tablespoon orange rind
    ½ cup fresh orange juice
    1 tablespoon fresh lemon juice
    1 cup whipping cream, whipped

Soften gelatin in water, place cup in hot water. Combine egg yolks, sugar (remove 2 tablespoons for egg whites) and salt. Add dissolved gelatin to yolk mixture. Stir in orange rind, orange and lemon juice. Cook in double boiler; when mixture thickens, remove from fire. While custard is cooling, beat egg whites until very stiff and dry. Fold in remaining 2 tablespoons sugar. Fold egg whites into cooled custard. Fill baked pie shell and place in refrigerator. Top with whipped cream.

PAINTING BY FREDERICK MALLOY

Lake Lawn Lodge

A year-round vacation spot, this resort has recently added a motel section and a heated swimming pool for use both summer and winter. Breakfast, lunch and dinner are served daily in the Frontier Room. The Lodge is on State Highway 50 on Delavan Lake, in Delavan, Wisconsin. H. Zilisch is the managing director of this delightful resort.

SWISS STEAK

    3 pounds round steak
    4 cups celery, diced
    4 cups onion, diced
    1 green pepper, chopped
    1 No. 2½ can tomatoes
    1 clove garlic
    2 cups beef stock
    2 tablespoons parsley, chopped
    1 No. 2 can mushrooms

Cut steak into 6 portions. Braise vegetables, except parsley and mushrooms, and when partially cooked add meat and braise. Add beef stock, cover and simmer slowly for 1½ hours. Thicken gravy to taste and sprinkle parsley and mushrooms over top. Serves 6.

PAINTING BY EDMUND G. ELSNER

Arizona Inn

On State Highway 15, in Delavan, Wisconsin, this restaurant is patterned after the rustic-style buildings of the ranch country of the West. Open weekdays 3:00 p.m. to 11:30 p.m.; Sunday, 11:30 a.m. to midnight. Kitchen inspection is welcomed, and guests are also taken to see the huge meat-aging cellar. Bill and Anna Huber are the owners.

Garmisch, U.S.A.

Patterned by owner Jean Funk on a Bavarian Lodge in Garmisch, Bavaria, this year-round resort is on Lake Namakagon, ten and a half miles east of Cable, Wisconsin, on County Road D. Breakfast and dinner served daily, family style; dining room open until 8:00 p.m. Overnight accommodations and excellent recreation facilities. Reservations preferred.

Hoffman House

One of the six dining rooms in this restaurant, the Paul Bunyan Room, contains a live trout stream and waterfall from which patrons net their own fish for immediate preparation. The seven Hoffman brothers own and operate this business. Lunch and dinner served daily; closed on Monday except July and August. The address is 512-514 East Wilson Street in Madison, Wisconsin.

DUTCH COCOA CAKE

1½ cups cake flour, sifted
1¼ cups sugar
3 teaspoons baking powder
1 teaspoon salt
¼ cup cocoa
½ cup vegetable shortening, unmelted
1 teaspoon vanilla
1 cup evaporated milk
2 eggs

Sift together flour, sugar, baking powder, salt and cocoa. Add shortening, vanilla and ⅔ cup of evaporated milk. Beat two minutes at high speed. Add remaining milk. Beat well, then add eggs and beat 2 minutes more at high speed. Pour into two 9-inch layer cake pans and bake in 350° oven for 35 minutes. Cool, split with sharp knife to make 4 layers. Fill with Whipped Cream Filling *(below)*, then frost with Chocolate Icing *(also below)*.

Whipped Cream Filling: Dissolve 1 teaspoon gelatin in 4 teaspoons of cold water. Begin to whip 1½ cups whipping cream in a chilled bowl; when half whipped add gelatin mixture. Beat 3 to 4 minutes longer. This filling holds its shape well.

Chocolate Icing: Melt ¼ cup butter or vegetable shortening mixed with ⅓ cup cocoa. Pour in 5 tablespoons scalding milk and 2 teaspoons vanilla; blend with 2 cups confectioners' sugar and ¼ teaspoon salt. Beat at high speed until stiff. Frosting will be thin at first.

TURKEY AND RICE

Brown 2 medium onions in 3 tablespoons butter and pour over 1 cup washed Uncle Ben's converted rice. Add 1 tablespoon marjoram, 1 tablespoon rosemary, ½ tablespoon summer savory and stir together. Add enough more butter to brown lightly a few minutes. Then pour 3 cups chicken stock or strong bouillon over mixture. Submerge the upper sections of 6 cooked turkey wings into rice and simmer over low fire until liquid is absorbed. Brown under broiler about 5 minutes. Serves 6.

FUDGE-BOTTOM
GRAHAM CRACKER PIE

Crust: Melt 3 ounces bitter chocolate. Boil together ¼ cup sugar and ⅓ cup water. Add melted chocolate and beat well. While hot, spread over bottom of 9-inch graham cracker crust.

Cream Filling: Combine 3 cups cold milk and 1 cup sugar over double boiler and bring almost to boil. Mix 5 tablespoons cornstarch and pinch of salt to 1 cup cold milk. Beat ⅓ cup egg yolks lightly and blend well into cold milk. Stir cold milk mixture into hot milk and cook until mixture comes to boil again. Stir constantly with whip to keep smooth. Cool, then add 2 teaspoons vanilla. Pour over chocolate in pie shell. Top with whipped cream and grated chocolate. Refrigerate until served.

HEAVENLY PIE CRUST

  1 cup sugar
  ½ teaspoon cream of tartar
  ¼ teaspoon of salt
  4 egg whites, beaten stiff

Beat sugar, cream of tartar, and salt into beaten egg whites, which hold soft peaks, until well blended and very stiff. Spread over well-greased 12-inch pie tin, make a depression in the center, and build up edges. Bake in 275° oven for 1 hour. Remove from oven and cool. Fill with Lemon Filling *(below)*, top with whipped cream.

Lemon Filling:
  4 egg yolks, slightly beaten
  ½ cup sugar
  ¼ cup lemon juice
    Pinch of salt
  1 cup whipping cream, whipped

Combine ingredients except whipped cream and cook in double boiler until thick, stirring constantly. When cooled, fold into whipped cream. Pour into pie shell and top with a thin layer of whipped cream. Let stand in refrigerator for 24 hours before serving.

PAINTING BY JOHN WARREN

The Simon House

Just two blocks from the State Capitol, this restaurant has been a part of Madison, Wisconsin, since it was established in 1883. Lunch and dinner served every day the year round. Open 11:30 a.m. to 10:20 p.m. Two blocks east of Capitol Square, it is at the corner of East Main and Butler streets. Reservations necessary. Deane Adams and Maurice Combs are the owners.

PAINTING BY JOHN WARREN

Eagle's Nest

Since pioneer days a wayside tavern has been in operation on the site of this eating place. In fact, part of the building is made of hand-hewn timber and is over 135 years old. In Verona, Wisconsin, a suburb west of Madison, it is located at the junction of U.S. Highway 18 and State Highway 69. Dinner is served 5:00 p.m. to 10:00 p.m. every day except Monday.

PAINTING BY CLARENCE KINCAID

4

SOUTH CENTRAL

The Creole cookery of New
Orleans and the many Dixie
gumbos make this region a
gourmet's delight. For variety,
add Spanish-Mexican dishes
found in Texas—such as
huevos rancheros, beef picadillo,
and chili con queso.
Charcoal-broiled steaks and
spicy barbecue sauces are
often found on menus. Look
for okra, shrimp, crab, and
rice in regional dishes.
Many seasonings grow in this
area and nowhere else, and
give native dishes a
flavor all their own.

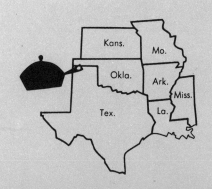

Burn's Gables

Perched atop Boston Mountain on U.S. 71, Burn's Gables is midway between Fort Smith and Fayetteville, near Winslow, Arkansas. The dining room is open daily 7:00 a.m. to 9:00 p.m. Vacation facilities are readily available. Closed from the first of December to the first of March. Mrs. Lavada Burns has been the owner and manager since 1936.

OZARK WILD HUCKLEBERRY PIE

2½ cups wild huckleberries
1¼ cups sugar
  3 tablespoons cornstarch or
    ⅓ cup flour
    Pinch of salt
  1 tablespoon lemon juice or generous sprinkle of green huckleberries

Combine all ingredients and mix well. Fill 9-inch pastry-lined pie pan. Cover with top crust, pinch top and bottom crusts together around pan; trim off excess. Bake in 450° oven 10 minutes; reduce heat to 350° and bake 35 minutes.

PIE CRUST

Melt ½ cup pure lard, add ¼ cup hot water and ¼ teaspoon salt; mix well. Add 1½ cups flour. Knead thoroughly by hand; chill overnight before using.

Cedar Grill

The address is 420 Main Street, Mountain Home, Arkansas, on U.S. 62 and State Highway 5. Mountain Home is located between Lakes Norfolk and Bull Shoals. Nearby is the White River, known all over the country for its fine trout fishing. The Cedar Grill, an exceptionally fine eating place, is owned and managed by M. O. and H. Nusch.

CHOCOLATE FUDGE CAKE

½ cup butter
  2 cups sugar
  4 squares bitter chocolate
  2 eggs
  2 cups cake flour
  2 teaspoons baking powder
1½ cups milk
  2 teaspoons vanilla
  1 cup pecans, chopped

Cream butter and sugar; melt chocolate and cool. Beat eggs slightly and add to butter and sugar mixture. Next, stir in cooled chocolate; add sifted dry ingredients alternately with the milk; blend in vanilla and pecans. Bake in two 9-inch round pans for 30 minutes at 350°.

Icing: Melt together ¼ cup butter and 2 squares bitter chocolate. Add 1½ cups powdered sugar, 1 egg, pinch of salt, then 1 tablespoon vanilla, 1 tablespoon lemon juice and 1 cup chopped pecans. Beat until ready to spread.

FROZEN PINEAPPLE SALAD

1 cup pineapple juice
2 tablespoons flour
½ cup butter
¼ cup sugar
   Pinch of salt
1 egg
2 tablespoons lemon juice
4 slices pineapple, cut fine
2 oranges, cut in sections
¼ cup chopped nut meats
8 maraschino cherries
10 marshmallows
½ pint whipping cream

Make paste of pineapple juice and flour. Add butter, sugar and salt. Cream together. Cook in top of double boiler for 10 minutes. Add egg, slightly beaten. Continue to cook for a few minutes, stirring continuously, then cool and add lemon juice, pineapple, orange, nuts, cherries and marshmallows. Whip cream and fold into mixture. Freeze and serve on crisp lettuce. Serves 6.

ROQUEFORT DRESSING

6 ounces Roquefort cheese
2 cups mayonnaise
1 cup sour cream
½ cup onion, ground
¼ cup sugar
1 ounce vinegar
1 tablespoon garlic powder

Pour all ingredients into mixing bowl and beat with electric mixer at high speed for 3 minutes. Refrigerate. Makes 1 pint.

EGG CUSTARD PIE

Cream ¼ pound butter or margarine with 1 cup sugar and pinch of salt. Beat 5 eggs into mixture. Add 2 cups milk and 1 teaspoon vanilla. Pour into 9-inch unbaked pie shell. Sprinkle nutmeg over top. Bake in 350° oven for 25 minutes or until filling is firm.

PAINTING BY BEN EARL LOONEY

Rose Inn and Lodge

A forty-year reputation for fine food and hospitality is maintained by Rodgers Heiss, manager of the Inn in Crossett, in the southeastern corner of Arkansas. Breakfast, lunch and dinner served daily. Overnight accommodations and complete vacation facilities. Reservations necessary. The address is 200 Main Street, on State Highway 133, one block south of U.S. 82.

PAINTING BY BEN EARL LOONEY

Anderson's Restaurant

Located at the junction of U.S. Highways 64 and 67 in Beebe, Arkansas, this restaurant and motel are just 28 miles north of Little Rock. Bruce Anderson owns and manages the restaurant and the adjacent Bel-Mar Motel. Meals served 5:00 a.m. to 10:00 p.m. every day. Reservations at motel advisable during summer. Playground for children; hunting and fishing nearby.

Spring Lake Restaurant

At Bellefonte, Arkansas, this restaurant is four miles southeast of Harrison near the intersection of U.S. Highways 62 and 65. Lunch and dinner served weekdays; dinner only served on Sunday after 4:00 p.m. Reservations preferred for special Chinese and Indian dishes. Faye and Ed Waddell own and manage this restaurant which is noted for its homemade bread and desserts.

A. Q. Chicken House

Roy C. Ritter owns and operates several large poultry farms which help supply the 100,000 broilers and many turkeys and stewing hens needed for his restaurant each year. Located in an Ozark vacationland area, the restaurant is open for breakfast, lunch and dinner daily. The A. Q. Chicken House is on U.S. Highways 71 and 62, a half-mile north of Springdale, Arkansas.

CHOCOLATE ANGEL DELIGHT

12 ounces semisweet chocolate chips
2 tablespoons water
3 eggs, separated
Pinch of salt
3 tablespoons sugar
1½ cups whipping cream
1 teaspoon vanilla
1 13-ounce angel food cake
Vanilla ice cream

Melt chocolate chips in water in top of double boiler. Stir in egg yolks and salt. Beat egg whites until stiff, add sugar and stir them into cooled chocolate and blend well. Whip cream, add vanilla; then fold into chocolate mixture. Break angel food cake (either fresh or stale) into bite-size chunks and place in 9x14-inch pyrex baking dish, then cover with chocolate sauce. Chill in refrigerator 6 hours before serving. Serve cold in squares; top each portion with a dip of ice cream. Makes 18 portions.

CHICKEN AND DUMPLINGS

Simmer a 5-pound stewing hen until tender. Remove meat from the bones. Strain broth hen was cooked in to use for dumplings. Combine 2 cups warm chicken broth, 1 tablespoon Ac'cent, 1 teaspoon salt and flour (about 5 cups) to make dough stiff. Roll out to about ⅛-inch thickness. Cut in small short strips and drop into boiling broth and let come to a boil. Turn heat low and simmer about 15 minutes with lid on. Combine dumplings, broth and chicken meat in soup bowls. Serves 20.

CLOVER LEAF ROLLS

Bring to boil 1 cup of milk, cool to luke-warm with 1 cup water, then add ½ cup melted Crisco. Dissolve 2 cakes compressed yeast in ¼ cup warm water, then combine with ½ cup sugar and 1 egg in mixer. Add milk and water and about 8 cups of flour and 1½ teaspoons salt. Mix for 8 minutes. Let dough rise. Then divide dough into small balls. Place three in each greased muffin cup and let rise again. Bake 20 minutes at 350°. Makes 2 dozen rolls.

CARAMEL DUMPLINGS

Sauce: Melt and burn ½ cup sugar in heavy skillet or pan. Add 1 cup sugar. 2 cups hot water, 2 tablespoons butter and ⅛ teaspoon salt. Cook 10 minutes, stirring occasionally.

Dumplings: Cream 2 tablespoons butter with ½ cup sugar. Sift 1½ cups flour with 2 teaspoons baking powder. Add alternately with ½ cup milk to sugar mixture. Season with ½ teaspoon vanilla. Drop batter by spoonfuls into hot caramel sauce *(above)*. Place on low flame and cook for 20 minutes without lifting cover. Serves 6-8.

GRINTER HOUSE PRUNE CAKE

```
  1 cup sugar
 ¾ cup vegetable shortening
  2 eggs
  2 teaspoons cinnamon
 ¼ teaspoon cloves
 ¼ teaspoon salt
  1 cup stewed prunes, chopped warm
2½ cups all-purpose flour
  3 teaspoons baking powder
 ¾ teaspoon soda, dissolved in
      1 cup hot prune juice
```

Cream sugar and shortening together by hand; add eggs, beat well. Stir in spices and prunes, beat batter again. Sift flour and baking powder together; combine soda and prune juice. Add these two mixtures alternately while continuing to beat. Pour batter into greased 12-inch sheet pan or two greased 8-inch layer pans. Bake 45 minutes at 350°. Spread with Orange Topping *(below)*.

Orange Topping: Cream 2 teaspoons butter with 1 cup sugar; beat in 1 egg. Add 2 tablespoons flour beating until smooth. Stir in ¾ cup prune juice and cook over medium heat until thick. Beat in 1 tablespoon orange juice and 1 tablespoon grated orange rind. Spread over cooled cake. A Christmas tradition at the Grinter House, the prune cake is often topped with whipped cream or vanilla ice cream.

PAINTING BY R. J. HUNT

Chuck Wagon Restaurant

Charcoal-broiled steaks and barbecued meats served in a Western atmosphere are featured in this Lawrence, Kansas, restaurant. Open 11:00 a.m. to 9:00 p.m. every day except Tuesday. Closed July 1 to August 1. On U.S. 59 South, two miles south of West Lawrence entrance to the Kansas Turnpike. John W. Dobbins and J. W. Wolfe are the owners of the Chuck Wagon.

PAINTING BY GRACE BILGER

Old Grinter House

Situated on Old Military Trail, which ran from the Oregon Trail to the Sante Fe Trail, this restaurant serves lunch from 11:30 a.m. to 2:30 p.m.; dinner, 5:00 p.m. to 8:00 p.m. on weekdays; on Sunday, 12:30 p.m. to 7:00 p.m. Closed on Monday. Reservations preferred. Located at 1420 South 78th Street (State Highway 32) in Muncie, Kansas.

The Red Barn

One of the historic old barns of Fort Scott, Kansas, was converted into this attractive restaurant which is decorated with antique hay hooks, horse collars and neck yokes. Dinner is served daily from 5:00 p.m. to 10:00 p.m.; on Sunday there is a special chuck wagon dinner served 11:30 a.m. to 8:00 p.m. Located a quarter of a mile east of the junction of U.S. Highways 54 and 69.

Stockyards Hotel

A landmark in Wichita, Kansas, the dining room is noted for its steaks which are selected from choice and prime beef and expertly cooked on charcoal broilers. Lunch and dinner are served on weekdays; lunch is not served on Saturday or Sunday. Reservations advisable. Four blocks east of U.S. 81, the hotel is at 659 East Twenty-first Street.

HEAVENLY HASH

1 No. 2½ can fruit cocktail, drained
1 or 2 bananas, sliced
2 tablespoons sugar
1 cup minature marshmallows
½ cup seeded grapes, halved
½ cup whipping cream, whipped
  Lettuce

Combine fruit, sugar and marshmallows. Fold whipped cream into fruit mixture and keep chilled until serving time. Makes a salad for 8 to 10 people.

CHARCOAL-BROILED STEAKS

From an establishment justly famous for its perfectly broiled steaks comes timely advice for the nation's outdoor cooks.

1. The charcoal bed should be thin, and the fire must be allowed to burn down until the surface shows considerable ash. This eliminates the Nero-like chefs who throw a fortune in beautiful steaks onto a roaring fire, then stand by as the steaks are carbonized.

2. The steaks should be cooked slowly to retain moisture in the meat. Ice cubes dropped onto the fire from time to time will control spots of flame. Caution is advised in this operation or the fire could be quenched.

3. Don't salt steak until it is removed from fire. Salt burns and gives the meat a bitter taste.

4. Use a good fast-acting meat thermometer until you can accurately time cooking periods for degrees of doneness.

5. Always turn steaks with a non-puncturing tool.

STUFFED HAM ROLLS
WITH CREAMED CHICKEN

    16 thin slices ham
    2 cups creamed chicken
Stuffing:
    ¾ cup cooked rice
    2 tablespoons parsley, chopped
    ¾ cup almonds or walnuts, chopped
       Salt and pepper, to taste
    3 tablespoons butter
       Pinch of poultry seasoning or
          mixed herbs

Mix stuffing ingredients thoroughly and spread over ham slices. Roll up ham slices and secure with toothpicks or twine. Place rolls in baking pan and cover with creamed chicken. Bake at 350° until thoroughly heated. Serve with spiced peaches or fruit salad. Makes 8 portions.

MAYNARD'S CHEESE CAKE

Crust: Mix thoroughly 1⅔ cups graham crackers or zwieback crumbs, 2 tablespoons sugar, 1½ teaspoons cinnamon and 6 tablespoons butter, melted. Pat into bottom and up sides of a 10-inch spring mold or 3-inch-deep pie pan.

Filling:
    1½ pounds cream cheese
    1 cup sugar
    3 eggs, well beaten
    ½ teaspoon vanilla

Beat cheese thoroughly in an electric mixer, then add sugar gradually, eggs one at a time and finally vanilla. Pour into pie shell and bake 20 minutes in 375° oven. Remove from oven and add topping.

Topping: Whip 1 pint sour cream, then add 3 tablespoons sugar and ½ teaspoon vanilla. Pour over baked pie and bake 5 minutes at 500°. Cool, then chill in refrigerator. Serve very cold. Makes 8 large portions.

PAINTING BY ALVIN PEARSON

Innes Tea Room

Situated in the Innes Department Store at 121 S. Broadway in downtown Wichita, the dining rooms are popular with men as well as women. Among culinary attractions are hot breads and homemade pastries. Lunch is served in the Men's Grill and tea room from 11:30 a.m. to 2:30 p.m. Dinner hours are from 5:30 p.m. to 8:30 p.m. Closed on Sundays and holidays.

PAINTING BY FREDERIC JAMES

Maynard's

Robert and Ida Lee Maynard opened a bakery at the corner of 8th and Jackson Streets, in downtown Topeka, in 1929 and the restaurant that grew out of it is still famous for cheesecake, pastries and homemade breads. Luncheon and dinner menus feature a roast beef special with oven baked potato, also salads and "New York" sandwiches. Open 8:00 a.m. (for pastry sales) to 9:00 p.m. daily.

Tujague's

This famous restaurant at 823 Decatur Street, across from the French Market in New Orleans, serves breakfast from 11:00 a.m. to 3:00 p.m. The meal starts with a hearty soup and goes through a full course meal in the French tradition that started when butchers and farmers were the only customers. Lunch, 11:00 a.m. to 3:00 p.m.; dinner, 5:00 to 9:00 p.m. Closed Friday.

TUJAGUE'S BOILED BEEF

3-4 pounds short ribs of beef
1 onion
2 carrots
3 sprigs parsley
2 stalks celery
2 tablespoons salt

Cut meat into good-size pieces. Measure 2 quarts water in large pot. Add meat and vegetables. Add salt when water begins to boil. Boil for 2½ hours; remove meat from water. Before serving remove bone. Serve with Tomato Horse-radish Sauce *(below)*.

Tomato Horse-radish Sauce: Combine 1 cup tomato ketchup, 2 teaspoons horse-radish, 1 teaspoon vinegar and ¼ teaspoon salt. Mix well and chill until ready to serve.

Mim's Restaurant

Breaux Bridge, Louisiana, is known as the Crawfish Capital of the World and one of its foremost purveyors of this Creole delicacy is Marie "Mim" Blanchard. Her restaurant has won cooking prizes at the biennial Crawfish Festival. Open for breakfast, lunch and dinner daily except Monday. Breaux Bridge is about nine miles from Lafayette by way of State Highway 94.

MIM'S CRAWFISH PATTIES

1 pound crawfish meat (lobster tails)
    or lobster, ground
1 cup salad oil
½ small onion, chopped
    Salt and pepper, to taste

Cook crawfish or lobster in oil over slow fire with onion and seasonings for about 20 minutes.

Crust:
½ cup shortening
2 cups flour
2 teaspoons baking powder
    Pinch of salt
    Milk, enough to form solid dough

Cut shortening into flour and add remaining ingredients; mix well. Add milk until it turns to a firm dough, not soft. Roll thin with rolling pin and cut into small circles. Form into 8 individual pie shells and fill with crawfish or lobster mixture. Bake in 350° oven 15 to 20 minutes. Serves 8.

SOUFLAKIA À LA TURK

2 pounds lean pork or beef tenderloin
1 large onion, chopped
1 clove garlic, finely chopped
½ cup olive oil
    Dash of oregano
½ cup dry sherry
6 peppercorns, crushed
1 teaspoon salt
    Thin slices onion, green pepper or tomato
4 each chicken livers and bread cubes
1 lemon, juice
    Rice pilaf

Cut tenderloin into pieces about 1½ inches thick and 2 inches square. Place them in a bowl with chopped onion, garlic, olive oil and oregano. Then sprinkle with sherry, crushed peppercorns and salt. Let marinate at least 4 hours at room temperature. Remove meat, dry each piece carefully, then brush with olive oil. Thread meat cubes on 4 long skewers separating them with slices of onion, green pepper or tomato. Place a piece of chicken liver in the center of each skewer. At the pointed end of each place a cube of bread brushed with oil to prevent meat from slipping off. Place under broiler flame basting frequently with drippings from the pan. Salt souflakia lightly and sprinkle with lemon juice just before serving on a garnished platter of rice pilaf. Serves 4.

LOBSTER À LA NEWBURG

1 cup mushrooms (pieces and stems)
4 tablespoons butter
2 cups milk
2 cups fresh heavy cream
    Salt and pepper, to taste
4 tablespoons cracker crumbs
½ cup sherry wine
4 boiled lobster tails, diced
    Dash of paprika

Sauté mushrooms in butter until brown. Add milk, cream and salt and pepper. Let mixture come to a boil, then add cracker meal until it thickens. Stir in sherry and lobster. Pour into casserole and sprinkle top with paprika. Put in 450° oven about 1 minute and serve piping hot. Makes 4 portions.

PAINTING BY BEN EARL LOONEY

The Rendezvous Restaurant

Excellent food is served at this Monroe, Louisiana, eating place, which is also an official tourist information center. Lunch and dinner served every day; dancing and floor show nightly, except Sunday, in the Carousel Room. The address is 1400 Louisville Avenue, on U.S. 80. Johnny Johnson and Bobby Pappas are the owners and Vicki Brown is the manager.

PAINTING BY BEN EARL LOONEY

Bilello's Restaurant

At the corner of St. Mary and Landry Streets in Thibodaux, Louisiana, this restaurant is especially noted for its seafood. Meals are served from 10:00 a.m. to 10:30 p.m. every day except Monday. Located right on State Highway 1, Bilello's is close to U.S. Highway 90. Sam Bilello is the manager of this outstanding Louisiana eating place.

Roussel's

For over thirty-five years, gourmets have been flocking to Warren Roussel's restaurant for seafood specialities such as crayfish bisque and its original and outstanding Trout Marguery. Just 25 miles north of New Orleans on Airline Highway (U.S. 61), it is at the junction of U.S. 51 at Laplace. Open daily for breakfast, lunch and dinner. Meals served until 11:00 p.m.

La Fiesta Theatre Restaurant

Efren and Mariano Valle own and manage this restaurant in Juarez, Chihuahua, Mexico, across the border from El Paso, Texas. Typical Mexican food is served, and the entertainment features native music and dances, and top-name American stars. Dinner served daily 5:00 p.m. to 3:00 a.m.; reservations necessary. At Mariscal and Ugarte streets, two blocks north of Pan American Highway.

TROUT MARGUERY

6 tablespoons butter
3 tablespoons flour
1 pound boiled shrimp, cleaned and chopped
1 bunch green onions
12 raw oysters or 1 cup clams, chopped
2 tablespoons dry white wine
6 pounds trout fillets
Salt and cayenne pepper, to taste

Melt butter in pan and blend in flour to form a smooth paste, then stir in chopped shrimp. When mixture begins to turn grayish, add chopped green onions and cook until wilted. Add chopped oysters or clams and simmer for 5 minutes. Thin with wine. Set aside. Sprinkle trout lightly with salt and pepper. Broil well on both sides. Arrange cooked trout on toast and cover well with sauce. Sprinkle with finely chopped parsley and serve immediately. Makes 12 portions.

CHILI CON QUESO

2 hot chili peppers, diced
2 green peppers, chopped
1 small onion, chopped fine
14½ ounces tomatoes, canned
14½ ounces tomato juice
1 small clove garlic, crushed
2 tablespoons cornstarch
½ pound Monterrey cheese, in 1-inch pieces

Boil chili peppers, green peppers, onion, tomatoes and tomato juice together for 15 minutes. Add garlic. Dissolve cornstarch in cold water and blend slowly into mixture. When it thickens add cheese pieces. Chile is spread on tortillas which are rolled up. 6 portions.

Mexican Rice: Melt 2 tablespoons Crisco in iron skillet and brown 1 cup uncooked rice over low heat. Mix ½ cup finely sliced onion and 1 crushed clove of garlic and cook for five minutes. Combine ½ cup tomato purée, 1½ teaspoons salt and 2½ cups boiling water; pour slowly into rice. Cover; simmer 40 minutes. Serves 6.

OYSTERS À LA FINELLIA

Bake 12 large oysters in the deep half of the shell in medium oven until edges curl. Melt ¼ pound butter, blend in 1 cup flour to form a smooth paste. Slowly add 1½ cups milk and ½ cup oyster liquor, if desired, keeping mixture smooth. Add 1 teaspoon Worcestershire sauce, 1 teaspoon sherry, and salt, pepper and paprika, to taste. Sauce must be thick. Add 1 cup cooked lobster meat, cubed. Divide sauce equally over top of each oyster, then top each with a thin slice of cheese, covering oyster well. Bake in medium oven until hot and cheese is melted. Sprinkle paprika on top. Serves 3.

TURKEY CUTLET WITH WILD RICE AND OLIVE SAUCE

Turkey: Salt and pepper 12 raw 2-ounce fillets of turkey breast. Beat 1 egg well and add to it 1 ounce of sherry and ½ cup of cream. Dip cutlet into mixture and then dredge in flour. Sauté in 1 cup butter until golden brown. Place turkey over wild rice and cover with Olive sauce *(both below)*. Makes 6 portions.

Wild Rice: Cook 1 cup wild rice like ordinary rice. Melt 1 tablespoon of butter in a pan and in it sauté 3 slices bacon, minced, 1 tablespoon chives and 1 small onion, minced. Add this to cooked rice. Mix two eggs into rice and blend well. Season with salt and pepper, to taste. Pour into greased bread pan and bake in 400° oven 15-18 minutes.

Olive Sauce: Melt 2 tablespoons butter in a saucepan. Blend in 3 tablespoons flour to make a smooth paste. Do not brown. Add 4 tablespoons of sliced stuffed olives and simmer for 5 minutes. Then add ½ cup chicken stock and cook for 10 minutes or until it becomes a smooth sauce. Add 1 cup of chicken stock and cook 15-18 minutes. Stir in 4 more tablespoons sliced olives and season to taste with salt and pepper. Remove from fire; add 3 ounces sherry.

PAINTING BY HAM EMBREE

Michael's Cafe

On U.S. Highway 61 North in Cleveland, Mississippi, this eating place is noted for its excellent seafood dishes. Open every day of the year from 6:30 p.m. to midnight. Closed July 4 and Christmas. Leo Michael is the owner of this popular restaurant. The area around Cleveland is known throughout the state of Mississippi for its fine fishing and hunting.

PAINTING BY DALE NICHOLS

Sun-N-Sand

A beautiful new motor hotel in Biloxi, Mississippi, the Sun-N-Sand is located on U.S. 90 (West Beach Boulevard) overlooking the Gulf of Mexico. Meals are served from 7:00 a.m. to 11:00 p.m. daily. Overnight accommodations and excellent vacation facilities, including two swimming pools, tennis courts and a children's playground. Open seven days a week, the year round.

Wurzburger's

On U.S. 66 and Meramee Caverns Road in Stanton, Missouri, this restaurant has been owned and operated by Mrs. Effie Wurzburger for the past forty-seven years. Superb food has made it popular with motorists who stop for lunch or dinner any day except Tuesday. Closed Thanksgiving and Christmas. No reservations are necessary at Wurzburger's.

LEMON CHEESE CAKE

Crust: Mix 1 box finely rolled zwieback, 1 cup granulated sugar, 6 tablespoons melted butter and 1 teaspoon cinnamon. Press firmly into the bottom and sides of a well-buttered spring form (6½ to 7-inch pan, 3 inches deep).

Filling: Rub 2 cups dry cottage cheese through sieve; add 4 beaten egg yolks, 1 cup sugar, ¼ teaspoon salt, 3 tablespoons lemon juice and grated rind of 1 lemon. Cook mixture in double boiler until thoroughly heated. Don't overcook. Dissolve 2 envelopes of gelatin in water, add to mixture. Whip 1 cup whipping cream flavored with ½ teaspoon vanilla; beat four egg whites sweetened with ¼ cup sugar. Fold into cooled cheese filling. Pour into crust. Chill in refrigerator for six hours.

Cheshire Inn

Shining armor and heraldic banners are just a few of the colorful decorative touches of this bit of England in St. Louis, Missouri, an exact replica of the Cheshire Cheese Restaurant on Fleet Street in London. Located at 7036 Clayton Avenue at Skinner, it is open daily for breakfast, lunch, dinner and after-theater supper until 1:30 a.m. Closed Christmas Day.

SPANISH ONIONS EN CASSEROLE WITH ALMONDS

    3 cups Spanish onions, cut
        in ¾-inch wedges
    2 tablespoons butter
    2 tablespoons flour
    1 cup chicken broth
    ½ cup light cream
    ½ cup blanched almonds, sliced
    ½ teaspoon salt
    ½ teaspoon pepper
    ½ cup Cheddar cheese, grated
    1 cup fine bread crumbs

Parboil onions in small amount of water. Drain well. Melt butter in saucepan, blend in flour, add chicken broth and cream, stirring constantly until thickened and smooth. Combine sauce, onions and almonds. Add seasonings and pour mixture into buttered casserole. Bake in water bath 350° oven for 35-45 minutes. Just before serving sprinkle cheese mixed with bread crumbs over top and brown under broiler. Serves 6-8.

SOUR CREAM NOODLE BAKE

Cook an 8-ounce package medium noodles in boiling salted water. Rinse and drain. Brown 1 pound ground beef in 1 tablespoon butter, then add 1 teaspoon salt, ⅛ teaspoon black pepper, ¼ teaspoon garlic salt and 1 cup tomato sauce or purée. Simmer 5 minutes. Combine 1 cup chopped green onions, 1 cup sour cream, 1 cup cream cottage cheese, and noodles. Alternate layers of noodle mixture and meat mixture in two-quart casserole, beginning with noodles and ending with meat. Top with 1 cup shredded sharp cheddar cheese. Bake at 350° in preheated oven 20-25 minutes, until cheese is brown. Serves 8.

WILL ROGERS SPECIAL

3 pounds beef tenderloin
  Marinade (below)
1 pound bacon, sliced
36 mushroom caps, lightly sautéed
6 ounces Roquefort cheese, grated
  Water cress and tomato wedges, for garnish

Cut beef into 30 inch-and-a-half cubes. They must be free of sinew and fat. Place in marinade overnight in refrigerator. Arrange ingredients on 6 ten-inch skewers or brochette needles. First place a mushroom cap on skewer, next a chunk of marinated beef, then a 1-inch slice of raw bacon; repeat until 5 chunks of beef are on each skewer. End each with a mushroom cap. Broil over a charcoal fire or under broiler of stove, turning occasionally until done (about 15 minutes for medium). Remove from fire and sprinkle each serving with 1 ounce of cheese. Return to broiler until cheese melts, about one minute. Serve hot with water cress and tomato wedges. Makes 6 portions.

Marinade: Crush 2 cloves garlic with 1½ teaspoons salt. Add 2 cups olive oil; 1 cup tarragon vinegar; 1½ teaspoons black pepper, freshly ground; ⅛ teaspoon each marjoram and oregano; 3 bay leaves; 1 teaspoon paprika; ¼ lemon, sliced thin and ¼ cup onion, chopped. Blend well.

PAINTING BY JAMES GREEN

Miss Hulling's Cafeterias

Here are two of the largest and most complete food services under single roofs to be found, with table and cafeteria service, a sandwich shop, carry-out and banquet facilities plus a bakery. Open 6:15 a.m. to 8:15 p.m. every day except Sunday and holidays. The cafeterias are in downtown St. Louis, Missouri, one at 1103 Locust Street, the other at 725 Olive Street.

PAINTING BY CHARLES BANKS WILSON

The Glass House

Diners have a fascinating view of traffic rolling beneath on the Will Rogers Turnpike. The Broiler Room is open daily 7:00 a.m. to 8:30 p.m.; summer, 11:00 a.m. to 9:00 p.m. The Express Buffet is open only during the summer season, 6:00 a.m. to 5:00 p.m. The Snack Shop is open 24 hours. The Glass House spans the new 88-mile toll turnpike south of Vinita, Oklahoma.

The Anna Maude Cafeteria

For 34 years this outstanding cafeteria has been famous in the Southwest. Meals are served continuously 10:45 a.m. to 7:30 p.m. on weekdays; Saturdays the cafeteria closes at 2:30 p.m.; closed on Sunday and holidays. The address is 119 North Robinson Avenue in the center of downtown Oklahoma City, Oklahoma. Owners are Robert N. Smith and Cooper Lyon.

Snug Harbor Restaurant

Ed Wright and his family built this eating place as an attraction to their fishing resort. Meals served 6:00 a.m. to 10:00 p.m. daily, year round. Cabins available for overnight or vacation; reservations advisable. On the shores of Fort Gibson Lake, the restaurant is reached by leaving U.S. 69 four miles north of Wagoner, Oklahoma, and proceeding east four miles as directed by signs.

GERMAN CHOCOLATE PUDDING

1 4-ounce bar German's sweet chocolate
¼ pound butter
3 eggs, separated
1 cup powdered sugar
1 teaspoon vanilla
1 pint whipping cream
  10-ounce box vanilla wafers

Melt chocolate and butter together. Add chocolate mixture to beaten egg yolks; then add ⅔ cup of powdered sugar and vanilla. Chill, then fold in whipped cream. Beat egg whites until they begin to stand in peaks. Add remaining ⅓ cup sugar into egg whites and fold into chocolate mixture. Grind vanilla wafers and line 9x9-inch deep dish with part of the crumbs. Spread 2 cups of chocolate mixture over crumbs, then add another layer of crumbs. Repeat until all the mixture is used. Top pudding with crumbs. Refrigerate 24 hours before using. Cut in portions 3x3 inches. Makes 9 servings.

HUSH PUPPIES

1 cup yellow or white corn meal
¼ cup flour
¼ cup onion, chopped
¼ teaspoon baking powder
¼ teaspoon paprika
1 teaspoon salt
1 teaspoon sugar
⅛ teaspoon red pepper (optional)
⅛ teaspoon garlic powder (optional)
1 cup and 2 tablespoons boiling water
  Hot fat for frying

Pour boiling water all at once into mixed dry ingredients. Stir mixture thoroughly. Drop by tablespoonsful into 350° fat. Deep fat may be used or hush-puppies may be fried in shallow fat and turned to brown. Makes 6 portions.

VEAL SCALOPPINE

Roll 1 pound thin veal cutlets, flattened and cut into about 4-inch strips, in flour and brown quickly in ¼ pound of butter. Sprinkle with salt and pepper. Mix ½ cup sweet sherry, 1 cup tomato sauce and 1 8-ounce can mushroom pieces. Cover and simmer over low heat about 10 minutes or until meat is tender. Serves 4.

PAINTING BY JAY O'MEILIA

Jack Sussy's Italian Restaurant

This popular dinner and evening spot at 4801 North Lincoln Road (U.S. 66 and U.S. 77, city routes) is a quarter-mile south of U.S. 66 by-pass in Oklahoma City. It opens every day at 2:30 p.m., closes at 1:00 a.m. on weekdays; at 3:00 a.m. Friday and Saturday. A special dining room for teenagers draws young patrons from all parts of the state.

SHRIMP CANTONESE
WITH LOBSTER SAUCE

1 pound fresh jumbo shrimp, cleaned
2 tablespoons vegetable oil
4 ounces minced pork
1 clove garlic, minced
1 tablespoon black fermented beans
    or soya sauce
1 teaspoon salt
¼ teaspoon black pepper
2 cups chicken broth, hot
½ teaspoon sugar
1 teaspoon monosodium glutamate
1 tablespoon cornstarch
2 eggs, beaten
¼ teaspoon sesame oil
2 tablespoons shallots
2 cups steamed rice

Heat oil in pan, sauté pork with garlic and beans. Add shrimp and brown at high temperature. Season with salt and pepper, to taste. Reduce heat, pour in broth, cover and let simmer for 10 minutes. Add sugar and glutamate. Dilute cornstarch with 2 tablespoons water and stir into mixture. Cut off heat, then stir in eggs and sesame oil. Pour into serving dish and sprinkle with chopped shallots. Serve with steamed rice. Makes 2 portions.

PAINTING BY A. PETER EMIG

Albert Gee's Ding How

Waiters in Mandarin garb add to the exotic and festive Oriental atmosphere here. Open every day from 11:00 a.m. to 1:30 a.m. The address is 6800 South Main (U.S. Highway 59) one block north of the Shamrock Hilton in Houston, Texas. Shrimp Cantonese with Lobster Sauce is a famous specialty of the house. Albert Gee is the owner and manager.

The Barn Door

Owner and manager Bill Tassos says that the interesting building which houses this restaurant was a country tavern over fifty years ago. It is located at 8400 North New Braunfels Avenue, east of U.S. 281 and west of U.S. 81 in San Antonio, Texas. Dinner is the only meal served. Closed on Monday, and from August 9 to August 31.

Eagle Coffee Shop

Located in a modernized old hotel in the historic border city of Eagle Pass, Texas, the coffee shop is close to U.S. 277. Meals are served 6:00 a.m. to 9:30 p.m. every day. Overnight accommodations. In addition to its regular menu, the coffee shop features a variety of border dishes. D. N. Ellis is the owner and Swannie D. Kilgore is the manager.

GARLIC DRESSING

4 raw eggs
1 teaspoon each salt and dry mustard
4 cups salad oil
4 hard-boiled eggs, chopped fine
4 cloves of fresh garlic, to taste, chopped
5 sprigs fresh parsley, chopped
4 whole green onions, chopped
3 stalks celery, chopped
½ cup mixed lemon juice and vinegar, to taste

Place eggs in mixer, while beating eggs add salt and mustard. Slowly add oil and then pour in remaining ingredients. Keep dressing in covered container. Makes 1 quart dressing.

SOUR CREAM SAUCE

1 pint sour cream
½ sweet green pepper, minced
3 whole green onions, chopped
Dash of Lawry's Seasoned Salt and Worcestershire Sauce
Salt, pepper and garlic salt, to taste

Blend ingredients and serve over hot potato. Here the potatoes are scrubbed and wrapped in aluminum foil. When half done, the potatoes are punctured with a pick to let moisture out.

HUEVOS RANCHEROS

6 dried chili peppers
1 teaspoon bacon drippings
1 small onion, chopped
½ cup tomatoes
Salt, to taste
4-6 eggs

Boil peppers in 1 cup water until tender. Mash through a sieve. Melt bacon grease in skillet and sauté onion lightly. Add chili paste, tomatoes and salt; simmer for a few minutes. Remove from burner and slip eggs into pan with sauce as if to poach. Cook over very low fire until eggs are done. Serves 4 to 6.

REMOULADE SAUCE

1 pint mayonnaise
1 level tablespoon prepared mustard
1 heaping tablespoon sweet relish
2 hard-boiled eggs, chopped fine
1 ounce tarragon vinegar
2 cloves garlic or 1½ tablespoons
   powdered garlic
1 teaspoon capers, minced (optional)
2 maraschino cherries, chopped
1 teaspoon maraschino cherry juice
1½ tablespoons parsley, chopped
1 large onion or 2 medium size,
   chopped fine
1½ teaspoons powdered thyme
   Salt and pepper, to taste

Mix all ingredients thoroughly. If fresh garlic is used, pulverize completely and use all the juice. Chill in refrigerator for at least 24 hours before using. Better if made several days before use. Serve with fish or meat. Makes about 3 cups.

PAINTING BY HELEN STAHL

Eddie's Covered Wagon

Since 1935, Eddie Thompson has operated this restaurant on U.S. 83 between McAllen and Pharr, Texas. The outdoor dining and dancing patio, beautifully landscaped with over a thousand flowers and shrubs, is more than an acre in area and has a children's play area. Open 5:00 p.m. to midnight; closed on Monday. Reservations necessary for groups and Saturday nights.

CHOCOLATE FUDGE PECAN PIE

4 whole eggs, room temperature
2 cups sugar
3 full tablespoons butter, melted
3 squares chocolate, melted
   Pinch of salt
½ teaspoon lemon juice
1 cup broken pecans
   10-inch unbaked pie shell

Beat eggs with spoon, add sugar. Blend in melted butter and chocolate, salt and lemon juice. Mix thoroughly. Stir in nuts and pour into pie shell. Bake at 375° for 30 minutes. Should be set but slightly shaky in the middle as it thickens when cool. Do not refrigerate. Serve with whipped cream or ice cream.

PAINTING BY SAM WAPLES

Green Parrot

This restaurant, owned by Mrs. Vira Fredericks, is in a lovely old mansion at 2314 MacGregor Way in Houston, Texas. Dinners served daily from 5:00 p.m. to 9:30 p.m.; on Sundays from noon to 8:30 p.m. Closed Monday, Tuesday, and Wednesday, and two weeks during Christmas and New Year's. Reservations recommended. Two new dining rooms overlook a garden waterfall.

Trade Winds Restaurant

This restaurant is part of a large 101-room motor hotel with 54 separate buildings on seven acres of land. The dining room is open for breakfast, lunch and dinner, from 6:00 a.m. to 10:00 p.m. Motel accommodations available; many vacation attractions nearby. On State Highway 9, (the corner of Leopard and Lexington Streets), it is in Corpus Christi, Texas.

STUFFED FLOUNDER WITH CRABMEAT DRESSING

1 large onion, minced
1 medium stalk celery, minced
6 cups cream
2 quarts rich chicken stock
2 pounds white flaked crabmeat
1 teaspoon salt
¼ teaspoon black pepper
½ pound butter
1 cup whipping cream
1 pound cracker meal
8 1-pound boneless flounders, cleaned

Sauté onion and celery. Boil cream separately, then combine with boiling chicken stock. Combine remaining ingredients, except cracker meal. Cook until crab is tender, then slowly stir in meal. Cook until thick but not stiff. Cool, then stuff flounder with crab mixture and garnish top with 3-4 shrimp. Dust with paprika and broil at 450° for 25 minutes. Serves 16.

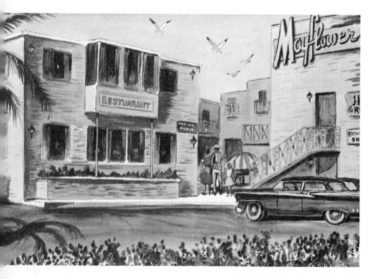

Mayflower Hotel Restaurant

One side of this modern motor hotel looks out on the bay where guests can watch ocean vessels and shrimp boats as they approach Corpus Christi; the other side faces the hotel swimming pool. Meals are served every day from 6:00 a.m. to midnight. Overnight accommodations and vacation facilities. The address is 1601 North Shoreline Boulevard in downtown Corpus Christi, Texas.

HUEVOS RANCHEROS
(Ranch-style Eggs)

3 eggs, scrambled or fried
1 whole fresh tomato, chopped fine
2 green onions, chopped fine
3 hot peppers, chopped
½ cup tomato purée
½ cup hot water
½ teaspoon salt
½ teaspoon black pepper
¼ teaspoon powdered garlic

Sauté tomato and onions together in hot greased skillet. Add hot peppers and sauté together. Stir in tomato purée and water, adding salt, pepper and garlic powder. Simmer for 8 minutes. Pour over eggs. Serves 4.

BARBECUED CHICKEN

3-pound frying chicken
3 medium-size onions, sliced thin

Cut chicken lengthwise or in quarters. Arrange in single layers skin side up in roasting pan. Sprinkle with salt and pepper. Pour in enough hot water to cover bottom of pan. Arrange onion slices over chicken, tuck some under wings and legs. Bake uncovered 30 minutes in a 350° oven. Then turn chicken pieces on other side and bake 30 minutes longer. Remove from oven and pour off all but ¾ cup of liquid in bottom of pan. Turn fryer skin side up and pour Barbecue Sauce *(below)* over chicken; return to oven and bake at 350° for one hour or until fork shows chicken is done. Baste frequently with sauce in pan.

Barbecue Sauce: Combine the following ingredients and simmer 10 minutes: 1½ cups tomato juice; ¼ teaspoon cayenne pepper; 2 teaspoons salt; ¼ teaspoon pepper; ¼ teaspoon powdered mustard; 4½ teaspoons Worcestershire sauce; 1 bay leaf; 1 teaspoon sugar; ½ cup cider vinegar; 3 peeled garlic cloves, minced; and 3 tablespoons butter.

PAINTING BY ED BEARDEN

Stage Coach Inn

Sam Houston and Robert E. Lee once signed their names in the guestbook of this "luxury stop-over" in Salado, about 40 miles from Waco. At that time the road was the Chisholm Trail; today it is Interstate 35 on the route to Mexico. The original building has been preserved, but now there is a modern motel with accommodations for 65. Open daily for lunch and dinner.

RUM PIE

Beat 3 egg yolks thoroughly while adding ½ cup of sugar, then bring mixture to a boil over hot water. Mix ½ teaspoon gelatin with 2 tablespoons water and add to boiling mixture. Flavor with 2 tablespoons rum flavoring or ½ cup dark rum. Set aside to cool and thicken. Crumble 9 graham crackers and mix with 2 teaspoons melted butter. Line 9-inch pie pan with this mixture. Whip ½ pint whipping cream and fold into filling. Whip 3 egg whites and fold into filling. Pour mixture into graham cracker shell and grate unsweetened chocolate over the top. Place in refrigerator until well set.

PAINTING BY CLYDE HORTON

Landrums Restaurant

In Brownsville, Texas, Landrums is located in one of the old residences typical of the early days in the city. Both Mexican and American foods are served from 11:30 a.m. to 2:30 p.m., and from 5:30 p.m. to 8:30 p.m. on weekdays; on Sundays, from noon to 8:00 p.m.. The address is 838 East Levee Street. Earle Brown, Jr., is the owner and manager.

PAINTING BY RALPH HULETT

5

WEST

Cooking with an international flare, yet adapted to local ingredients and palates, gives Western cuisine a distinctive, regional taste. Dishes such as coq au vin, shrimp sauté marsala, enchilada casserole, and rabbit sauté sec are indicative of the cosmopolitan tastes of the area. Look for salmon from Alaska, cranberries from Washington, pinto beans from New Mexico, potatoes from Idaho, and garden-fresh fruits and vegetables from California as specialties of the region.

Hotel Hälsingland

In buildings that were once part of Fort William Steward, the first American army post in the far north, the hotel is in Port Chilkoot, Alaska, near Haines and north of Juneau. Delicious Swedish meals featuring baked Alaska salmon and native strawberries are served daily, family style. Breakfast served 7:00 a.m. to 9:30 a.m.; lunch at noon and dinner at 6:00 p.m. Reservations necessary.

BAKED MACARONI LUNCHEON

Spread 1 cup cooked macaroni on the bottom of a buttered baking dish. Arrange the contents of a No. 2 can of green asparagus tips (save juice) on top of macaroni and a No. 303 can of whole tomatoes, drained, on top of asparagus. (Fresh tomato slices may be used in season.) Melt 2 tablespoons butter in a pan and blend in 1 tablespoon flour. While stirring, add asparagus juice, ¾ cup of canned milk and 1 cup grated American cheese; bring to a boil. Season with salt and pepper, to taste. Pour sauce over casserole and sprinkle top with ½ cup of bread crumbs. Pour 2 tablespoons melted butter over crumbs and bake in 350° oven until slightly brown. Makes 6 portions.

Baranof Western Hotel

William S. Bryant is manager of this fine hotel in Juneau, Alaska. It is located in one of the largest buildings in the center of town, at 2nd and Franklin streets. The Bubble Room is open every day for lunch and dinner until 3:00 a.m. After 9:00 p.m., there is music and entertainment nightly. The walls are hung with fine paintings depicting Alaska's early history.

SPARERIBS À LA SARABIA

4-5 pounds spareribs
2 cups celery, diced
1 green pepper, diced
1 large onion, diced
3 slices lemon
1 clove garlic, minced
1 cup chili sauce
1 cup catsup
½ cup vinegar
¼ cup liquid smoke
½ cup Worcestershire sauce
1 teaspoon dry mustard
   Pinch of white pepper
   Salt, to taste
1 teaspoon Ac'cent
1 whole bay leaf

Combine vegetables and seasonings; cook over medium heat until vegetables are tender. Wash spareribs in hot water, then bake in 350° oven until browned and half-cooked. Drain off fat; add barbecue sauce and finish cooking. Makes 6 portions. At the hotel, the spareribs are cooled and reheated over a charcoal fire before serving.

STEAK SAUCE

1 cup catsup
1 cup chili sauce
2 tablespoons onion, minced
2 tablespoons green pepper, minced
2 tablespoons celery, minced
1 tablespoon Worcestershire sauce
1 tablespoon A-1 sauce

Mix ingredients in order listed and refrigerate until ready to use. Serve with
steak or as a relish dip.

GARLIC TOAST

This restaurant bakes its own French
bread in extra-large loaves. These are
sliced about one inch thick and are
painted with a thin layer of butter
mixed with garlic oil. Then two kinds
of grated cheese are sprinkled on the
slices, Parmesan and a sharp yellow
cheese, and then they are dusted with
paprika. The slices are left in the refrigerator covered with wax paper for at
least 24 hours, then put into a hot oven
to heat thoroughly a few minutes before serving.

BANANA CHANTILLY

Beat 3 egg whites nearly stiff; gradually add ¾ cup granulated sugar, beating constantly. Add ½ teaspoon vanilla
and ¼ teaspoon vinegar. Beat until well
blended. Divide meringue into two parts
and place each part shaped to fit refrigerator tray on buttered baking sheet.
Bake in slow (275°) oven for 40-45
minutes or until delicately browned.
Remove from oven, cool.

Combine 1 cup banana pulp with ¼
teaspoon salt and 1½ tablespoons lemon
juice. Whip 1 cup whipping cream,
sweeten with ¼ cup confectioners' sugar.
Fold whipped cream into banana mixture. Place one baked meringue in refrigerator tray and cover with filling.
Top with second meringue. Freeze about
3 hours. Slice into 6-8 portions and top
each with mint leaves and a red cherry.
This is a favorite Christmas season
desert at the Lodge.

PAINTING BY WILLIAM SCHIMMEL

Green Gables

When Robert E. Gosnell built his restaurant in Phoenix,
Arizona, he set out to re-create the mood of the Middle
Ages in England. Arriving guests drive into the grounds
through a wrought-iron gate topped with flaming torches,
and are met by an armor-clad "Sir Lancelot" on his
charger. Meals are served from 11:30 a.m. to 1:00 a.m.
daily. Located at the corner of 24th and Thomas Road.

PAINTING BY PEGGY SCHOLER

Lodge on the Desert

A friendly, homelike atmosphere is the distinctive feature
of this vacation resort which is also noted for its excellent
food. The lodge is only ten minutes away from downtown
Tucson, Arizona, at 306 North Alvernon Way at Poe.
Dining room closed May 15 to November 15. Overnight
accommodations and recreation facilities the year round.
Schuyler W. Lininger is the owner and manager.

Christmas Tree Inn

Russell and Erma Bromaghim greet their guests in the small and friendly dining room of their restaurant on U.S. Highways 93 and 466, fifteen miles northwest of Kingman, at Santa Claus, Arizona. Open 7:00 a.m. to 4:00 p.m. on weekdays and until 7:00 p.m. on Sunday. Closed on Mondays. Reservations are recommended for weekday dinners at this popular restaurant.

Paul's

People come from miles around for dinner in this quaint family-style restaurant which specializes in excellent Italian cuisine. John Gaudenzi is the chef-owner. Open 11:30 a.m. to 10:00 p.m. weekdays; 4:00 p.m. to 9:00 p.m. on Sunday; closed Monday and most holidays. The address of the restaurant is 1521 Alhambra Avenue in Martinez, California.

CRANBERRY WALDORF

1 pound fresh cranberries
2 cups sugar
1 cup water
1 package lemon gelatin dessert
1 tablespoon plain gelatin
1 cup apples, chopped
1 cup celery, chopped
1 cup nuts, chopped

Combine cranberries with sugar and water and cook over medium heat until berries stop "popping." Dissolve gelatin dessert, and gelatin dissolved first in cold water, in 1 cup hot water, then mix with cooked cranberries and allow to cool. Stir remaining ingredients into oiled 9-inch square pan or molds. Chill thoroughly. Serve as a relish or on crisp lettuce with Pineapple Cream Dressing: Melt ¼ pound butter in top of double boiler, blend in ⅔ cup of flour. Add 1 cup sugar and 2 egg yolks. Mix well, then stir in 2½ cups pineapple juice and cook until thick. Fold in beaten whites of 2 eggs. Store in refrigerator and thin with whipped cream as used.

RABBIT SAUTÉ SEC

1 3-pound rabbit
4 tablespoons oil
2 sprigs parsley
1 clove garlic
8 large mushrooms, sliced
1 medium tomato
3 tablespoons butter
2 ounces white wine
  Pinch each thyme and rosemary
  Salt and pepper, to taste
4 ounces chicken or beef consommé
  (optional)

Wash rabbit in salt water. Dry thoroughly. Halve, then cut each half into six pieces. Brown rabbit in hot oil in iron skillet. Chop parsley, garlic, thyme and rosemary very fine. When rabbit is browned, drain oil and add chopped spice and mushrooms. Add butter and finely chopped tomato. Braise ingredients together for 3-4 minutes. Add wine and remaining seasonings. Cook until tender with lid partly sealed, about 20 minutes. If more moisture is desired add chicken or beef consommé. Serves 4.

CHOCOLATE APPLESAUCE CAKE

Sift 3 times: 2 cups flour, 1½ cups sugar, 2 teaspoons soda, pinch of salt, ½ teaspoon nutmeg, 1 teaspoon cinnamon, ½ teaspoon allspice and 3 tablespoons cocoa. Combine this sifted mixture with 1 cup raisins and 1 cup walnuts. Add 1½ cups unsweetened applesauce, ½ cup milk, ½ cup melted shortening and 2 teaspoons vanilla. Pour batter into greased 9 x 9 x 2-inch pan; bake 45 minutes in 350° oven.

PAINTING BY ANDREW CORLEY

Heritage House

Traces of old cables and secret caves still exist around this quiet country inn as a reminder of the days when it was a smuggler's headquarters. Breakfast and dinner served daily during the season. Closed from the first of December to the first of February. The inn is on State Highway 1 near Little River, California, seventeen miles south of Fort Bragg.

FILET OF BEEF PROVENÇALE

    6 6-ounce portions of beef filet
    4 ounces carrots, sliced ⅛-inch thick
   10 ounces onions, chopped coarse
    1 bay leaf
    1 pinch sweet basil
    1 small sprig fresh oregano
    1 pinch salt
    1 pinch ground black pepper
    1 ounce sherry
    7 ounces peeled tomatoes, chopped
    3 ounce can mushrooms and liquid
    2 ounces sliced black olives
    5 ounces supreme sauce (purchase
         in can or use cream of
         mushroom soup)
    6 toast rounds

Sauté carrots and onions a few minutes. Add the bay leaf, sweet basil, fresh oregano, salt and pepper. Stir and blend them. Add sherry and cook until carrots are tender but not soft. Add tomatoes, mushrooms and liquid, then olives. Continue cooking until completely done. Add required amount of supreme sauce to thicken. Cut ¼-inch slices of filet and cut in two. Sauté 6 ounces per person, add to Provençale sauce and serve on toast.

PAINTING BY RALPH HULETT

Sycamore Inn

In the Gold Rush days of 1849, this was the site of a trailside inn where Pony Express and Butterfield Stagecoach riders stopped for rest. Today, the Inn is a favorite stopping spot of motorists enroute to Palm Springs. Located on U.S. Highway 66 (8318 Foothill Blvd.) at Bear Gulch, Cucamonga. The Sycamore Inn is 19 miles west of San Bernardino. Lunch and dinner served daily.

The Beach Broiler

To reach this shore restaurant, you follow Pier Avenue from U.S. Highway 101 to the ocean, and then to 1215 Strand in Hermosa Beach, California. Picture windows overlook the Pacific. Lunch and dinner are served daily. A luncheon specialty is the charburger, charcoal-broiled beef on a toasted French roll. Woody Kaplan is the owner of The Beach Broiler.

Kan's Chinese Restaurant

Each dish is individually cooked on the *wok lo* (Chinese range) by expert chefs. Weekdays, lunch is served from 12:00 to 3:00 p.m., and dinner from 4:00 to 10:30 p.m. Saturday, Sunday and holidays, dinner is served from 5:00 to 10:30 p.m. Closed Thanksgiving and Christmas. Reservations accepted for eight or more. The address is 708 Grant Avenue, San Francisco, California.

BEACH BROILER BEANS

    ½ cup green pepper, chopped
    1 cup onion, chopped
    1 can pork and beans (about
        1 pound)
    ⅓ cup brown sugar
    ½ teaspoon oregano, ground
    ½ teaspoon black pepper, coarse
    ½ teaspoon dry mustard

Mix all the above ingredients together, then top with bacon. Bake uncovered in 300° oven for 2½ hours. Makes 6 portions.

MOTHER KAN'S STEAMED EGGS WITH MINCED CLAMS

        8-10 ounce can minced clams
    2½ cups cold water
        4 large eggs
    ¼ teaspoon salt
    ½ teaspoon Ac'cent
    1 tablespoon soy sauce
        Finely chopped green onions
        Steamed or fried rice

Drain clam juice from can (which will yield about ½ cup) and mix with water in a saucepan. Heat until hot, then cool. Beat eggs well with fork; add clams, salt and Ac'cent. Mix well and add clam juice and water mixture. Pour into oiled shallow baking dish or casserole. Place casserole elevated on a trivet in large cooking utensil, such as Dutch oven or chicken fryer which has a tight-fitting lid. Add enough water so that 2 inches of water surrounds casserole. Add boiling water to pan as needed. This is the Chinese method of steaming food. Cover and cook over moderate heat, removing cover of utensil frequently to drain moisture which will collect on inside of cover. This will prevent excess water from going into eggs. Cook 15-20 minutes or until knife blade comes out clean when inserted. Remove casserole from Dutch oven and sprinkle with soy sauce. Garnish with chopped green onions. Serve immediately over steamed rice. Makes 4 portions.

SHRIMP SAUTÉ MARSALA

25 jumbo shrimp
¼ pound butter
3 ounces green onions, chopped
3 ounces white onions, chopped
Pinch of garlic, chopped
Whole rosemary, to taste
Salt, to taste
Black pepper, to taste
1 cup Marsala wine
1 cup brown sauce (S&W or Hunt's
Brown Gravy)

Peel and fantail jumbo shrimp. Heat butter to smoking point and sauté shrimp. Then add onions, garlic, rosemary, and salt and pepper. Pour in Marsala and brown sauce. Simmer for 10 minutes and serve with Rice Pilaf (below). Serves 5.

RICE PILAF

Melt 2½ ounces butter and into it stir 2 ounces of broken vermicelli; brown. Add 1 cup cooked rice and 2 cups boiling chicken broth. Simmer for 20 minutes. Top with sour cream.

SAUCE PHILIPPET

2 onions, minced
1 tablespoon butter
⅓ cup dry white wine
1 tablespoon vinegar
1 cup brown sauce
2 tablespoons tomato sauce
1 tablespoon dry English mustard
(or to taste)
1 teaspoon parsley, minced
Salt, pepper and monosodium
glutamate, to taste

Sauté onion in butter until onion is golden; add wine and vinegar; reduce one half. Add brown sauce and a little tomato sauce; simmer about 10 minutes. When ready to serve, stir in mustard, parsley and seasonings. If necessary correct consistency with brown stock or wine. Sauce should be fairly thin. At the Shadow-Brook, this sauce accompanies ground beef steaks served under a glass bell. Also excellent with roasts, steaks or spareribs. Serves 8.

PAINTING BY PARKER EDWARDS

International Room

Over half the diners at this restaurant atop San Francisco's spectacular International Airport are not travelers but natives who come to enjoy the food and watch planes. A twenty-minute drive from the heart of town, the restaurant specializes in seafood and delicacies from its charcoal broiler. Lunch and dinner served daily except Saturday lunch. Reservations advisable.

PAINTING BY JAMES WARREN

Shadow-Brook

This unique restaurant is on Wharf Road in Capitola-by-the-Sea, near Santa Cruz, California. The dining room is reached by cable car or winding garden paths. Dinner served daily 5:30 p.m. to 10:00 p.m. Summer, Sunday and holiday hours are 2:00 p.m. to 9:00 p.m. Closed January through March, and Mondays in April and May. Open weekends only October through December.

PAINTING BY JAMES A. LAWRENCE

Squaw Valley Lodge

This lodge is located at an outstanding new ski development at Squaw Valley, California, site of the 1960 Winter Olympics. Breakfast, lunch and dinner served daily; dinner only during winter; continuous service at the snack bar. Overnight accommodations. Closed September 15 to December 15, and April 30 to June 15. Leave U.S. 40 at Truckee and take State 89 to the turnoff.

PAINTING BY JAMES WARREN

Sportsmen's Lodge

In 1946 David Harlig and Raymond Fine opened their unique restaurant at 12833 Ventura Boulevard (U.S. 101) at Coldwater Canyon, in North Hollywood, California. Through huge picture windows in all of the dining rooms, guests may look out onto five acres of trout-filled lakes and streams. Trout caught in the lakes are served in the dining room. Dinner daily, 5:00 p.m. to 2:00 a.m.

TOURNEDOS OF BEEF TENDERLOIN

Place ½ cup sherry wine in shallow pan over low heat. Slowly add 8 well-beaten egg yolks, then the juice of 1 lemon and ½ teaspoon tarragon. Simmer for 1 minute. Place pan in double boiler to keep mixture hot while adding ½ pound melted butter. Stir constantly. Place 12 ¾-inch-thick slices filet mignon in broiler and broil to taste. When done, place 1 tablespoon sauce mixture on each steak and top each with a fried mushroom. Serves 6.

BEEF STROGANOFF

1½ pounds tenderloin tips, sliced
4 tablespoons butter
4 shallots, chopped fine
1 clove garlic
1 medium onion, chopped
6 button mushrooms, sliced
1 bay leaf
1½ tablespoons flour
2 cups consommé
3 ounces tomato purée
1 tablespoon Lea and Perrin Sauce
½ cup sherry wine
4 tablespoons sour cream
2 tablespoons chives
2 cups uncooked rice
   Dash of Tabasco
   Crushed black pepper and salt,
      to taste

Combine 2 tablespoons butter, shallots, garlic, onion, mushrooms and bay leaf; sauté until transparent. Add flour, mix until well blended; add heated consommé, tomato sauce; simmer for 10 minutes. Season sliced tenderloin tips with salt and freshly crushed pepper; sauté in remaining 2 tablespoons butter until brown. Add Lea and Perrin Sauce, sherry and Tabasco. Combine sauce with meat. Just before serving add sour cream and chives until well blended. Serve with steamed white rice. Makes 4 portions.

FILET TIPS SAUTÉ

3 pounds beef filet
4 tablespoons olive oil
1½ green peppers
1 medium onion, sliced
½ cup mushrooms, canned
½ teaspoon parsley, chopped
½ teaspoon beef soup base
½ teaspoon chicken soup base
5 tablespoons water
1 tablespoon sauterne
½ teaspoon soy sauce

Cut filet ¼-inch thick and into 1½-inch pieces. Brown in olive oil. Sauté green peppers, onion, mushrooms and parsley in oil with meat. Dissolve soup bases in water. Combine all ingredients together with the meat and cook for 1½ minutes. Serve immediately. Makes 5 portions.

PINEAPPLE ICEBOX CAKE

¼ pound butter
2 cups confectioners' sugar
4 eggs, separated
2 cups well-drained pineapple, crushed
2 cups vanilla wafers, crushed
½ cup nuts, chopped

Blend butter and sugar. Add beaten egg yolks and mix. Stir in pineapple and fold in beaten egg whites. Spread half of crumbs and nuts over bottom of 24 x 12-inch pan and pour pineapple mixture over them. Cover with remaining nuts and crumbs. Chill in refrigerator overnight before serving. Makes 24 portions.

ROYAL CHICKEN SOUP

Braise together in 2 tablespoons chicken fat: ½ cup ground carrots, ½ cup ground onions and ½ cup ground celery. Blend in ½ cup flour. Add 2 cups chicken stock and boil gently 30 minutes. Then add 2 cups powdered milk; ½ cup cooked chicken, chopped; and 1 pimento, chopped. Season to taste with salt and pepper and heat but do not boil. Makes 6 portions.

PAINTING BY W. STANLEY PEARCE

Mission Ranch

Located at the south end of Dolores Street, the Ranch is a fifteen-minute walk from Carmel, California, and is adjacent to the 1771 Carmel Mission, the second-oldest in the state. Dinner served from 5:00 p.m. to 1:00 a.m. Overnight accommodations and recreation facilities. Reservations advisable. Mail address: Manager, Charles Heebner; Route #2, Box 88; Carmel, California.

PAINTING BY ED VON BARTHELD

The Williams Wayside Inn

Fried chicken served with all the mashed potatoes, gravy, hot rolls and honey you can eat is the specialty of the house. Steak, mountain trout and shrimp are also on the menu. About forty-two miles from Denver, the Inn is at 505 Mountain Avenue (U.S. 287) in Berthoud, Colorado. Lunch and dinner served; closed Monday and from December 23 to January 2. Stan Williams is the owner.

The Blue Jay Inn

On Route 126 in the quiet mountain village of Buffalo Creek, Colorado, in Pike National Forest, this resort is 50 miles southwest of Denver. Closed Labor Day to June 15. Reservations required for meals; overnight and vacation accommodations. Mrs. Katherine Ramus is the owner. Attractions at The Blue Jay Inn include trout fishing, a gift shop and antiques.

Red Rock

A Friday night seafood buffet is a feature of this restaurant at 1304 North Main Street (U.S. 30) in Pocatello, Idaho. Breakfast, lunch and dinner are served every day of the year, 7:00 a.m. to 2:00 a.m.; no reservations necessary. R. C. Fowler is the owner as well as the manager of this fine eating place. The Butter Rum Sauce is particularly outstanding.

BROCCOLI AND HAM CASSEROLE

1 fresh broccoli, or 10 ounces frozen
1 cup cooked ham, chopped
1 tablespoon parsley, chopped
2 tablespoons green pepper, chopped
2 hard-boiled eggs, chopped
¼ cup American cheese, grated
1 teaspoon onion, chopped
4 teaspoons lemon juice
1½ cups light cream sauce
1 cup buttered bread crumbs

Cook broccoli; cut into 1-inch pieces and place in buttered casserole. Combine ham with parsley, green pepper, eggs, cheese, onion and lemon juice. Cover broccoli with ham mixture. Top with cream sauce. Sprinkle buttered crumbs on top. Bake in 350° oven for 20 minutes. (Green beans or asparagus may be substituted for broccoli.) Serves 5-6.

BUTTER RUM SAUCE

2 tablespoons cornstarch
½ teaspoon salt
1 cup sugar
2 cups boiling water
2 tablespoons butter
1 teaspoon rum flavor
1 ounce rum
Juice of ½ lemon

Mix cornstarch, salt and sugar together. Add boiling water gradually, stirring constantly. Boil 5 minutes and remove from fire. Add butter, rum flavor, rum and lemon juice. Serve warm over hot mince or apple pie. Also makes a delicious topping for fruit cake or ice cream.

CHICKEN IN FOIL

Cook ¾ cup rice in salted water until done. Drain and rinse rice in cold water. Add 2 tablespoons melted butter, ⅓ teaspoon curry powder, pinch of cayenne, pinch of nutmeg, 1½ tablespoons blanched chopped almonds and ¼ cup shredded coconut. Make a cream sauce by blending 2 tablespoons butter with 3 tablespoons flour and 3 cups of milk. Cook over low heat until sauce thickens. Sauté small green pepper, chopped, and 1 small onion, also chopped, and add to cream sauce. Then add 1 ounce pimentos, ¾ teaspoon salt and ¾ pound cooked chicken, diced. Cut aluminum foil into 12 12-inch squares and place 2 tablespoons rice mixture in center, then add 3-4 tablespoons chicken mix on top. Fold foil to make envelope and bake 30 to 40 minutes in a 350° oven. Makes 12 small servings or 6 large portions.

PAINTING BY LEON BEROTH

Templin's

Half a million visitors annually visit the recreation areas in the northern part of Idaho which surround this restaurant. It is at 112 West Sherman in Coeur d'Alene, Idaho, at the intersection of U. S. Highways 10 and 95. Open every day 7:00 a.m. to 1:00 a.m. Closed Christmas. Overnight accommodations at the adjoining motel. R. C. Templin is the owner and Jim Taylor is the manager.

LEMON PIE

Filling:
- 1½ cups sugar
- 1½ cups water
- ¼ teaspoon salt
- 5 tablespoons cornstarch
- 2 tablespoons flour (mixed with ⅓ cup water for paste)
- 3 egg yolks (save whites)
- 1½ lemons, juice
  Grated rind of 1 lemon
- 1 tablespoon butter
- 9-inch pie shell, baked

Bring sugar and water to rolling boil. Add salt, cornstarch and flour paste. Stir until clear and smooth. Then add beaten egg yolks, lemon juice, grated rind and butter. Cook 1 minute. Cool; pour into 9-inch cooked pie shell and top with meringue.

Meringue: Beat the whites of the 3 eggs left from filling until stiff. Add 2 tablespoons sugar, stir in well. Spread over filled pie. Place in 350° oven for 3 minutes or until golden brown.

PAINTING BY DON BENNETT

Shady Nook Inn

In the beautiful and rugged north central section of Idaho, set against a backdrop of the Bitterroot Mountains, this restaurant is located in the town of Salmon on U.S. 93. During the summer (July to September) dinner is served daily 5:00 p.m. to 1:00 a.m. The rest of the year the restaurant is closed on Sunday. Reservations are not required. The Shady Nook Inn is owned by Spencer Sheets.

Bud Lake Cafe

On U.S. 10 and 93, it is three miles west of Missoula, Montana. W. E. Hainline, Jr., is the owner and manager of this eating place which is open every day of the year— 24 hours a day. There are year-round facilities for sportsmen in this area. Abundant game and fish are available and pack horse trips for big game hunting may be made into Idaho's Clearwater County and other areas.

Brooks Hotel

This hotel has been a favorite eating place in western Montana since 1915, when it was founded by Mr. and Mrs. Louis N. Brooks. It is now owned by their daughters. Surrounding poplar trees were planted in 1890. It is two miles east of U.S. 93 in Corvallis. Breakfast, lunch and dinner weekdays; Sunday dinner, 1:30 p.m. by reservation. Overnight accommodations.

BAKED PORK CHOPS SOUTHERN STYLE

6 extra-thick center cut pork chops
2 tablespoons shortening
1 large onion sliced
½ cup uncooked rice
   Salt and pepper, to taste
1 No. 2½ can tomatoes

Brown pork chops on both sides in shortening. Place in baking dish and cover chops with onion slices. Sprinkle rice over dish and season well with salt and pepper. Cover with tomatoes and bake for two hours in preheated 300° oven. Makes 6 servings.

APPLE PUDDING

2 eggs, beaten
1 cup sugar
1 teaspoon each: soda and cinnamon
¼ teaspoon each: clove and salt
1 cup flour
4 tablespoons butter, melted
½ cup nuts
½ cup raisins
3 cups apples, grated

Beat eggs until light, add sugar gradually. Beat in sifted dry ingredients. Add butter, grated apples, and floured nuts and raisins. Spread mixture about 1½-2 inches thick in buttered 8 x 12-inch pan. Bake 40 minutes in 375° oven. Serve with Butterscotch Sauce (below).

Butterscotch Sauce: Mix together 1 cup light brown sugar; 1 cup water; 1 tablespoon cornstarch and 3 tablespoons butter. Cook until thick. Add ½ teaspoon vanilla and serve warm over pudding.

BEEF STEAK STROGANOFF

1 pound sirloin steak, in ¾-inch
  strips
¼ cup flour
1 tablespoon paprika
½ teaspoon salt
⅛ teaspoon pepper
2 tablespoons fat
½ cup onion, chopped
1 clove garlic, minced
  6-ounce can mushrooms
  10-ounce can mushroom soup
1 tablespoon Worcestershire sauce
1 cup sour cream
2 cups hot cooked rice

Combine flour, paprika, salt and pepper. Roll meat strips in flour mixture and then brown in hot fat. Remove meat when browned, then add onion, garlic and mushrooms. Cook gently until onions are golden—*don't scorch!* Add remaining ingredients except cream and rice. Cook until thickened and bubbly. Return meat to pan and simmer about 1 hour or until meat is tender. Stir occasionally. Add cream 15 minutes before serving—*don't boil!* Serve over hot rice and sprinkle with Parmesan cheese, if desired.

DATE NUT BREAD

½ cup butter, melted
2 yeast cakes
5 cups flour
2 eggs
1 tablespoon salt
1 tablespoon cinnamon
2 cups dates, chopped
1½ cups walnuts, chopped
1 cup sugar

Put 2 cups lukewarm water in a mixing bowl; add butter, yeast and 2 cups flour. Make a sponge by mixing and let stand in warm place until dough doubles in size. Add remaining ingredients, mixing well, and then knead; again let mixture double in size. Shape into 3 loaves 4½x8x2½ inches; let rise again and bake at 350° for 1 hour. Makes 3 eight-ounce loaves of nut bread.

PAINTING BY JAMES DEW

Lake McDonald Lodge

In Glacier National Park, Montana, this was once a hunting lodge, but in more recent years it has been a comfortable vacation spot for families. Breakfast, lunch and dinner served daily. Overnight accommodations and excellent recreation facilities. Open every day during the season, June 15 to September 15. Reservations necessary for lodging only. Grill open between meals.

PAINTING BY JAMES A. LAWRENCE

El Capitan

One block north of U.S. Highway 95, at 541 F Street in Hawthorne, Nevada, this resort motel offers a heated swimming pool, baby sitters and a guide- and boat-booking service for trout fishing on nearby Walker Lake. The dining rooms are open twenty-four hours a day the year round. George Goodall is the manager and host of this Nevada vacation spot.

The Christmas Tree

Steaks and chops are the only main courses served here; they are broiled in the dining room over an open fire of mountain mahogany. Eighteen miles south of Reno, Nevada, on the Mount Rose Highway, this restaurant is adjacent to both the Reno Ski Bowl and the Mount Rose Ski Area. Nearby in California is Squaw Valley, site of the 1960 Winter Olympics. Dinner served every day.

Sharon House

This dining room is located at the corner of C and Taylor streets in Virginia City, Nevada, a town which has become a mecca for tourists interested in the Old West. Lunch and dinner served every day in summer; summer hours, 12:00 noon to 11:00 p.m.; winter hours, 5:00 p.m. to 11:00 p.m. Closed Tuesday starting December 1. Overnight accommodations. Reservations.

CHRISTMAS TREE ROQUEFORT DRESSING

14 ounces Roquefort cheese
4 tablespoons wine vinegar
1 tablespoon salt
½ teaspoon ground white pepper
   Pinch of Coleman's dry mustard
   Dash of Tabasco sauce
1½ teaspoons Lea and Perrin Sauce
4 tablespoons salad oil
5⅓ cups mayonnaise
   Milk, to desired consistency

Crumble cheese, then add all ingredients in order listed, except mayonnaise and milk. Mix ingredients thoroughly, then add mayonnaise. Mix again and thin to desired consistency by adding milk. Store in refrigerator in covered jar. Makes about 2 quarts of dressing.

ALMOND CHICKEN

4-4½ pounds uncooked frying chicken
2 cloves garlic, minced
½ cup salad oil
3 cups water
2 cups water chestnuts, diced
2 cups bamboo shoots
1 cup Chinese or button mushrooms, diced
2 cups celery, diced
1 cup onion, diced
1 cup peas, fresh or frozen
1 teaspoon salt
½ teaspoon white pepper
¾ teaspoon monosodium glutamate
1 teaspoon Kitchen Bouquet
2 tablespoons cornstarch in ½ cup water
2 cups toasted almonds
   Steamed rice

Bone and dice chicken. Sauté garlic in hot salad oil until soft. Add chicken, cook for 5 minutes. Blend in water, water chestnuts, bamboo shoots, mushrooms, celery and onion. Cover and cook five minutes. Add peas and seasonings, except Kitchen Bouquet. Bring to a boil. Then add Kitchen Bouquet. Thicken with cornstarch. Garnish with toasted almonds. Serve over steamed rice. Serves 4-6.

OLD-FASHIONED BEEF STEW

    2 pounds beef chuck, 1½-inch cubes
    2 tablespoons fat
    4 cups boiling water
    1 tablespoon lemon juice (optional)
    1 teaspoon Worcestershire sauce
    1 clove garlic
    1 medium onion, sliced
    1 to 2 bay leaves
    1 tablespoon salt
    1 teaspoon sugar
    ½ teaspoon pepper
    ½ teaspoon paprika
      Dash allspice or cloves
    6 carrots
    18-24 small white onions

Heat fat and thoroughly brown meat on all sides. Add water, lemon juice, Worcestershire, garlic, sliced onion, bay leaves and other seasonings. Cover pot and simmer for 2 hours, stirring occasionally to keep from sticking. Remove bay leaves and garlic clove. Add carrots and onions. (If desired, cubed potatoes may be added.) Cover and continue cooking 30 minutes, or till vegetables are done. Remove the meat and vegetables and thicken liquid for gravy. Serves 6-8.

ENCHILADA CASSEROLE

    1 pound ground beef
    2 tablespoons shortening
    2 tablespoons chili powder
    6 tablespoons flour
      Garlic, salt and pepper, to taste
    1 quart water
    12 corn tortillas
    1½ cups onion, chopped
    1½ cups longhorn cheese, grated

Braise ground beef in shortening; add chili, flour and other seasonings. Cook 5 more minutes, add water and bring to a boil. Cook 8-10 minutes. Dip tortillas in hot deep fat. Build up alternate layers of tortillas, onion, cheese and chili in an 8-inch-deep casserole. Heat in 375° oven for 20-25 minutes until bubbly. Makes 6 servings.

PAINTING BY CLARENCE E. KINCAID

The Trails Restaurant

This excellent highway restaurant is popular with tourists as well as natives. It is adjacent to the Pioneer Motor Lodge which offers a heated swimming pool, air conditioning and extra-length beds for six-footers. Located on U.S. Highways 60, 70 and 84 East at Clovis, New Mexico, the restaurant is open for breakfast, lunch and dinner every day. Owned and operated by the Peter Millers.

PAINTING BY JOSEF BAKOS

Sagebrush Inn

Taos, New Mexico, a world-famous art colony located at the foot of the beautiful Sangre de Cristo Mountains, is the home of this spacious Spanish-style inn. Breakfast and dinner served daily; Sunday brunch served from 8:30 a.m. to 2:30 p.m. Overnight accommodations are also available. The Sagebrush Inn is located on U.S. Highways 64 and 85.

Albert's Lodge

On Oregon's famous McKenzie River, the Lodge is in Vida, Oregon, 27 miles east of Eugene on U.S. Highway 126. Dinner is the only meal served to non-resident guests, and reservations should be made; closed Monday. Each meal is cooked to order in the Lodge's small kitchen. Overnight accommodations and excellent white-water boating and trout fishing in the area.

STUFFED BAKED POTATOES

6 large baking potatoes
  Cream
1 tablespoon onion, grated
¼ teaspoon monosodium glutamate
  Salt, to taste
6 pats of butter

Scrub potatoes well and bake. Cut off tops and scoop out cooked potato and mash. Then add remaining ingredients, except butter, and beat well. Heap seasoned potato into shells and at serving time heat in 400° oven for 15 minutes. Top each potato with a pat of butter.

The Pantry

Chicken bisque, served steaming hot in a gleaming copper tureen, toasted nippy cheese bread and crisp greens with French-Caesar dressing are a favorite light meal combination. Across from the Lloyd Shopping Center, at 1025 N.E. Broadway in Portland, the dining room is open weekdays from 11:30 a.m. to midnight; Sundays from 4:00 p.m. to 10:00 p.m.

CHICKEN BISQUE

8 cups rich chicken stock
1 cup finely chopped chicken
¼ cup green peppers, chopped
¼ cup pimientos, chopped
  Salt and pepper, to taste
  Dash of Ac'cent
½ cup butter
½ cup flour

Combine chicken stock, chicken, green peppers and pimientos. Simmer for 30 minutes and season to taste. Melt butter over low flame, then add flour a little at a time, stirring constantly. When roux is lightly browned, add a few tablespoons of hot soup and blend into a smooth paste. Stir into simmering soup and continue stirring until it thickens. Makes 8 portions.

SPARERIBS À LA HILLVILLA

Cut 4 pounds of spareribs into 2-3 rib portions. Apply Figaro or Liquid Smoke on each side of ribs and brown lightly in a 450° oven. Pour off grease.

Sauce:

2 cups catsup
2 cups water
1 ounce Worcestershire sauce
½ cup brown sugar
1 tablespoon salt
1 ounce Figaro or Liquid Smoke
1 small clove garlic, cut fine
1 medium onion, sliced
¼ cup red wine

Combine all of the above sauce ingredients and pour over spareribs which have been placed in a heavy baking pan. Cover and bake in 325° oven for about 1½ hours or until ribs are tender. Serves 4.

PAINTING BY JOHN WADDINGHAM

Palaske's Hillvilla

Perched high above the Willamette River, diners at this restaurant have a magnificent view of seven great mountains of the Cascade Range. The address is 5700 S. W. Terwilliger in Portland, Oregon. Lunch and dinner served every day throughout the year. Reservations not required but recommended. E. Palaske is the owner and manager of this scenic spot.

OYSTER LOAF

Sauté 3 dozen small Pacific oysters in 2 tablespoons butter with 1 cup chopped celery until the oysters are plump, about 8-10 minutes over medium heat. Cut the top crust from 1-pound loaf of French bread (or 6 individual loaves), hollow out the interior and brush the inside and top crust generously with ½ cup melted butter. Brown bread in 450° oven for 4-5 minutes. Add 2 cups medium cream sauce and 1 cup toasted bread crumbs to oysters. Pour mixture into browned loaf of bread, replace top, and heat in 450° oven for 8-10 minutes. Makes 6-8 portions.

PAINTING BY ERNEST RICHARDSON

Poor Richard's

The era of Benjamin Franklin is reflected in the décor of this delightful restaurant in Portland, Oregon. Two blocks north of U.S. 30 at 3907 N.E. Broadway, it is open weekdays 11:30 a.m. to 1:00 a.m. Closed on Sundays, Christmas Day and Labor Day. Owners Stan Prouty and Hal Hulburt are particularly proud of their West Coast seafood.

PAINTING BY ERNEST RICHARDSON

Sky Room Lounge

Located at the Municipal Airport in Pendleton, Oregon, this restaurant affords diners an excellent view of the arriving and departing planes. Breakfast, lunch and dinner served daily. The airport is three and a half miles west of the city, a mile off U.S. Highway 30. Fred T. Hall is the owner and manager of the Sky Room Lounge. The clam chowder is a delectable treat here.

CLAM CHOWDER

1 cup potatoes, diced
1 small onion, diced
1 ounce butter
2 tablespoons flour
3 cups whole milk
  Pinch of pepper
½ teaspoon salt, or to taste
1 8-ounce can minced clams

Simmer potatoes and onion together in small amount of water until tender. Melt butter in small pan, then blend in flour making a smooth paste. Drain juice from clams and blend into butter and flour mixture. Add to cooked potatoes and onions, then stir in milk and clams. Heat to serving temperature—do not boil. Season to taste and serve. Makes 6-8 portions.

PAINTING BY HAROLD CRAIG

The Pancake House

A popular place to stop for breakfast on the way to Oregon's beaches, this specialty restaurant features thirteen kinds of pancakes—each a different national favorite. Pancakes are favorites for light lunches and dinners, too. The Pancake House is open from 6:00 a.m. to 8:00 p.m. every day except Monday. It is on Barbur Boulevard (U.S. 99) at S.W. 24th in Portland, Oregon.

OLD-FASHIONED GERMAN PANCAKES

4 eggs
1 cup cream
1 cup hard wheat flour
3 tablespoons confectioners' sugar
  Dash of freshly grated nutmeg
¼ teaspoon salt
  Lemon juice and confectioners' sugar

Break eggs in mixing bowl, then add remaining ingredients, except lemon juice and confectioners' sugar. Whip to a smooth batter with a wire whip and pour ½ cup batter into a well-buttered 11-inch pan. Place over burner until set. Then turn over and put in 500° oven for 3 to 5 minutes. Follow same procedure with remaining batter. Coat with confectioners' sugar and serve with lemon juice. Serves 2-4.

CHICKEN LIVERS HOMESTEAD

3½ cups chicken livers
1 cup seasoned flour
8 tablespoons butter

Roll chicken livers in flour and brown in butter. Pour Bordelaise Sauce *(below)* over browned livers. Cover and simmer 15 minutes. Turn occasionally to prevent burning. Makes 4 portions.

Bordelaise Sauce: Sauté ¼ cup chopped onion and 2 tablespoons chopped green pepper in 2 tablespoons vegetable oil. Add 2 cups rich brown beef gravy, ¼ cup mushroom buttons and 6 tablespoons sherry.

ROQUEFORT DRESSING

Combine 1 cup sour cream, 1 cup mayonnaise, 2-ounce wedge of Roquefort (or to taste), 2 teaspoons lemon juice, 1 teaspoon horse-radish, few drops of Worcestershire sauce, dash of Tabasco sauce and 2 tablespoons sherry.

SWEDISH APPLE PIE

2 cups apple slices, cooked
2 tablespoons flour
¾ cup sugar
Pinch of salt
1 egg
1 teaspoon vanilla
1 cup sour cream
9-inch pie shell, unbaked

Mash apples slightly; add flour, sugar, and salt. Beat eggs and vanilla, add to apple mix. Beat sour cream until stiff and fold into apple mixture. Pour into pie shell and bake at 350° for 40 minutes. Remove and sprinkle with Topping *(below)*, return to oven for 15 minutes.

Topping: Rub the following ingredients together like pastry dough with fork or fingers: ⅓ cup sugar, ⅓ cup flour, 1 teaspoon cinnamon and ¼ pound soft butter or margarine.

PAINTING BY CHRISTIAN JENSEN

The Homestead

Formerly called Schneitter's Hot Pots, this hotel is located in one of the high cool valleys in the Wasatch Mountains, about an hour's drive from Salt Lake City, Utah. To reach the resort, turn west on U.S. 40 at Heber, Utah, and follow signs to The Homestead in Midway. From Memorial Day through Labor Day, the hotel is open daily for meals and accommodations.

PAINTING BY V. DOUGLAS SNOW

Andy's Smorgasbord

Over seventy dishes are offered to diners from the smorgasbord table at this Salt Lake City, Utah, restaurant. Dinner served every day; reservations necessary on weekends. Stephen B. Anderson is the manager of this eating place at 3350 Highland Drive. The Swedish apple pie recipe, the restaurant's specialty, has been a carefully kept secret until now.

PAINTING BY CHRISTIAN JENSEN

Maddox Ranch House

Twelve years ago this restaurant started out as a small drive-in, but it was popular from the first day and today it has expanded to three dining rooms *and* a drive-in. Meals served from 11:00 a.m. to 11:00 p.m. daily; closed on Monday and January 2 to January 21. Two miles south of Brigham City, Utah, it is on U.S. Highways 30S, 91, 89 and 191, in the shadow of the mountains.

PAINTING BY VERA ERICKSON

Illahee Ranch

The aroma of oven-fresh bread greets guests at this delightful restaurant midway between Tacoma and Seattle, just off U.S. Highway 99, at 30602 Pacific Highway South, Federal Way, Washington. Open 4:30 p.m. to 10:00 p.m. daily, the ranch features individual loaves of old-fashioned bread every day. Mary Jarrett owns this establishment which overlooks Steele Lake.

WESTERN POTATO SOUP

1 gallon fresh, rich beef stock
1 small bunch green onions, chopped fine
½ green pepper, chopped fine
¼ teaspoon black pepper
1 teaspoon salt
1 teaspoon Ac'cent
3 freshly boiled potatoes, mashed
1 generous tablespoon butter
1 cup milk

Simmer onions and green pepper and seasonings in beef stock until vegetables become soft. Add freshly mashed potatoes and butter and simmer. Combine milk with flour to a smooth mixture and blend into soup. Serve with golden brown toast or your favorite cracker.

INDIVIDUAL LOAVES OF HOMEMADE BREAD

1 quart lukewarm water
¼ cup sugar
1 packet Fleischmann's powdered yeast
1⅓ cups powdered milk
10 cups Gold Medal hard wheat or all-purpose flour
2 tablespoons salt
1 cup salad oil

Quickly stir together lukewarm water, sugar, yeast, powdered milk and 4 cups of flour. Place in bread raiser or bowl and set in warm place with lid on pan. In one hour this mixture, which is the old-fashioned bread starter, will be bubbly. Add salt, salad oil and remaining 6 cups of flour and knead this mixture for 5 minutes to get a good rubbery dough. Put dough back in bread raiser, replace lid, and again set in warm place. When it has more than doubled its bulk, knead to remove all air. Do not pat—only knead and squeeze. Place dough in individual (children's size—1½ inches deep, 2 inches wide and 3½ inches long) greased bread pans. Fill pans half full. Let rise again until double. Place loaves in pre-heated 350° oven. Bake 10 minutes. Remove bread from oven and pans; butter top crust and eat. Makes 20 individual loaves.

TOSSED GREEN SALAD

1 head romaine
2 carrots, grated
4 stalks celery, diced
½ cup red cabbage, shredded
4 shallots, chopped
1 tomato, cut in wedges
1 hard-boiled egg, grated
½ cup crabmeat or shrimp
   Dash of Parmesan cheese
   Fresh bread croutons

Combine vegetables in a chilled bowl. Add dressing *(below)*, grated egg and crabmeat or shrimp. Add touch of cheese and serve with croutons which have been buttered and toasted with Parmesan cheese.

Dressing: Combine 1 cup wine vinegar, 3 cups oil, salt and pepper to taste, 1 teaspoon dry mustard, dash of Tabasco and Worcestershire, 1 teaspoon paprika and ¼ cup tomato purée. Shake well and use on salad. Store in refrigerator.

PAINTING BY HARRY BONATH

Top o' the Town—Hotel Sorrento

Guests dining here are treated to a magnificent view of Puget Sound and the city of Seattle. A special prime ribs dinner is the only meal featured in this dining room which is open weekdays 5:30 p.m. to 1:00 a.m. It closes at midnight on Saturday. Closed on Sunday. The hotel is at the corner of Terry and Madison streets in downtown Seattle, Washington.

HOT ROLLS

1 cup boiling water
¼ cup shortening
1½ teaspoons salt
3 tablespoons sugar
1 egg, beaten
1 yeast cake
½ teaspoon sugar
3½ cups flour, approximately

Combine boiling water, shortening, salt and sugar; let mixture cool. Combine yeast cake with half teaspoon sugar and just enough lukewarm water to soften. When mixture has cooled, put in egg, yeast mixture and about 2 cups of flour. Mix and continue to add flour until dough can be easily handled. Knead lightly and let rise in warm place until double in size. Push down and form into Parker House rolls. Let rise until double again. Bake in 375° oven for 15-20 minutes. Makes 30 rolls.

PAINTING BY PHIL KOOSER

Trout Lodge

Just 21 miles from the White Pass ski area, the Lodge is on State Highway 5 seventeen miles from Naches, Washington. Breakfast, lunch and dinner are served daily. Motel accommodations and recreational facilities in the area the year round. Closed on Wednesday during the slow season. Ralph and Barbara Von Weller are the owner-managers of this scenic vacation spot.

PAINTING BY F. L. MC KENNA

Hotel Emerson

In the heart of clam and cranberry country, this hotel at 701 Simpson (U.S. 101) is on the Hoquiam River in Hoquiam, Washington. Breakfast, lunch and dinner served in the dining room and coffee shop daily. Closed Sunday. Vacation facilities are also in the area. J. James Lesko is the manager. Wild huckleberry pie is one of the many favorites that come from the Emerson's kitchen.

WILD HUCKLEBERRY PIE

4 cups fresh huckleberries
3 tablespoons granulated tapioca
1½ cups brown sugar
⅛ teaspoon salt
1 tablespoon lemon juice
1 tablespoon butter
2 9-inch pie crusts

Stem and wash berries. Mix together tapioca, sugar and salt. Sprinkle over berries. Sprinkle with lemon juice. Line pie tin with bottom crust, pour in filling and dot with butter. Cover with top crust. Bake in 450° oven for 10 minutes. Reduce heat to 350° and bake 35 minutes more or until berries are tender.

PAINTING BY JAMES HAUGHEY

Cassie's Supper Club

On U.S. Highway 20, just a mile and a half west of Cody, Wyoming, right in the heart of Buffalo Bill's territory. This restaurant is open weekday evenings for dinner from 5:00 p.m. to 11:00 p.m. Closed Sunday. Owners Ole and Mable Nelson greet all guests. Chicken Cream Salad is a great favorite with the diners. Seafood specialties are also very popular.

CHICKEN CREAM SALAD

2 cups cooked chicken, minced
1 tablespoon gelatin
2 tablespoons cold water
½ cup mayonnaise
½ cup heavy cream, whipped
¼ tablespoon lemon juice
½ cup celery, minced
¼ cup stuffed olives, minced
   Shredded lettuce
6 tomato slices

Soak gelatin for 5 minutes in cold water. Set over hot water until it melts, add to mayonnaise. Fold mixture into whipped cream, then add remaining ingredients. Pour into six individual molds greased with butter and chill in refrigerator until firm. Arrange shredded lettuce on individual salad plates with tomato slice in center.

Turn mold out onto tomato. Garnish with mayonnaise and pickle fans, if desired. Makes 6 portions.

BARBECUED RIBS

6 pounds of pork loin ribs or
  short ribs of beef
2 tablespoons celery salt
1 tablespoon chili powder
2 tablespoons garlic salt
½ cup brown sugar
¼ teaspoon black pepper
¼ teaspoon allspice
3 tablespoons salt
1 tablespoon cloves, ground
½ cup sweet pickle relish
1 quart catsup
1 pint pork meat stock
1 cup onion, chopped
½ cup vinegar

Braise ribs until light brown. Combine remaining ingredients and pour over ribs and cook at 350° for 2½ hours. Makes 12 portions.

PAINTING BY ROBERT ATWOOD

Sheridan Inn Dining Room

Long ago Buffalo Bill held forth on the veranda of this Sheridan, Wyoming, inn. Today it is owned and managed by Bob and Margueritte Lepper. Open for breakfast at 6:00 a.m. to 10:00 a.m.; and for dinner 5:30 p.m. to 9:30 p.m. Modern overnight accommodations. Closed December 24 and January 1. Turn east off Main Street (U.S. 14 and 87) at Fifth, go two blocks to Broadway.

BEEF AND TURKEY TENDERLOIN

8 ounces tenderloin steak, sliced
8 ounces cooked turkey breast,
  sliced
2 tablespoons butter
4 pieces of toast
4 tablespoons mushrooms
½ cup cream sauce
2 tablespoons cream
2 tablespoons white wine
  Parsley, freshly chopped

Sauté beef and turkey in butter. Trim toast to circle shapes. Remove meat from butter and sauté mushrooms lightly. Add mushrooms to warm cream sauce; then blend in butter, cream and wine. Place one piece each of beef and turkey on toast circles and top with sauce. Garnish with parsley. Serves 4.

PAINTING BY A. THERNES KASTLE

Hitching Post

Located on the western side of Cheyenne, Wyoming, at 1600 West Lincolnway (U.S. 30), the Hitching Post is a complete stop for motorists, with dining facilities, shops and a motel. There is also a heated swimming pool and children's play area. The dining room is open 5:00 a.m. to 1:00 a.m. daily. Harry P. Smith is the owner. Reservations advisable for the dinner hour.

Travelers' Guide to Restaurants

ALABAMA

Blue Moon Inn. 1816 Goode St. (U.S. 80W), Montgomery. Lunch, dinner. Closed Sun., Mon., and the month of Aug. **R**

The Coffee Pot. U.S. 29 and 331, 1 mile south of Luverne. Closed Christmas Day. (See page 34.)

The Colonial Inn. 201 S. Mobile Ave. (U.S. 98), Fairhope. **O–V–R** (See page 35.)

Constantine's. 9-11 N. Royal St., Mobile. (See page 35.)

The Cotton Patch. U.S. 11 and 43, Eutaw. Lunch, dinner. **R**

Dale's Cellar. 1927 Seventh Ave., Birmingham. Lunch, dinner. Closed Sun.

Grand Hotel. U.S. 98, Point Clear (25 miles southeast of Mobile). **O–V–R** (See page 34.)

Meme's. 10 miles south of Foley, Bon Secour. Lunch, dinner. Closed Mon. and from Dec. 15 thru Dec. 30 and the first two weeks in May. **R**

The Ranch Restaurant. 3118 Mobile Rd. (U.S. 80W and Alt. U.S. 82 and 31), Montgomery. Closed Christmas Day. (See page 36.)

The Town Club. 612 N. Wood Ave., Florence. Lunch, dinner. Closed Sun. **R** (See page 36.)

ALASKA

Baranof Western Hotel. Second and Franklin Sts., Juneau. Lunch, dinner. (See page 104.)

Hotel Hälsingland. Port Chilkoot. **O–R** (See page 104.)

ARIZONA

Camelback Inn. 5402 E. Lincoln Dr., Phoenix. Closed May 6 to Oct. 8. **O–V–R**

Christmas Tree Inn. U.S. 93 and 466, Santa Claus (15 miles northwest of Kingman). Open 7 a.m. to 4 p.m. weekdays, until 7 p.m. Sun. Closed Mon. **R** for weekday dinner. (See page 106.)

El Tovar Hotel. State Hwy 64, Grand Canyon. Closed Nov. 1 to May 1. **O–V**

Frontier Inn. 466 E. Center St., Wickenburg. Lunch, dinner. Closed Tues., Christmas Day, and the months of July and Aug.

Green Gables. 24th and Thomas Rd., Phoenix. Lunch, dinner. (See page 105.)

Lee's Restaurant. 2310 E. McDowell Rd., Phoenix. Open 4 p.m. to 10 p.m. Closed Mon.

Lodge on the Desert. 306 N. Alvernon Way, Tucson. Dining room closed May 15 to Nov. 15. **O–V** (See page 105.)

Lulu Belle. 14 E. Main St., Scottsdale. Lunch, dinner to 1 a.m. daily.

Pink Pony Restaurant. 1 E. Main St., Scottsdale. Lunch, dinner.

ARKANSAS

A. Q. Chicken House. U.S. 71 and 62, ½ mile north of Springdale. (See page 86.)

Anderson's Restaurant. Junction of U.S. 64 and 67, Beebe. **O–V–R** (See page 85.)

Bruno's Little Italy. 3400 W. Roosevelt Rd., Little Rock. Lunch, dinner. Closed Tues., the last week in May, and 2 weeks during Christmas and New Year's.

Burn's Gables. U.S. 71, near Winslow. Closed Dec. 1 to March 1. **V** (See page 84.)

Cedar Grill. 420 Main St. (U.S. 62 and State Hwy 5), Mountain Home. (See page 84.)

Crescent. U.S. 62, Eureka Springs. Closed Nov. 15 to April 1. **O–V**

Davy Crockett. U.S. 67, Walnut Ridge. **O–V**

Hotel-Motel Sam Peck. Capitol and Gaines Sts., Little Rock. **O–V**

Mexico Chiquito. 201 Jacksonville Hwy (U.S. 67 and 70), N. Little Rock. Dinner only. Closed Mon. **R**

Rose Inn and Lodge. 200 Main St., Crossett. **O–V–R** (See page 85.)

Spring Lake Restaurant. Near intersection of U.S. 62 and 65, Bellefonte. Lunch, dinner; dinner only on Sun. (See page 86.)

CALIFORNIA

Alexis Restaurant. 1001 California St. (on Nob Hill), San Francisco. Dinner to 2 a.m. Closed Sun.

Anderson's Pea Soup Restaurant. U.S. 101, Buellton.

Apple Valley Inn. State Hwy 18, Apple Valley. **O–V–R**

The Beach Broiler. 1215 Strand, Hermosa Beach. Lunch, dinner. (See page 108.)

Cathay House. 718 California St., San Francisco. Lunch, dinner. Closed Thanksgiving Day and Christmas Day. **R**

Chasen's. 9039 Beverly Blvd., Hollywood. Dinner. Closed Mon. **R**

Cliff House. 1090 Point Lobos (Great Hwy at Seal Rocks), San Francisco.

The Cock 'n Bull. 9170 Sunset Blvd., Hollywood. Lunch, dinner, snacks noon to 2 a.m. Hunt breakfast 10 a.m. to 2:30 p.m. **R** for dinner.

Breakfast, lunch, and dinner served daily unless otherwise noted.
O—overnight accommodations **V**—vacation facilities **R**—reservations necessary or advisable

Colonial House. 711 N. Oxnard Blvd., Oxnard. **O**

Del Monte Lodge. Seventeen-Mile Drive, Pebble Beach. **O–V–R**

Don the Beachcomber. 1727 N. McCadden Place, Hollywood. Dinner. Closed Thanksgiving Day and Christmas Day. **R**

El Paso Inn. 20 Olvera St., Los Angeles. Lunch, dinner. **R**

Ernie's Restaurant. 847 Montgomery St., San Francisco. Dinner. **R**

The Fox and Hounds. 2900 Wilshire Blvd., Santa Monica. Lunch, dinner.

Frank Torres Beach Hotel. State Hwy 1, Montara. Closed Mon. and Tues. unless a holiday. **R**

The Garden Room. Sheraton West Hotel, 2961 Wilshire Blvd., Los Angeles. Lunch, dinner. Closed Sat. from noon and all day Sun. **O–V–R**

Gwinn's Restaurant. 2915 E. Colorado Blvd., Pasadena. Closed Christmas Day.

The Harbor Restaurant. Foot of State St. on Stearns Whay, Santa Barbara. Lunch, dinner. Closed Christmas Day. **R**

Heritage House. State Hwy 1, 5 miles north of intersection with State Hwy 128, Little River. Breakfast, dinner. Closed Dec. 1 to Feb. 1. **R** for dinner. (See page 107.)

Holiday House. 1270 Prospect St., La Jolla. Lunch, dinner. Closed Mon. and Tues.

Hotel Bel-Air. 701 Stone Canyon Road, Los Angeles. **O–V**

Hotel Claremont. Off U.S. 101 at Ashby Ave., Berkeley. **O–V–R**

Hotel del Coronado. Oceanfront, Coronado. **O–V–R**

Idle Spurs. 29557 U.S. 466, Barstow. Dinner. Closed Sun. and Mon., and from Oct. 1 to Nov. 15. **R**

India House. 629 Washington St., San Francisco. Dinner. Closed Sun. **R**

International Room. International Airport, San Francisco. Lunch, dinner; dinner only on Sat. **R** (See page 109.)

Kan's Chinese Restaurant. 708 Grant Ave., San Francisco. Lunch, dinner. Closed Thanksgiving Day and Christmas Day. **R** for 8 or more. (See page 108.)

Knott's Berry Farm. State Hwy 39, Buena Park. Closed Christmas Day.

Kover's Bull Pen. 14649 Ventura Blvd., Sherman Oaks (Los Angeles). Open 24 hours. Closed Mon. **R** on holidays.

La Avenida Cafe. 1301 Orange Ave., Coronado. **O–V–R**

Lawry's, The Prime Rib. 55 N. La Cienega Blvd., Beverley Hills. Dinner to midnight.

Lazio's Seafoods. Humboldt Bay at the foot of #4 C Street, Eureka. Lunch, dinner. Closed Sun. from Oct. to May.

L'Omelette French Restaurant. 4170 El Camino Real (U.S. 101), Palo Alto. Dinner. Closed Mon., Tues., and the first 2 weeks in July.

Manuel's. 2616 San Diego Ave., San Diego. **R**

Marty Cable's Plands. 265 W. MacArthur at Broadway, Oakland. Open 24 hours.

Mission Ranch. South end of Dolores St., Carmel. Dinner. **O–V–R** (See page 111.)

Mom's Italian Village. 421 E. Cota St., Santa Barbara. Dinner. Closed Mon.

My Old Kentucky Home. 802 E. Huntington Dr. (U.S. 66), Monrovia. Dinner. Closed Mon., Tues., and the last 2 weeks in July. **R** for 8 or more.

Nikko Sukiyaki Restaurant. Van Ness and Pine Sts., San Francisco. Dinner from 4 p.m. to 11 p.m. **R**

Nut Tree. U.S. 40, Vacaville. Closed Thanksgiving, Christmas, and New Year's Days.

Omar Khayyam's. 196 O'Farrell St. at Powell, San Francisco. Dinner to midnight; from 2 p.m. on Sun. and holidays.

Owl 'n Turtle. 615 Washington St., San Francisco. Dinner. Closed Sun. and Mon.

Padua Hills Restaurant. Padua Hills, Claremont. Lunch, dinner. Closed Mon. and last 2 weeks in Sept.

Paul's. 1521 Alhambra Ave., Martinez. Lunch, dinner. Dinner only on Sun. Closed Mon. and holidays. (See page 106.)

Pedens' Cafe. 119 W. Seventh St. (State Hwy 198), Hanford. Closed Christmas Day.

Perino's. 4101 Wilshire Blvd., Los Angeles. Lunch, dinner. **R**

The Pioneer. West on Woodside Road in Redwood City on way to Woodside. Lunch, dinner; breakfast on Sun. only.

Rainbow Tavern. U.S. 40, Cisco. **O–V**

Rickey's Hyatt House. 4219 El Camino Real (U.S. 101), Palo Alto. **O–V**

Santa Maria Inn. 801 S. Broadway (U.S. 101), Santa Maria. **O–V–R**

Santa Ynez Inn. 17310 Sunset Blvd., Pacific Palisades. **O–V–R**

Schroeder's Cafe. 240 Front St., San Francisco. Lunch (men only; women invited after 1:30 p.m.), dinner. Closed Sat. and Sun.

Sea Shanty. 630 E. 31st St., Newport Beach. Open 6 a.m. to 2 a.m. **R**

Shadow-Brook. Wharf Rd., Capitola-by-the-Sea. Dinner. Closed Jan. 1 through March, and Mon. during April and May. Open weekends only from Oct. through Dec. (See page 109.)

Shelter Island's Bali Hai. 1325 Yacht Harbor Drive, San Diego. Lunch, dinner. Closed Christmas Day. **R**

Sheraton-Palace Hotel. Market and New Montgomery Sts., San Francisco. **O–R**

Skipper Kent's. 1040 Columbus St., San Francisco. Lunch on weekdays only, dinner daily. **R**

Spenger's. 1919 Fourth St. (near University Ave.), Berkeley. Lunch, dinner. Closed Thanksgiving Day and Christmas Day.

Sportsmen's Lodge. 12833 Ventura Blvd. (U.S. 101), Coldwater Canyon, North Hollywood. Dinner. (See page 110.)

Squaw Valley Lodge. Squaw Valley. Closed Sept. 15 to Dec. 15, and April 30 to June 5. **O–V** (See page 110.)

Stuft Shirt Restaurant. 2241 W. Coast Hwy (U.S. 101), Newport Beach. Lunch, dinner. Closed Mon. **R**

Swedish Farmhouse. State Hwy 28, Tahoe City. Dinner. Closed Labor Day to Jan. 20. **O–V**

Sycamore Inn. 8318 Foothill Blvd. (U.S. 66), Bear Gulch, Cucamonga. Lunch, dinner. (See page 107.)

Breakfast, lunch, and dinner served daily unless otherwise noted.

O—overnight accommodations **V**—vacation facilities **R**—reservations necessary or advisable

Tagus Ranch Restaurant. U.S. 99, four miles north of Tulare. Open 6 a.m. to midnight daily.

Tail o' the Cock. 477 S. La Cienega Blvd., Los Angeles. Lunch, dinner.

Taix French Restaurant. 321 E. Commercial St., Los Angeles. Lunch, dinner.

Tarantino's Restaurant. 206 Jefferson St., Fisherman's Wharf, San Francisco. Lunch, dinner.

Trader Vic's. 6500 San Pablo Ave., Oakland. Lunch on weekdays only; dinner daily. Closed Thanksgiving Day and Christmas Day. **R**

The Victor Hugo Inn. 361 Cliff Drive, Laguna Beach. Lunch, dinner.

Wilson's. 13136 Sierra Hwy (U.S. 6), Saugus. Open 24 hrs. **O**

Yamato Sukiyaki House. 717 California St., San Francisco. Lunch, dinner. Closed Mon. **R**

CANADA

Chantecler. Provincial Hwy 11, Ste.-Adele-en-Haut, Quebec. Also serves tea. **O–V–R**

Chateau Frontenac. 1 des Carrieres St., Quebec City. Also serves tea. **O–V–R**

Chateau Laurier. Confederation Square, Ottawa. **O–V**

Kerhulu Restaurant. 22 Rue de la Fabrique, Quebec City. **R**

COLORADO

The Blue Jay Inn. Rte 126, Buffalo Creek. Closed Labor Day to June 15. **O–V–R** (See page 112.)

Brown Palace Hotel. 17th and Tremont Sts., Denver. Lunch, dinner. **O–V–R**

Copper Kettle. 4 blocks north of State Hwy 82 at Aspen Meadows, Aspen. Closed Mon. evening and from Oct. 1 to Dec. 20 and from April 5 to June 10. **R** for dinner.

Craftwood Inn. 404 El Paso Blvd., Manitou Springs. Lunch, dinner. Closed Nov. 1 to April 15. **O**

Daven Haven Lodge. Grand Lake. Closed Sept. 20 to June 1. **O–V**

Holiday Inn. U.S. 24, Hartsel. Closed May 20 to Oct. 15. **O**

The Northwood Inn. U.S. 85 and 87, Littleton. Lunch, dinner. Closed Mon. and Sept. 10 to March 31.

The Old Plantation. 140 E. Elkhorn Ave. (U.S. 34 and State Hwys 7 and 66), Estes Park. Breakfast in July and Aug. only; lunch and dinner from June 1 to Sept. 20. Closed Mon. in July and Aug.

The Ranchouse Restaurant. State Hwy 7, 1½ miles south of Estes Park. Closed from Oct. thru May.

Redstone Lodge. State Hwy 133, Redstone. **O–V–R**

Riverside Lodge and Ranch. State Hwy 7, Lyons. Chuck Wagon dinner on Thursday evening. Closed Sept. 15 thru June 14. **O–V**

Ruth's Oven. 220 N. Tejon St., Colorado Springs. Closed Christmas Day.

Stagecoach Inn. 702 Manitou Ave. (U.S. 24), Manitou Springs. Lunch, dinner. Closed Mon. and from Sept. 25 to May 26.

Toklat Wilderness Lodge. Castle Creek Road, Ashcroft. Closed Wed. in summer. **R**

The Village Inn. 217 E. Pikes Peak Ave., Colorado Springs. Lunch, dinner.

The Williams Wayside Inn. 505 Mountain Ave. (U.S. 287), Berthoud. Lunch, dinner. Closed Mon. and from Dec. 23 to Jan. 2. (See page 111.)

Zietz Buckhorn Restaurant. 1000 Osage St., Denver. Lunch, dinner. Closed Sun. **R** for large parties.

CONNECTICUT

Charpentier Steak and Lobster House. 232 East Ave., East Norwalk. Lunch, dinner. Closed Christmas Day.

Cooke's Tavern. New Britain Ave. at Cook St. (State Hwy 72), west of New Britain. Lunch, dinner. Closed Mon. **R** on Sat. and holidays.

Country Squire Inn. State Hwy 80, Killingworth. Lunch, dinner. Closed Mon. unless a holiday, and from Dec. 1 to May 1.

Dorlon's Shore House. Gregory Blvd. (Dorlon's Point), East Norwalk. Lunch, dinner. Closed Tues. and from Nov. 1 to April 21.

Fox Hill. U.S. 7, Ridgefield. Closed Mon. from Labor Day to Memorial Day. **O–V–R**

Lighthouse Inn and Keepers' Lodge. Off Rte 95 to Ocean Beach, New London. **O–V–R**

Lime Rock Lodge. State Hwy 112, Lime Rock. Closed Tues. and from Jan. 1 to March 28.

Manero's. 559 Steamboat Rd., Greenwich. Lunch, dinner. (See page 7.)

The Mayflower Inn. State Hwy 47, Washington. **O–V–R**

Old Riverton Inn. State Hwy 20, Riverton. Breakfast for houseguests and fishermen only; lunch, dinner. **O–V–R** on Thanksgiving Day and Christmas Day.

The Old Well. Tarifville Road, Simsbury. Open noon to 1 a.m. weekdays, Sun. til 9 p.m. Closed Tues., Christmas Day, and the first week in Aug. **R**

Pier Restaurant. 144 Water St. (Rte 136), South Norwalk. Lunch, dinner. Cocktail lounge open to midnight. Closed Oct. 1 to May 1.

The Red Barn. 290 Wilton Road (Merritt Pkwy, exit 41), Westport. Lunch, dinner. Closed Christmas Day. **R**

Silvermine Tavern. Perry and Silvermine Aves., (Merritt Pkwy, exit 38), Norwalk. Closed Tues. from Thanksgiving to Easter. **O–R** on holidays.

Skipper's Dock. Front St., Noank. Lunch, dinner. Closed Oct. 15 to May 1. **R**

The Spinning Wheel. Merritt Pkwy, exit 45, Redding Ridge. Lunch, dinner. Closed Mon. and Jan. 1 to March. **R** on holidays and weekends.

Stonehenge. U.S. 7, Ridgefield. Lunch, dinner. Closed Mon. **O–V–R**

Tode's Inn at Ridgefield. 4 West Lane (State Hwy 35), Ridgefield. Lunch, dinner. Closed Tues. during winter. **O–R**

Breakfast, lunch, and dinner served daily unless otherwise noted.

O—overnight accommodations   **V**—vacation facilities   **R**—reservations necessary or advisable

Waverly Inn. Exit 61 from Wilbur Cross Pkwy, north on State Hwy 10 to Cheshire. Lunch, dinner. Closed Mon. **R** (See page 6.)

Werner's. 36 Elm St., Westport. Lunch, except Sun.; dinner. **R** (See page 6.)

Westleigh Inn. U.S. 25, Litchfield. **O–V**

White Hart Inn. Fork of U.S. 44, State Hwy 41, Salisbury. **O–V**

Yankee Pedlar. 93 Main St., Torrington. **O–V**

DELAWARE

Angler's Restaurant. Off Savannah Rd. near Canal Bridge, Lewes. Closed Easter, Thanksgiving, Christmas, and New Year's Days. **O–V**

Dinner Bell Inn. 121 S. State St., Dover. Lunch weekdays only; dinner. Closed Sun. and from Christmas Day to New Year's Day.

Holiday Inn. 1843 Marsh Rd., Wilmington. Lunch, dinner. Closed Christmas Day. **R** on weekends. (See page 37.)

Naaman's on the Delaware. U.S. 13, Claymont. Lunch, dinner. Closed Christmas Day. **O**

The Surrey. 1101 Philadelphia Pike (U.S. 13 going south) and Holly Hill Rd., Wilmington. Lunch, dinner. (See page 37.)

Winkler's. 1419 French St., Wilmington. Lunch, dinner. Closed Sun.

DISTRICT OF COLUMBIA
(Washington, D. C.)

Blackie's House of Beef. 1217 22nd at M St., N.W. Lunch, dinner. Closed Sun. **R** (See page 31.)

Cannon's. 1270 5th St., N.E. Closed Sun. **R**

The Genghis Khan Restaurant. 1805 Connecticut Ave., N.W. Lunch, dinner. **R**

Golden Parrot. 1701 20th St., N.W. Lunch, dinner. Closed Sun. and holidays. **R**

Hall's Restaurant and Garden. 2121 First St., S.W. Lunch, dinner, late supper. Closed Thanksgiving and Christmas Days. **R**

Iron Gate Inn. 1734 N St., N.W. Lunch, dinner. **R**

Mayflower Hotel. Connecticut Ave. and De Sales St., N.W. **O–V–R** (See page 31.)

O'Donnell's Sea Grill. 1221 E St., N.W. Lunch, dinner. Closed Christmas Day.

Water Gate Inn. Potomac River at 2700 F St., N.W. Lunch, dinner.

FLORIDA

Black Caesar Forge Gourmet Club. Coral Reef and Ludlam Rds., Miami. Dinner. Closed Christmas Day and Mon. during the season. **R**

Candlelight Inn. 3131 Commodore Plaza, Miami. Lunch, dinner, late supper.

Chalet Suzanne. U.S. 27A, Lake Wales. **O–V–R**

Chandler's. 220 21st St., Miami Beach. Dinner, supper.

Chesler's. 235 Worth Ave., Palm Beach. Lunch, dinner. Closed May 1 to Oct. 1. **R** (See page 38.)

Columbia Restaurant. 2117 E. Broadway, Tampa. **R** in winter.

Creighton's—Johnston's Coffee Shop. 200 Magnolia at Palmetta, Daytona Beach. Lunch, dinner. (See page 40.)

The Cypress Gardens Inn Restaurant. 4 miles west of U.S. 27 on Cypress Gardens Rd., Winter Haven. Open 8 a.m. to 4 p.m. weekdays. Sundays and holidays 9 a.m. to 4:30 p.m.

Dolphin Restaurant. State Hwy A1A, Marineland. **O–V**

Fred Abood's Steer Room. 1780 W. Beaver St., Jacksonville. Closed Sun. (See page 40.)

The Garden. 2235 S.W. Eighth St., Miami. Lunch, dinner.

Grandma's Kitchen. 5240 S.W. Eighth St., Miami. Dinner only.

The Grill. U.S. 98, Apalachicola. Closed Christmas Day. (See page 38.)

Hanley's Waterfront Restaurant. U.S. 1, Marathon. Open noon to 11 p.m. **O–V–R** during winter season.

Island Hotel. U.S. 19 to State Hwy 24, Cedar Key. **O–V**

Jamaica Inn Restaurant. 320 Crandon Blvd., Key Biscayne. Dinner only. (English Pub open for breakfast, lunch, and dinner.)

Las Novedades. 1430 E. Broadway, Tampa. Lunch, dinner.

Lauderdale Beach Hotel. U.S. A1A, Fort Lauderdale. **O**

Lighthouse Seafood Restaurant. Baker's Haulover (Rte A1A), Miami Beach. Lunch, dinner.

Loffler Brothers' Oyster House. 280 Alhambra Circle, Coral Gables. Lunch, dinner. **R**

Louis Pappas' Riverside Cafe. 785 Anclote Blvd. at Sponge Boat Docks, Tarpon Springs. Lunch, dinner.

Maison LaFitte. 15 Via Parigi, Palm Beach. Lunch, dinner. Closed Sun. and from Easter to Thanksgiving. **R**

Marco Island Inn. Off U.S. 41 to State Hwy 92, Marco Island. Closed June 1 to Nov. 15. **O–V**

The Old Cove. 1195 8th St., S. (U.S. 41), Naples. Lunch, dinner. Closed Sun. **R**

Outrigger Inn. North end of Sunshine Skyway Bridge and Causeway (U.S. 19), St. Petersburg. **O–V**

Robert Clay Hotel. 129 S.E. Fourth St., Miami. **O–V**

The Rod and Gun Club. State Rd. 29, Everglades. Closed June 1 to Oct. 31. **O–V** (See page 41.)

Sea Grape Lodge. 20 miles from Fort Myers across Pine Island, Matlacha. Closed May 1 to Oct. 31. **O–V–R**

Siple's Garden Seat. 1234 W. Druid Rd., Clearwater. Lunch, dinner. (See page 39.)

Spanish Park Restaurant. E. Broadway at 36th St., Tampa. (See page 41.)

Tides Hotel and Bath Club. 16700 Gulf Blvd., North Redington Beach, St. Petersburg. **O–V–R**

Wedgewood Inn. 4th St. and 18th Ave., S., St. Petersburg. Lunch, dinner. **O**

Breakfast, lunch, and dinner served daily unless otherwise noted.
O—overnight accommodations   **V**—vacation facilities   **R**—reservations necessary or advisable

Zinn's. 6101 N. Tamiami Trail (U.S. 41), near Sarasota. Dinner; from noon on Sun. (See page 39.)

GEORGIA

The Alpine Restaurant. 718 W. 7th (U.S. 82 and 319), Tifton. Closed Dec. 25-26.

Aunt Fanny's Cabin. 375 Campbell Rd., Smyrna. Dinner; lunch also on Sun. Closed Christmas Eve and Day. (See page 42.)

Callaway Gardens Clubhouse. Near Pine Mountain (30 miles north of Columbus). **O—V** (See page 43.)

Davis Brothers Suburban Restaurant. 101 N. Slappey (U.S. 19 and 82), Albany. (See page 42.)

Franklin D. Roosevelt State Park Inn. 4 miles south of Pine Mountain, Pine Mountain. Open 10:30 a.m. to 10:30 p.m. Closed Mon. **O—V—R**

Georgian Tea Room in the Pink House. 23 Abercorn St., Savannah. Lunch, tea, dinner. Closed Sun. and holidays.

Goo Goo Restaurant and Drive Inn. 700 Linwood Blvd., Columbus. Closed Sun. **O—V**

Hotel Warm Springs. Alt. U.S. 27, Warm Springs. **O—V**

Luau Restaurant. 1999 Peachtree Rd., Atlanta. Lunch, dinner. Closed Sun. (See page 43.)

Mammy's Shanty. 1480 Peachtree St., N.W., Atlanta. Also has a coffee shop.

New Perry Hotel. 800 Main St. (U.S. 341), Perry. **O—V**

The Pirates' House. 20 E. Broad St., Savannah. Lunch, dinner. Closed Christmas Day. (See page 44.)

Riegeldale Tavern. U.S. 27, south of Trion. Lunch, dinner. Closed July 4th and Christmas Day. **R**

HAWAII

Canlis' Charcoal Broiler. 2100 Kalakaua Ave., Honolulu. Dinner. **R**

Duke Kahanamoku's. Waikiki Beach, Honolulu. Dinner until 1 a.m. Closed Sun. **R**

Ishii Garden. 1720 Huna St., Honolulu. Dinner. **R**

The Willows. 901 Hausten St., Honolulu. Lunch, dinner. Closed Sun. **R**

IDAHO

Challenger Inn. Sun Valley. Dinner. Closed Oct. 15 to Dec. 16. **R**

Hurschell's Lighthouse. Lake Pend Oreille, Hope. Open 8 a.m. to midnight. Closed during Jan.

Red Rock. 1304 N. Main St. (U.S. 30), Pocatello. (See page 112.)

Shady Nook Inn. U.S. 93, Salmon. Dinner. Closed Sun. from Oct. thru June. (See page 113.)

Shore Lodge. State Hwy 15, McCall. Open 7 a.m. to 10 p.m.

Sun Valley. U.S. 93, 1 mile northeast of Ketchum. Closed month of April and from Oct. 15 to Dec. 16. **O—V—R**

Templin's. 112 W. Sherman, Coeur d' Alene. Closed Christmas Day. **O** (See page 113.)

ILLINOIS

Azuma Sukiyaki Restaurant. 5116-20 N. Broadway, Chicago. Dinner, from 1 p.m. on Sun. Closed Mon. and Christmas week. (See page 60.)

The Beau Nash Club. State and Goethe Sts., Chicago. Lunch, dinner. Open to women 4 p.m. to 7 p.m. and Sat. lunch. Closed Sun. **O—V—R**

Boston Oyster House. Morrison Hotel, Chicago. Open 11 a.m. to midnight. **O**

The Brick House. 402 Lincolnway West, Morrison. Lunch, dinner. Closed all day Sat., Sun. evenings, Christmas week, and the first week in Aug.

The Country Squire. State Hwy 120 (off U.S. 45), Grayslake. Lunch, dinner. Closed Mon. **R** (See page 61.)

Fanny's. 1601 Simpson St., Evanston. Dinner. Closed Christmas Day. **R**

The Imperial House. 50 E. Walton Place, Chicago. Lunch, except Sat., and dinner. Closed Sun. and holidays. **R**

Jul's Danish Farm. U.S. 30, ½ mile west of Rock Falls. Lunch, dinner. **O**

Julion's. 103 E. Chicago Ave., Chicago. Mon.-Sat., all meals; Sun., brunch only.

Klas' Restaurant. 5734 W. Cermak Rd., Cicero. Lunch, dinner. Closed Mon. and the last 2 weeks in July.

Mathon's Sea Food Restaurant. 6 E. Clayton St., Waukegan. Lunch, dinner. Closed Mon., Thanksgiving Day, and Christmas Day.

Mickleberry's Log Cabin. 2300 W. 95th St. (U.S. 12 and 20), Chicago. Lunch, dinner; Sun. breakfast. Closed Mon.

The Milk Pail. Fin 'n Feather Farm, State Hwy 25, between Elgin and Dundee. Lunch, dinner. Closed Mon. and Dec. 22 to Jan. 2. **R** (See page 60.)

Mill Race Inn. 4 E. State St., Geneva. Lunch, dinner. Closed July 4th and from Dec. 15 to Mar. 11.

Nielsen's Restaurant. 7840 S. Western Ave., Chicago. Lunch, dinner, after-theater supper. **R** for large groups.

Old Spinning Wheel. 421 E. Ogden Ave., Hinsdale. Lunch, dinner; also Sun. breakfast. **R**

The Pantry. 718 Garden St., Park Ridge. Lunch, dinner. Closed Mon. and Tues. and from Jan. 2 to the last Sat. in Jan. **R**

The Plantation. 3701 7th St., Moline. Lunch, dinner.

Plentywood Farm. 130 S. Church Rd., Bensenville. Closed Mon. (See page 61.)

Polynesian Village. 5349 N. Sheridan Rd., Chicago. Dinner. **O—V**

Pump Room. Hotel Ambassador East, 1300 N. State Pkwy, Chicago. Lunch, dinner. Closed Dec. 23-30. **O—V—R**

Breakfast, lunch, and dinner served daily unless otherwise noted.

O—overnight accommodations   **V**—vacation facilities   **R**—reservations necessary or advisable

Ridgeland Farm. 110th and Ridgeland Aves., Worth. Dinner. **R** on weekends.

Southern Air. 3045 Clearlake Ave., Springfield. Dinner; from noon on Sun.

Stock Yard Inn. 4178 S. Halsted St., Chicago. Lunch, dinner. **O–R**

Urbana-Lincoln Hotel. 209 S. Broadway, Urbana. **O–V**

The Wagon Wheel. Junction of State Hwys 2 and 75, Rockton. **O–V–R**

Well-of-the-Sea. Hotel Sherman, Randolph St. at Clark, Chicago. Lunch, dinner. **O**

Yesteryear. Harrison Ave. at the river, Kankakee. Lunch, dinner.

INDIANA

Clifty Inn. Clifty Falls State Park (State Hwys 56 and 62 or State Hwy 107), Madison. **O–V** (See page 62.)

Corner Cupboard. State Hwys 46 and 135, Nashville. Open 11:30 a.m. to 8 p.m. Closed Mon. and Oct. 25 to March 21.

Hawthorn Room. N. Meridian at 16th St. (U.S. 31), Indianapolis. Lunch, dinner. Closed Christmas Day.

The Keys. N. Meridian St. (U.S. 31), Indianapolis. Lunch, except Sat.; dinner. Closed Sun. **R**

Kopper Kettle. U.S. 52, Morristown. Lunch, dinner. Closed Christmas Day. **R**

Nashville House. Main and Van Buren Sts., Nashville. Lunch, dinner. Closed Tues. and from Dec. 24 to Jan. 7.

Pritchett's Steak House and Smorgasbord. 2701 W. Lexington (U.S. 20 at State Hwy 112), Elkhart. Lunch, dinner.

Smitty's Holiday Inn Restaurant. 2508 U.S. 41 N., Evansville. Lunch, dinner. Closed Sun. (See page 62.)

Turkey Run Inn. Turkey Run State Park, Marshall. **O–V**

IOWA

Bill Zuber's Restaurant. Homestead. Lunch, dinner. Closed July 4, Dec. 24, 25, 31, and Jan. 1. (See page 63.)

Canary Cottage. 207 High Ave. E., Oskaloosa. Lunch, dinner. Closed Mon.

Carver's Restaurant. U.S. 218 and State Hwy 3, Waverly. **O**

Hotel Manning. Keosauqua. **O–V**

Johnny and Kay's. Fleur Dr., Des Moines. Dinner.

The Lark Restaurant. Tiffin (U.S. 6). Dinner. Closed Sun. and Dec. 22 to Jan. 3. (See page 63.)

Lloyd's Restaurant. U.S. 30 (Lincoln Hwy), 4 miles west of Marshalltown. Lunch, dinner. Closed Mon. and Dec. 18 to March 5. (See page 64.)

Ox Yoke Inn. Amana (west of Iowa City). Lunch, dinner. (See page 64.)

Stone's Restaurant. 507 S. Third Ave., Marshalltown. Lunch, dinner. Closed Christmas Day.

Swiss Valley Chalet. U.S. 151, Dubuque. Lunch, dinner. Closed Mon. and the week of July 4th.

Tiny's Horse 'n' Buggy Dining Room. State Hwy 90, Adel. Lunch, dinner. Closed Mon.

Tony's Famous Restaurant. 502 Kenyon Rd. (U.S. 20 and 169), Fort Dodge. Lunch, dinner. Closed July 4th, Thanksgiving Day, and Christmas Day. **R**

KANSAS

Brookville Hotel. U.S. 40, Brookville. Dinner, from noon on Sun. Closed Mon., Thanksgiving Day, and Christmas Day. **O–V–R**

Chuck Wagon Restaurant. U.S. 59S, Lawrence. Lunch, dinner. Closed Tues. and from July 1 to Aug. 1. (See page 87.)

Cohen's Chicken House. Grandview Plaza (U.S. 40), Junction City. Lunch, dinner. Closed Thanksgiving Day and Christmas Day.

Innes Tea Room. Innes Department Store, 121 S. Broadway, Wichita. Lunch, dinner. Closed Sun. and holidays. (See page 89.)

Maynard's. 8th and Jackson Sts., Topeka. Open 8 a.m. to 9 p.m. (See page 89.)

Old Grinter House. 1420 S. 78th St. (State Hwy 32), Muncie. Lunch, dinner. Closed Mon. **R** (See page 87.)

The Red Barn. ¼ mile east of junction of U.S. 54 and 69, Fort Scott. Dinner. (See page 88.)

Stockyards Hotel. 659 E. 21st St., Wichita. Lunch on weekdays; dinner. **O–R** (See page 88.)

KENTUCKY

Beaumont Inn. U.S. Hwy 127, Harrodsburg. Closed Dec. 1 to March 1. **O–V–R**

Boone Tavern. Berea College Campus, Berea. **O–V–R**

Campbell House Hotel. U.S. 68S (Old Harrodsburg Rd.), ¼ mile s. of Lexington. **O–V** (See page 45.)

The Coach House. 855 S. Broadway (U.S. 68), Lexington. Lunch, dinner. Closed Sun., Thanksgiving Day, and Christmas Day.

Indiana Cafe. U.S. 41, Crofton. (See page 45.)

Oelsner's Colonial Tavern. Dixie Ave., Covington. Lunch, dinner.

The Old House Restaurant. 432 S. Fifth St., Louisville. Lunch, dinner. Closed Sun. and holidays. **R**

Old Talbott Tavern. Court House Square, Bardstown. **O–R** for lodging.

Stagecoach Inn. Intersection of U.S. 41 and 79, near Guthrie. Closed Dec. 24-25.

Village Inn Restaurant. U.S. Hwys 641 and 62, Kentucky Dam State Park near Gilbertsville. **O–V** (See page 44.)

Wilbur Hotel. U.S. 25W (corner of Laurel and Center Sts.), Corbin. Dining room closed Sun. evening from Oct. to June. **O–V** (See page 46.)

Breakfast, lunch, and dinner served daily unless otherwise noted.

O—overnight accommodations **V**—vacation facilities **R**—reservations necessary or advisable

LOUISIANA

Antoine's. 713 St. Louis St., New Orleans. Lunch, dinner. Closed Sun. **R**

Arnaud's Restaurant. 801-829 Bienville St., New Orleans. Open 11 a.m. to 12:30 a.m. daily.

Bilello's Restaurant. St. Mary and Landry Sts., Thibodaux. Closed Mon. (See page 91.)

Brennan's Patio Royal. 417 Royal St., New Orleans. Open 9 a.m. to midnight. Closed Christmas Day and Sun. unless by reservation, except the Sun. before New Year's and Mardi Gras.

Brocato's Stopmoor Restaurant. 189 E. Kings Hwy, Shreveport. Lunch, dinner. Closed Mon.

The Coffee Pot. 710 St. Peter St., New Orleans.

Commander's Palace. 1403 Washington Ave., New Orleans. Lunch, dinner.

Court of Two Sisters. 613 Royal St., New Orleans.

Don's Seafood and Steak House. 301 E. Vermillion St. (U.S. 90E), Lafayette. Lunch, dinner. Closed Christmas Day. **R**

Galatoire's Restaurant. 209 Bourbon St., New Orleans. Lunch, dinner. Closed Mon.

Kolb's Restaurant. 125 St. Charles St., New Orleans. Closed Sun.

Maylié's. Poydras and Dryades Sts., New Orleans. Lunch, dinner. Closed Sun.

Mim's Restaurant. Breaux Bridge. (See page 90.)

The Rendezvous Restaurant. 1400 Louisville Ave. (U.S. 80), Monroe. Lunch, dinner. (See page 91.)

Roussel's. Junction of U.S. 51 and 61 at Laplace, 25 miles north of New Orleans. (See page 92.)

Tujague's. 823 Decatur St., New Orleans. Closed Fri. (See page 90.)

MAINE

Augusta House. 170 State St., Augusta. **O–V** (See page 7.)

Bar Harbor Motor Inn. New Port Drive, Bar Harbor. Closed mid-Sept. to mid-June. **O–V** (See page 8.)

Barbara Dean's. U.S. 1A (Shore Rd.), Ogunquit. Closed Sept. 15 to June 15. **O–V**

County Fair. U.S. 1, Damariscotta. Closed Oct. 15 to May 25. **O–V**

Jordan Pond House. Seal Harbor. Lunch, dinner. Closed Sept. 15 to June 20.

Lakewood Inn. U.S. 201, Lakewood. Closed Sept. 10 to mid-June. **O–V–R**

Mary Jane Restaurant. Main St. (State Hwy 3), Bar Harbor. Closed Oct. to May 30.

The Mount Kineo. Rockwood (by boat to peninsula in Moosehead Lake). Closed Labor Day to June 19. **O–V–R** (See page 8.)

Shawmut Inn. Kennebunkport. Closed Oct. 1 to May 25. **O–V–R**

Sky Lodge. U.S. 201, Jackman. Closed Dec. 1 to May 25. **O–V–R**

The Yardarm. U.S. 1 near Searsport. Closed Oct. 15 to May 15. **O** (See page 9.)

MARYLAND

The Butlers' Canvasback Motor Inn. Hwys 40 and 222, Perryville. **O–V** (See page 46.)

Chesapeake Restaurant. 1707 N. Charles St., Baltimore. Lunch, dinner. Closed Mon. and 2 weeks in July. **R** (See page 47.)

Francis Scott Key Hotel. W. Patrick and N. Court Sts., Frederick. **O** (See page 47.)

Haussner's Restaurant. 3236-3244 Eastern Ave. at Clinton St., Baltimore. Closed Sun. and Christmas Day.

Kitty Knight House. U.S. 213, Georgetown. Breakfast on weekends only; lunch, dinner daily. **O–R**

Maison Marconi. 106 W. Saratoga St., Baltimore. Lunch, dinner. Closed Sun.

Normandy Farm. State Hwy 189 (Falls Rd.), Rockville. Lunch, dinner. **R**

Olney Inn. Columbia Pike (State Hwy 97), Olney. Lunch, dinner. Closed Mon. **R**

Peter Pan Inn. State Hwy 355, south of Frederick. Dinner. Closed Mon. and from Dec. 1 to April 1.

The Tidewater Inn. Harrison and Dover Sts., Easton. **O**

MASSACHUSETTS

Alwin and Olga. 16 Federal St., Greenfield. Lunch, dinner. Closed Mon.

Andover Inn. Chapel Ave., Andover. **O**

The Belmont. Belmont Rd., West Harwich-by-the-Sea, Cape Cod. Closed from mid-Sept. to late June. **O–V–R**

The Blacksmith Shop. On Harbor Front, Rockport (Cape Ann). Closed Oct. to April. **R**

The Christopher Ryder House. Rte 28, Chathamport. Lunch, dinner. Closed Oct. 1 thru June 15. (See page 13.)

Colonial Inn. 11 Monument Square, Concord. **O**

The Drum. Intersection of State Hwys 2A and 78, Orange. Lunch, dinner. Closed Mon. and from Dec. 1 to May 1. **R** on Sun.

Durgin Park. 30 N. Market St., Boston. Closed Sun. and holidays. (See page 10.)

The 1812 House. Rte 9 (Worcester Tpke), Framingham Center. Lunch, dinner. **R**

Fieldstones. 400 S. Main St. (State Hwy 28), Andover. **R** (See page 9.)

Four High Road. 4 High Rd., Newbury. Lunch, dinner. Closed Sun. and Mon. from Dec. thru Feb. **R** for dinner.

General Glover Inn. U.S. 1A, Swampscott. Open noon to 9 p.m.

Grey Gull Inn. Liberty St., Nantucket. Closed after Labor Day to June 24. (See page 12.)

Hartwell Farm. Virginia Rd., Lincoln. Lunch, dinner. Closed Mon. and Christmas Day. **R**

Jack August's Restaurant. 5 Bridge St., Northampton. Lunch, dinner. Closed Mon. (See page 10.)

Latham's on Cape Cod. U.S. 6A, Brewster. Dinner. Closed Mon. and from Labor Day to June 15. **O–V–R**

Breakfast, lunch, and dinner served daily unless otherwise noted.
O—overnight accommodations **V**—vacation facilities **R**—reservations necessary or advisable

Longfellow's Wayside Inn. U.S. 20, South Sudbury. Also tea. **O–R**

The Lord Jeffery. 30 Boltwood Ave. (Rtes 9–166), Amherst. **O–V**

The New Meadows. 167 Worcester Rd. (State Rte 9), Framingham. Lunch, dinner. Closed Christmas Day. **R**

The Northfield Inn. Off State Hwys 10 and 63 to East Northfield. **O–V–R**

Old Chase House. State Hwy 28, West Harwich, Cape Cod. Open noon to 10:30 p.m. Closed Sept. 15 to June 15. **O–V**

Old Grist Mill. 390 Fall River Ave., Seekonk. Lunch, dinner. Closed Mon. **R**

The Old Mill. State Hwy 2A, Westminster. Closed Christmas Day. **O**; **R** on weekends and holidays.

The Opera House. 4 S. Water St., Nantucket Island. Dinner. Closed mid-June. **R** (See page 11.)

The Overlook Hotel. 3 Step Lane, Nantucket Island. Breakfast daily; after Labor Day dinner for hotel guests only. Closed Nov. 1 to May 13. **O–V** (See page 11.)

Parker House. 60 School St. at Tremont, Boston. **O**

Peg Leg. 18 Beach Street, Rockport. Closed Dec. 1 to April 1. **O–V–R**

Provincetown Inn and Motel. 1 Commercial St., Provincetown. Closed Nov. 1 to March 31. **O–V** (See page 13.)

Publick House. Main St., Sturbridge. **O–R**

Schine Inn. On the Massachusetts Tpke at Chicopee. **O–V** (See page 12.)

Ship's Haven. 24-26 Broadway (Hwy 128), Lynnfield. Lunch, dinner. Closed Tues. unless a holiday. **R**

The Springs. U.S. 7, New Ashford. **O–V**

Toll House. Junction of Rtes 18 and 14, Whitman. Lunch, dinner. Closed Mon. unless a holiday and during the month of Jan. **O–R**

Towne Lyne House. Newburyport Tpke, Lynnfield. Lunch, dinner. **R**

Wequassett Inn. State Hwy 28, East Harwich, Cape Cod. Closed Oct. through May. **O–V–R** (See page 14.)

Wiggins Old Tavern. 36 King St., Northampton. **O–V**; **R** on holidays and Oct. and June weekends.

Williams House. Williams St., Williamsburg. Dinner; from noon on Sun. Closed Mon. and from Dec. 20 to Dec. 30. **R**

Williams Inn. College Place, Williamstown. **O–V–R**

MEXICO

La Fiesta Theatre Restaurant. Mariscal and Ugarte Sts., Juarez, Chihuahua (near El Paso, Texas). Dinner. **R** (See page 92.)

MICHIGAN

Al Green's. 15301 E. Jefferson Ave., Grosse Pointe Park. Lunch, dinner; also Sun. brunch.

Botsford Inn. 28000 Grand River (U.S. 16), Farmington. **O–V**

Caucus Club. Penobscot Bldg., 150 W. Congress St., Detroit. Lunch, dinner. Closed Sun. **R**

Chimney Corner. Intersection of U.S. 31 and State Hwy 131N, Petoskey. Lunch, dinner. (See page 66.)

Colonial Inn. Near State Hwy 131 and U.S. 31, Harbor Springs. Dining room closed from Oct. 1 to June 1; hotel open all year. **O–V–R** (See page 67.)

Dearborn Inn, Colonial Homes and Motor House. 20301 Oakwood Blvd., Dearborn. **O–V**

Devon Gables. U.S. 24, Bloomfield Hills. Lunch, dinner.

The Doherty Hotel. 604 McEwan St. (near junction of U.S. 27 and 10), Clare. **O–V**

The Embers. 1217 S. Mission St., Mt. Pleasant (½ mile west of U.S. 27). Lunch, dinner; closes at 8 p.m. Sun.

Fox and Hounds Inn. 1560 N. Woodward (U.S. 10), Bloomfield Hills. Lunch, dinner. **R**

Hillside Inn. 41661 Plymouth Rd., east of Plymouth (25 miles west of Detroit). Lunch, dinner. Closed Sun. and holidays. (See page 66.)

Hotel Dilworth. Water and East Sts. (State Hwy 75), Boyne City. Breakfast, dinner. **O–V**

Hotel Mayflower. 827 W. Ann Arbor Trail, Plymouth (midway between Ann Arbor and Detroit). **O**

House of Ludington. 223 Ludington St., Escanaba. Closed Sun. Also serves brunch in summer. **O–V–R**

Indian River Inn. State Hwy 27, Indian River. **O–V** (See page 65.)

Joe Muer's. Corner of Gratiot and Vernor Hwy East, Detroit. Lunch, dinner weekdays; dinner only Sat. Closed Sun. and holidays. **R**

Old Hickory House. 3626 N. Saginaw Rd., Midland. Dinner. Closed Sun. and holidays. **R**

Phil de Graff's Lodges. State Hwys 48 and 123, Trout Lake. Closed Oct. 16 to June 25. **O–V–R**

Pontchartrain Wine Cellars. 234 W. Larned, Detroit. Lunch, dinner. Closed Sun., holidays, and the first 2 weeks in July. **O**

Red Brick Tavern. Old U.S. 131 (N. Tenth St.), Plainwell. Lunch, dinner. Closed Mon., July 4th, and from Jan. 15 to March 15.

St. Clair Inn. 500 N. Riverside Ave., St. Clair. **O–V**

Schweizer's. 260 Hastings, Detroit. Lunch, except Sat. Closed Sun.

Sid's on the Seaway. 9715 St. Clair River Dr., Algonac. Lunch, dinner.

The Surf. U.S. 2 (Lake Shore Dr.), 2 miles east of Manistique. Closed Nov. 25 to April 15. **V** (See page 67.)

Topinka's. 2968 W. Grand Blvd., Detroit. Lunch, dinner. Closed Sun. (with exception of Lions' football games and Fisher Theater matinees.) **R**

Topinka's Country House. Corner of Seven Mile and Telegraph Rds. (U.S. 24), Detroit. Lunch, dinner to 2 a.m. weekdays; Sun. from 2 p.m. to 10 p.m. **R**

Weber's Supper Club. 3050 Jackson Rd. (U.S. I-94), 2 miles west of Ann Arbor. Lunch, dinner. Closed holidays. (See page 65.)

MINNESOTA

The Bungalow Inn. 6221 56th Ave. North, Minneapolis. Closed Sun. **O–V**

Breakfast, lunch, and dinner served daily unless otherwise noted.

O—overnight accommodations **V**—vacation facilities **R**—reservations necessary or advisable

Charlie's Cafe Exceptionale. 701 Fourth Ave., Minneapolis. Lunch, dinner. Closed Sun. and legal holidays. **R**

Crystal Waters Lodge. State Hwy 38, 15 miles north of Grand Rapids. Open May 30 to Sept. 20. **O—V—R** (See page 71.)

Eibner's. 108 N. Minnesota St., New Ulm.

The Flame. 353 S. Fifth Ave. West, Duluth. Lunch, dinner. Closed Sun.

The Frederick Martin Hotel. 403 Center Ave. (U.S. 10), Moorhead. Tree Top Room closed on Sun. **O**

Gaslight. 1420 Washington Ave., S., Minneapolis. Lunch, dinner. Closed holidays. **R**

Hollands. 216 First Ave., Rochester. Closed Sun. (See page 68.)

Hotel Albert. 335-337 S. Broadway (U.S. 65), Albert Lea. **O**

Hubbel House. 3 miles north of U.S. 14 on State Hwy 57, Mantorville. Dinner, from noon on Sun. Closed Mon.

Lowell Inn. 102 N. Second St., Stillwater. **O—V—R** (See page 68.)

Lutsen Resort. U.S. 61, Lutsen. **O—V**

The Oaks. Off U.S. 61 to Minnesota City. Lunch, dinner.

Otis Lodge. Sissebakwet (Sugar) Lake, Grand Rapids. Closed Oct. to mid-May. **O—V** (See page 69.)

Port's Restaurant and Coffee Shoppe. 1046 Grand, St. Paul. Lunch, dinner. Closed Mon. and the first 2 weeks in July.

St. James Hotel. 406 Main St. (U.S. 61), Red Wing. Closed Sun. **O—V**

Shorewood Terrace. U.S. 61, 16 miles northeast of Duluth. Closed Mon. and Nov. 1 to May 15. **R** (See page 69.)

Timber Bay Lodge. Birch Lake, Babbitt. Closed Oct. 1 to May 14. **O—V—R** (See page 70.)

Van's Cafe. Sixth and Washington (U.S. 371 and 210), Brainerd. Closed Tues. (See page 70.)

MISSISSIPPI

Angelo's. 3206 W. Beach, Gulfport. Lunch, dinner. Closed Christmas Day.

The Carriage House Restaurant. Pearl and High Sts., Natchez. Lunch, dinner. Closed Sun. evenings and Christmas Day.

Evangeline Restaurant. 947 Telephone Rd. (1 block north of U.S. 90), Pascagoula. Closed Christmas Day.

Friendship House. U.S. 90, Biloxi. **O—V—R**

Gulf Hills Dude Ranch. 1 mile north of Ocean Springs and U.S. 90, Ocean Springs. **O—V; R** in busy season.

Michael's Cafe. U.S. 61N, Cleveland. Dinner. Closed July 4th and Christmas Day. (See page 93.)

Old Southern Tea Room. 1201 Monroe St., Vicksburg. Closed Christmas Day. **R** for large groups.

Paradise Point Restaurant. U.S. 90, Mississippi City. Open to midnight.

Sun-N-Sand. West Beach Blvd. (U.S. 90), Biloxi. **O—V** (See page 93.)

Weidman's Restaurant. 208-210 22nd Ave. (U.S. 45), Meridian. Open 24 hrs.

MISSOURI

Arrow Rock Tavern. Arrow Rock. Lunch, dinner. No hot meals on Mon. **R**

Big Spring Inn. 320 Spring St., Neosho. **O—V**

Chalet DeNormandie. 9748 Manchester Rd., St. Louis. Open noon to 1 a.m. except Sun. and Mon.

Cheshire Inn. 7036 Clayton Ave. at Skinner Blvd., St. Louis (See page 94.)

Kentwood Arms Motor Hotel. 700 St. Louis St. (Business Loop 44), Springfield. **O—V**

McDonald Tea Room. State Hwys 6 and 13, Gallatin. Lunch, dinner.

Miss Hulling's Cafeterias. 1103 Locust St. and 725 Olive St., St. Louis. Closed Sun. and holidays. (See page 95.)

Riverside Inn. U.S. 65, Ozark. Dinner only. Closed Christmas Day.

Sherman House. Main and First Sts., Gideon.

Wurzburger's. U.S. 66 and Meramee Caverns Rd., Stanton. Lunch, dinner. Closed Tues., Thanksgiving Day, and Christmas Day. (See page 94.)

MONTANA

Brooks Hotel. 2 miles east of U.S. 93, Corvallis. No breakfast or lunch on Sun.; dinner by reservation. **O—R** (See page 114.)

Bud Lake Cafe. U.S. 10 and 93, 3 miles west of Missoula. Open 24 hours. **V** (See page 114.)

The Crossroads Inn. U.S. 10 and 12, east of Miles City. Dinner only.

The Diamond Bar Inn. 48 miles west of U.S. 91 at Dillon, Jackson. **O—V**

Hotel Florence. 111 S. Higgins Ave., Missoula. **O**

Lake McDonald Lodge. In Glacier National Park. Closed Sept. 15 to June 15. **O—V—R** (See page 115.)

Swansons' Mountain View Lodge. U.S. 2, southeast of Troy. Smorgasbord on Sun. Closed Nov. 1 to May 1. **O—V—R**

Thompson River Ranch. Thompson River Road (off U.S. 10A), 5 miles east of Thompson Falls. Dinner until 2 a.m.

NEBRASKA

Caniglia's Pizzeria and Steak House. 1114 S. Seventh St., Omaha. Lunch, dinner. Closed Mon.

The Compass Room. Municipal Airport, Lincoln. Lunch, dinner. (See page 72.)

Dillon's Town House. 7000 Dodge St. (U.S. 6), Omaha. Open 24 hours. Also has coffee shop. **O—V**

Gorat's Steak House, Inc. 4917 Center St. (State Hwy 38), Omaha. Lunch, dinner. Closed Sun. **R**

Hilltop House. 49th and 4901 Dodge Sts. (U.S. 6, 275, and Alt. 30), Omaha. Lunch, dinner. Closed Mon. and the last 2 weeks in July.

Breakfast, lunch, and dinner served daily unless otherwise noted.

O—overnight accommodations   **V**—vacation facilities   **R**—reservations necessary or advisable

Hotel Cornhusker. 301 S. Thirteenth and N Sts., Lincoln. **O**

Johnny's Cafe. 4702 S. 27th St. (U.S. 275), Omaha. Closed Sun.

Ross' Steak House. 909 S. 72nd St. (U.S. 275), Omaha. Lunch, dinner. Closed Sun. (See page 71.)

Sam Nisi's Sparetime Cafe. 703 S. 72nd St., Omaha. Dinner to 1 a.m. Closed Sun.

Steinhart Park Lodge. South of U.S. 73 and 75, Nebraska City. Dinner. Special lunch for groups; smorgasbord on Sun. Closed Mon. and from Jan. 1 to April 1. **R**

Tillman's Plaza Restaurant. 2110 Winthrop Rd., Lincoln. Dinner. Closed Mon. (See page 72.)

NEVADA

The Christmas Tree. Mount Rose Hwy, 18 miles south of Reno. Dinner. **V** (See page 116.)

El Capitan. 541 F St., Hawthorne. **O–V** (See page 115.)

Golden Nugget. Second and Fremont Sts., Las Vegas. Open 24 hours.

Sharon House. C and Taylor Sts., Virginia City. Lunch, dinner in summer; dinner only in winter. Closed Tues. thru winter months. **O–R** (See page 116.)

NEW HAMPSHIRE

Christmas Farm Inn. Off State Hwy 16B, north of Jackson. Closed Nov. 1 to Dec. 15. **O–V–R**

Eastern Slope Inn. Main St., North Conway. **O–V–R** (See page 15.)

The Eating House. Cranmore Mountain Rd. (off State Hwy 16), North Conway. (See page 14.)

Green Ridge Turkey Farm Restaurant. U.S. 3, south of Nashua. Lunch, dinner.

The Hanover Inn and Motor Lodge. Dartmouth College Campus, State Hwy 10, Hanover. **O–V**

Hoffman House. Intervale Road (U.S. 302), North Conway. Closed Nov. 1 to Dec. 23 and April 1 to May 15. **O–R**

The Inn at Steele Hill. Sanbornton (off U.S. 3). Lunch, dinner. **O–V–R** (See page 16.)

Lovett's by Lafayette Brook. Junction of State Hwys 18 and 141, Franconia. Closed Oct. 4 to Dec. 25 and April 5 to June 15. **O–V–R**

New England Inn. Rte 16A, Intervale. **O–V**

The Ox-Yoke. State Hwy 12, Westmoreland Depot. Lunch, dinner. Closed Mon. unless a holiday and from Jan. 1 to Feb. 22. **R** on Sun. and holidays.

Palmer Lodge. Concord Road (State Hwy 9), northeast of Keene. Closed Tues. from Oct. 30 to Jan. 1 and entirely from Jan. 1 to May 1. **O–V**

Peckett's-on-Sugar Hill. Off State Hwy 117, Franconia. Closed Oct. 15 to June 15. **O–V–R**

Pinkham Notch Inn. State Hwy 16, Jackson. **O–V**

Stonehurst Manor and Hotel. U.S. 302, 1½ miles north of North Conway. Closed Oct. 17 to June 10. **O–V–R**

Wentworth-by-the-Sea. Portsmouth. **O–V–R**

Whitney's. Five Mile Circuit Rd., Jackson. **O–V–R**

Ye Cocke and Kettle Inn. Lafayette Rd. (U.S. 1), Seabrook. **O–V–R** (See page 15.)

NEW JERSEY

The Afton. South Orange Ave., Florham Park. Lunch, dinner. Closed Mon. and the month of Feb.

Angelo's Closter Manor. 411 Piermont Road, Closter. Dinner to 2 a.m. Closed Mon. **R** on Sat.

Bottle Hill Restaurant. Main St. (State Hwy 24), Madison. Lunch, dinner. **R**

Bruno's. 161 Summit Ave., Jersey City. Lunch, dinner.

China Chalet. Corner of Piermont and Ruckman, Closter. Lunch, dinner. Closed Mon.

Clinton Inn. 6 E. Clinton Ave., Tenafly. Lunch, dinner. **O** (See page 18.)

Colligan's Stockton Inn. Bridge and Main Sts., Stockton. Lunch, dinner. Closed Christmas Day.

The Country Garden Town House. 37 W. Ridgewood Ave., Ridgewood. Lunch, dinner. Closed Mon. and the month of Aug.

Franklin Arms Tea Room. 409 Franklin St., Bloomfield. Lunch, dinner. Closed Mon. and last two weeks of Aug. (See page 16.)

Gruning's "The Top". 616 W. South Orange Ave., South Orange. Lunch, dinner.

The Harbor. U.S. 46, Parsippany. Lunch, dinner. Closed Mon.

Ho-Ho-Kus Inn. Sheridan Ave. and Franklin Tpke, Ho-Ho-Kus. Dinner only. Closed Tues. **R**

Lambertville House. 32 Bridge St. (U.S. 202), Lambertville. **O–V–R** (See page 17.)

Molly Pitcher Hotel. 88 Riverside Ave. (State Hwy 35), Red Bank. **O–V**

The Newarker. Newark Airport, Newark. Lunch, dinner. (See page 17.)

Old Mill Inn. U.S. 202, Bernardsville. Lunch, dinner. Closed Christmas Day. **O–V**

Pals Cabin. Corner of Prospect and Eagle Rock Aves., West Orange. Lunch, dinner, late supper.

Princeton Inn. 115 Alexander St., Princeton. Also serves tea. **O–V**

Red Lion Inn. Main St. and Euclid Ave., Hackensack. Lunch, dinner.

Robin Hood Inn, Inc. 1129 Valley Road, Clifton. Lunch, country-style dinner. Closed Mon. and 4 weeks in Aug.

Saddle Inn. State Hwy 17, Upper Saddle River. Dinner to midnight. **R**

Swiss Chalet. State Hwy 17, Ramsey. Lunch, dinner. **O–V–R**

Tony Yonadi's Homestead Restaurant and Golf Club. Allaire Rd. (west of Rte 71 and east of Rte 35), Spring Lake. Lunch, dinner. Closed Mon. except holidays and during winter season. (See page 18.)

The William Pitt. 94 Main St., Chatham. Lunch, dinner. Closed Mon. and from Aug. 1 to Aug. 15.

Breakfast, lunch, and dinner served daily unless otherwise noted.

O—overnight accommodations   **V**—vacation facilities   **R**—reservations necessary or advisable

NEW MEXICO

The Bishop's Lodge. Bishop's Lodge Rd., 3 miles north of U.S. 64, 84, and 285, at the north end of Santa Fe. **O–V–R**

El Rancho Hotel and Courts. 1000 U.S. 66E, east of Gallup. **O**

Hacienda Dining Room. Old Town Plaza, Old Albuquerque. Lunch, dinner. Closed Christmas and New Year's Days.

La Dona Luz. Kit Carson Rd. (U.S. 64), Taos. Lunch, dinner. Closed Sun. during July and Aug. and from Dec. 1 thru Feb.

The Pink Adobe. 406 College St., Santa Fe. Lunch, except Sun.; dinner daily. Closed Tues. during the winter. **R**

The Pink Garter Saloon. U.S. 285, Lamy. Closed Sun. **R** on weekends.

Sagebrush Inn. U.S. 64 and 85, Taos. Breakfast, dinner; brunch on Sun. **O** (See page 117.)

The Trails Restaurant. U.S. 60, 70, and 84E, at Clovis. (See page 117.)

NEW YORK

Avon Inn. U.S. 20 and 5, Avon. Lunch, dinner. **R**

Beau Sejour. Stewart and Central Aves., Bethpage, Long Island. Lunch, dinner. Closed Tues. and Dec. 24-25.

The Beekman Arms. State Hwy 308 and U.S. 9, Rhinebeck. **O** (See page 23.)

Bird and Bottle Inn. Albany Post Road (U.S. 9), Garrison. Lunch, dinner. Closed Tues. **R** on weekends.

Blue Spruce Inn. 1480 Northern Blvd., Roslyn, Long Island. Lunch, dinner, supper.

Canoe Place Inn. State Hwy 27, Hampton Bays, Long Island. Closed Tues.

Chambord. 5 E. 55th St., New York City. Lunch, dinner. Closed Sun.

Dahlstrom's Green Tree Lodge. 93 W. Jericho Tpke, Huntington Station, Long Island. Lunch, dinner; also smorgasbord. Closed Tues. and the first 2 weeks in Feb.

Deer's Head Inn. U.S. 9 and 9N, Elizabethtown. **O** (See page 19.)

Emily Shaw's. State Hwy 137, Pound Ridge. Lunch, dinner. Closed Mon. **R**

Fraunces Tavern. 54 Pearl St. at Broad, New York City. Lunch, dinner. Closed Sat. night and Sun.

Gage and Tollner's. 372-4 Fulton St., Brooklyn. Lunch, dinner. Closed Sun. **R**

Grand Central Oyster Bar. Grand Central Terminal (lower level), New York City.

Gripsholm Restaurant. 324 E. 57th St., New York City. Lunch, dinner; also smorgasbord. **R**

Gurney's Inn. Old Montauk Hwy, Montauk, Long Island. **O–V–R**

Hampshire House. 150 Central Park South, New York City. **O–R**

Hereford House-Hotel Gramatan. 2 blocks from Bronx River Pkwy, Bronxville. Dinner. Closed Mon. **O–R** (See page 20.)

The Homestead Inn. 16 Main St. (State Hwy 86), Lake Placid. **O–V–R** (See page 21.)

Hudson Shore Club. Kings Ferry Road, Montrose. Closed Nov. 1 to April 15. **O–V–R**

Keen's English Chop House. 72 W. 36th St., New York City. Lunch, dinner. Closed Sun. **R**

The Krebs. 39 W. Genessee St., Skaneateles. Dinner only. Closed Fri. and from the last Sun. in Oct. to Mother's Day. **R**

La Cremaillere. (Merritt Pkwy, Exit 31), Banksville. Lunch, dinner except Monday. Closed first 3 weeks in Feb.

Land's End. 80 Brown's River Rd., Sayville. Lunch, dinner. Closed Mon. during the winter. **O–V–R** (See page 19.)

Leighton's Woodlands Lake Restaurant. Saw Mill River Pkwy, Ardsley. Lunch, dinner, late supper. Closed Mon. **R**

Lingnan Restaurant. 2512 Broadway, New York City. Lunch, dinner.

The Lobster Box. 34 City Island Ave., Bronx. Dinner only. Closed Mon. and the month of Jan. **R** for large parties.

Lüchow's Restaurant. 110 E. 14th St., New York City. Lunch, dinner. Closed Mon. (See page 20.)

The Maine Maid. State Hwys 106-107, Jericho, Long Island. **R**

Mammy's Pantry. 122 Montague St., Brooklyn. Lunch, dinner. Closed Memorial Day, Fourth of July, and Christmas Day.

Mark Twain Hotel. W. Gray St. and Main, Elmira. **O–V–R**

McCarthy's. Bowden Square, Southampton, Long Island. Lunch, dinner, late supper. **R** (See page 24.)

Memory Inn. New Hackensack Rd., Wappingers Falls. Breakfast for houseguests only; dinner. **O–V–R**

Mirror Lake Inn. 35 Mirror Lake Drive, Lake Placid. **O–V**

Nelson House. 28-42 Market St. (Rte 9), Poughkeepsie. Closed Sun. except for breakfast. **O**

O'Brien's Inn, Inc. Waverly Hill, State Hwy 17, Waverly. Lunch, dinner.

The Old Homestead. 56 Ninth Ave., New York City. Lunch, dinner. **R** during rush hours.

Perkin's Inn. Main St., Riverhead, Long Island. **O–R** (See page 22.)

Red Coach Inn. Main St. and Buffalo Ave., Niagara Falls. **O**

Sloppy Louie's. 92 South Street, New York City. Lunch, dinner. Closed Sat. and Sun.

Sportsman's Tavern. State Hwys 28 and 80, Cooperstown. Closed Oct. 15 to May. **O**

The Spring House. 3001 Monroe Ave. (Rte 31), Rochester. Lunch, dinner. Closed Mon. **R**

Sweet's Restaurant. 2 Fulton Street, New York City. Lunch, dinner. Closed Sat., Sun., holidays, and the first 2 weeks in July.

Taughannock Farms Inn. Rte 89, 8 miles north of Ithaca, in Trumansburg. Dinner only. Closed Thanksgiving to Easter. **O**

Tavern on the Green. 67th St. and Central Park West, New York City. Lunch, dinner, supper; Sun. brunch.

Breakfast, lunch, and dinner served daily unless otherwise noted.

O—overnight accommodations   **V**—vacation facilities   **R**—reservations necessary or advisable

Three Village Inn. Rte 25A, Stony Brook, Long Island. Closed during the Christmas season. **O—V—R**

The Treasure Chest. 568 South Rd., south of Poughkeepsie. Lunch, dinner. Closed Tues. **R** on weekends. (See page 21.)

The Virginian. 72 Palmer Ave., Bronxville. Lunch, dinner. Closed Tues. (See page 23.)

Waldorf-Astoria. Park Ave. and 50th St., New York City. **O—R**

The White Inn. 52 E. Main St. (U.S. 20), Fredonia. No breakfast on Sun. **O—V** (See page 22.)

Ye Olde Chop House. 101 Cedar Street, New York City. Lunch, dinner. Closed Sat. and Sun.

NORTH CAROLINA

Boundary Tree Motor Lodge. U.S. 441, at entrance to Great Smoky Mountains National Park, Cherokee. **O—R** (See page 48.)

Carolina Inn. Cameron Ave., southwest of Durham, in Chapel Hill. Dining room open mid-Sept. to mid-June; cafeteria open all year. **O**

The Carolinian. U.S. 158, Nags Head. Lunch, dinner. **O—V** (See page 49.)

The Colonial Inn. 153 W. King St., Hillsboro. **R** on Sun.

Fergus' Ark. Cape Fear River at the foot of Princess St., Wilmington. Lunch, dinner. Closed Christmas Eve and Christmas Day. (See page 48.)

High Hampton Inn. State Hwy 107, Cashiers. Closed Oct. 30 to May 10. **O—V**

Holly Inn. Pinehurst. **O—V**

Nu-Wray Inn. U.S. 19E (Village Green), Burnsville. Closed Sun. night. **O—V—R**

The Old Station. U.S. 158, Kitty Hawk. Closed Oct. 31 to April 30.

The Ramshead Rathskeller. 153 E. Franklin St. (U.S. 70 and 15), Chapel Hill. Lunch, dinner. Closed Sun.

The Ranch House. Airport Rd. (State Hwy 86, ½ mile north of Chapel Hill). Dinner only; roundup buffet on Sun. Closed Mon. **R**

Sunset Farm. Sunset Farms Road, Whittier. Closed Nov. 3 to April 1. **O—V—R**

Tapoco Lodge. U.S. 129, Tapoco. Closed Dec. 1 to Jan. 1. **O—V—R**

The Towne House. 460 N. Main St. (U.S. 19A and 23), Waynesville. Lunch, dinner. (See page 49.)

NORTH DAKOTA

The Dutch Mill. U.S. 2, Minot. Dinner. Closed Sun.

Grand Pacific Hotel and Steakhouse. 205 Fourth St., Bismarck. Dinner. **O** (See page 73.)

The Ranch. State Hwy 20, Devils Lake. Dinner. Closed Sun. and most holidays.

Riverside Lodge. U.S. Hwy 2, southeast of Minot. Dinner. Closed Sun. **O—R** (See page 73.)

OHIO

Antioch Inn. N. College St., Yellow Springs. Lunch, 11:30 a.m. to 1:30 p.m.; dinner, 5:30 p.m. to 7:30 p.m. Closed Dec. 24 to Jan. 7. **O—V** (See page 74.)

Arne Nissen's Tivoli. 5060 Monroe St., Toledo. Lunch, dinner. Closed Sun. and Christmas Day. **R**

Bessie Miller's Restaurant. 6048 Broadview Rd., Parma. Dinner only. Closed Mon. and from a few days prior to Christmas to the Sat. before Easter. **R**

The Betsey Mills Dining Room. 4th and Putnam Sts., Marietta. Lunch, dinner. Closed Mon. **O** for women only.

Frontier Steak House. 5th and Race Sts., Cincinnati. **O**

The Golden Lamb. S. Broadway (U.S. 42 and State Hwy 48), Lebanon. Closed Christmas Day. **O—V—R**

Gourmet Restaurant. 15 W. Sixth St. (Terrace Hilton Hotel), Cincinnati. Cocktails and dinner. Closed Sun. and the month of July. **O**

Grammer's. 1440 Walnut St., Cincinnati. Lunch, dinner. Closed Sun. and holidays. (See page 76.)

Grandview Inn. 1127 Dublin Rd. (U.S. 33), Columbus. Lunch, dinner. Closed Sun. (See page 75.)

Greenfield-Mills Restaurant. 77 South High St. (Rte 23), Columbus. Closed Sun. and holidays.

Gruber's. 20120 Van Aken Blvd., Shaker Heights. Lunch, dinner. Closed Sun. **R**

Hotel Phoenix Coffee Shoppe. 305 S. Main St., Findlay. **O**

Jai Lai Cafe. 1421 Olentangy River Rd., Columbus. Lunch, dinner, late supper. Closed Sun. and holidays except Easter and Mother's Day. (See page 74.)

Jim's Steak House. 1800 Scranton Rd., Cleveland. Lunch, dinner. Closed Sun. and holidays. (See page 76.)

King Cole Restaurant. 34 W. Second St. (3 blocks west of U.S. 25), Dayton. Closed Sun. and major holidays.

Luccioni's. 4213 Euclid Ave., Cleveland. Lunch, dinner. Closed Sun. **R**

Mecklenburg's Garden. 302 E. University Ave., Cincinnati. Lunch, dinner.

Motor Hotel Lafayette. 101-111 Front St. (on the banks of Ohio River), Marietta. Closed Christmas Day. **O—V—R**

Mrs. Wagner's Colonial Kitchen. 122 E. Main St. (U.S. 35), Eaton. Lunch, dinner. Closed Mon., Christmas week, and first 2 weeks in Feb.

The Peerless Pantry. 317 S. Second St., Miamisburg. Lunch, dinner. Closed Mon. and Christmas Day. **R** on Sun.

Pete's Wayside Inn. Brookpark and Ridge Roads, Cleveland.

Red Brick Tavern. U.S. 40, Lafayette. Lunch, dinner. Closed Mon. and from Dec. 24 to March 1.

Smorgasbord. 3983 Darrow Road (State Hwy 91), Stow. Lunch, dinner. Closed Mon. **R**

Spanish Inn. 15 E. Eighth St., Cincinnati. Lunch, dinner. Closed Sun. and holidays. **R** for dinner only.

Terrace Hilton Hotel. 15 W. Sixth (at Vine St.), Cincinnati. Dinner, cocktails. **O—R**

Breakfast, lunch, and dinner served daily unless otherwise noted.
O—overnight accommodations   **V**—vacation facilities   **R**—reservations necessary or advisable

Valerio's Italian Restaurant. 114 E. Sixth St. (2nd floor), Cincinnati. Lunch, dinner. Closed Tues. and the last 2 weeks in Aug., including Labor Day. **R**

Village Inn. State Hwy 229, Gambier. Closed Mon., the last 2 weeks in July, and from Dec. 26 to Jan. 2.

West Milton Inn. 136 N. Miami St., West Milton. Closed Nov. 1 to March 15. (See page 75.)

Young's. 2744 Manchester Rd. (State Hwy 93), south of Akron. Lunch, dinner. (See page 77.)

OKLAHOMA

The Anna Maude Cafeteria. 119 N. Robinson Ave., Oklahoma City. No dinner on Sat. Closed Sun. and holidays. (See page 96.)

The Glass House. Will Rogers Tpke, south of Vinita. Snack shop open 24 hours. (See page 95.)

Jack Sussy's Italian Restaurant. 4801 N. Lincoln Rd. (U.S. 66 and 77, city routes), Oklahoma City. Lunch, dinner. (See page 97.)

Louisiane Restaurant. 116-118 E. 18th St., Tulsa. Lunch, dinner. Closed Thanksgiving Day and Dec. 24-25.

Pete's Place. U.S. 270 and State Hwy 31, Krebs (1 mile east of McAlester). Dinner only. Closed Mon. and from July 1 to Sept. 1.

Snug Harbor Restaurant. On Fort Gibson Lake, 4 miles north of Wagoner. **O–V–R** (See page 96.)

OREGON

Albert's Lodge. U.S. 126, Vida. Dinner only to other than guests. Closed Mon. **O–V–R** (See page 118.)

The Country Inn. 4100 Country Farm Road, Eugene. Dinner only. **R**

Crab Broiler. U.S. 101 at Cannon Beach Junction, Seaside. Lunch, dinner. Closed Thanksgiving Day and the middle 2 weeks of Dec. **R**

Dan Lewis Oyster Bar. 208 S.W. Ankeny St., Portland. Lunch, dinner. Closed Thanksgiving Day and Christmas Day.

Davey's Locker. 800 S.W. Broadway, Portland. Lunch, dinner.

Oregon Caves Chateau. Oregon Caves. Open 7:30 a.m. to 10 p.m. Closed Sept. 16 to May 28. **O**

Palaske's Hillvilla. 5700 W. Terwilliger, Portland. Lunch, dinner. **R** (See page 119.)

The Pancake House. Barbur Blvd. (U.S. 99) at S.W. 24th, Portland. Closed Mon. (See page 120.)

The Pantry. 1025 N.E. Broadway, Portland. Open weekdays 11:30 a.m. to midnight; Sun. 4 p.m. to 10 p.m. (See page 118.)

The Par-Tee Room. 451 Avenue U., Seaside. Dinner to midnight. Closed Dec. 1 to March 1.

Pine Tavern. Foot of Oregon Ave., Bend. Closed Sun. Smorgasbord Sat. eve. during skiing season.

Poor Richard's. 3907 N.E. Broadway, Portland. Lunch, dinner. Closed Sun., Christmas Day, and Labor Day. (See page 119.)

Sky Room Lounge. Municipal Airport, Pendleton. (See page 120.)

PENNSYLVANIA

Belmont Mansion. Off Belmont Ave., Philadelphia. Dinner 5 p.m. to 8 p.m. Open May 1 to Nov. 1. **R** for large groups.

The Black Bass Hotel. Lumberville, in Bucks County. Lunch, dinner. Closed Christmas Day. **O–R** (See page 24.)

The Briar Patch. 3 miles from Somerset interchange of the Penn. Tpke on Rte 2, off U.S. 219 N. Lunch, dinner. Closed Oct. 15 to June 15. **O–V–R** (See page 25.)

Bryn Mawr College Inn. Morris and Lombaert Sts., Bryn Mawr. Closed during the summer. **R** for large groups.

The Bull Tavern. Rte 23W, Phoenixville. Lunch, dinner. **R** (See page 28.)

Chez Odette. S. River Road (U.S. 202), New Hope. Lunch, dinner, supper.

Conti Cross Keys Inn. U.S. 611 and State Hwy 313, Doylestown. Lunch, dinner. Closed Sun. **O–R**

Cuttalossa Inn. River and Cuttalossa Roads, Lumberville. Lunch, dinner (no lunch in off season). Closed Sun. **R**

The Dutch Pantry. U.S. 11 and 15, north of Selinsgrove. Closed Christmas Day.

Green Gables. ¼ mile north of U.S. 30 on U.S. 219, Jennerstown. Lunch, dinner. **R** on summer weekends. (See page 26.)

The Homestead Restaurant of Lavender Hall. State Hwy 532, north of Newtown. Lunch, dinner. Closed Christmas Day. **R** on Wed., Thurs., and Sat. (See page 25.)

Kugler's. 1339 Chestnut St., Philadelphia. Lunch, dinner. Closed Sun., July 4th, and Christmas Day.

Logan Inn. 10 W. Ferry St. (opposite Bucks County Playhouse), New Hope. Lunch, dinner. Sandwiches served til midnight during theater season. Closed Sun. and from Dec. 23 to Jan. 22. **O**

Old Covered Wagon Inn. Lancaster Tpke and Old Eagle School Road (U.S. 30), Strafford. Lunch, dinner. Closed Sun. **R**

Old Original Bookbinder's Restaurant. 125 Walnut St., Philadelphia. Lunch, dinner.

The Penn-Wells Hotel. 62 Main St. (Rte 287), Wellsboro. **O–V** (See page 26.)

Playhouse Inn. New Hope, Bucks County. Lunch, dinner daily to 2 a.m. **O–V**

Pocono Manor. Rte 940, Pocono Manor. **O–V–R**

Red Rose Inn. On U.S. 1, Jennersville. Closed Tues. **O** (See page 27.)

Shartlesville Hotel. U.S. 22, Shartlesville. **O**

The Stock Yard Inn. 1147 Lititz Ave., Lancaster. No breakfast Sun. Closed Christmas Day. (See page 27.)

The Tavern. 261 Montgomery Ave., Cynwyd. Lunch, dinner. Closed Sun. and the week of July 4th.

Tow Path House. Mechanic St. at the Canal, New Hope. Lunch, dinner. Closed Mon.

Water Wheel Inn. Old Eastern Road (off U.S. 611), Doylestown. Lunch, dinner. Closed Christmas Day.

Breakfast, lunch, and dinner served daily unless otherwise noted.

O—overnight accommodations   **V**—vacation facilities   **R**—reservations necessary or advisable

RHODE ISLAND

Gautreau's. Putnam Pike (U.S. 44), Chepachet. Lunch, dinner. Closed Mon. **R** (See page 28.)

Great House. 2245 Post Road (U.S. 1), Warwick. Dinner only. Closed Mon. **R**

Johnson's Hummocks Grill. 245 Allens Ave. (Rte 1A), Providence. Lunch, dinner.

Lindsey Tavern. 609 Smithfield Ave., Lincoln. Dinner 5 p.m. to 1 a.m. weekdays; Sun. and holidays, noon to 1 a.m. Closed Mon. during July and Aug.

SOUTH CAROLINA

Brewton Inn and Tea Room. 75 Church St., Charleston. Breakfast to houseguests only; lunch, dinner. Closed Sun. and from the end of May to Oct. 15. **O—V**

The Cleveland Hotel. 178 W. Main St. (U.S. 29A), Spartanburg. **O—V**

Gardens Corner Restaurant. Junction of U.S. 17 and U.S. 21, Gardens Corner. Closed Christmas Day and Memorial Day.

Henry's. 48-54 N. Market St., Charleston. Lunch, dinner.

Jack Tar Francis Marion Hotel. Charleston. Lunch, dinner. Closed Sun. **O—V** (See page 50.)

La Brasca's Spaghetti House. 975 King St., Charleston. Lunch, dinner. (See page 50.)

Perdita's. 10 Exchange St., Charleston. Dinner only. Closed Sun. and legal holidays. **R**

The Pink House. North 43rd (U.S. 17N), Myrtle Beach. No lunch Sun. Closed Nov. and Dec. **R** for dinner.

Poinsett Hotel. S. Main St., Greenville. **O—V**

South of the Border. U.S. 301 and U.S. 501, 6 miles north of Dillon. **O** (See page 51.)

The White Heron. U.S. 17, Myrtle Beach. Dinner only.

SOUTH DAKOTA

The Black Steer Restaurant. 3rd and Pine Sts., Yankton. Dinner from 4 p.m. to midnight. (See page 77.)

Capitol Cafe and Lounge. 420 S. Main St., Aberdeen. Closed Memorial Day, July 4th, Thanksgiving, Christmas, and New Year's Days. (See page 78.)

The Derby Cafe. 204 Main St., Chamberlain. Closed Dec. 15 to March 1. **V**

Latchstring Inn. Lead. Closed Oct. 1 to May 1. **O—V**

State Game Lodge. U.S. 16A in Custer State Park. Closed Oct. 1 to May 15. **O** (See page 78.)

TENNESSEE

Alpine Lodge. Natural Bridge (off U.S. 64), Waynesboro. Closed Sept. 15 to May 15. **O—V—R**

Blackberry Farm. Millers Cove Road, Walland. Closed Mon. and Nov. 16 to March 14. **O—V** (See page 52.)

Buckhorn Inn. R.F.D. #1, Gatlinburg. Closed Nov. 1 to April 1. **O—V—R**

Chilhowee Inn. State Hwy 73, Walland. Lunch, dinner; picnic lunches to take out. Closed Mon. and from Nov. 1 to May 1.

Dixie Hotel Dining Room. Public Square (1 block off U.S. 231), Shelbyville. Closed Sat. and Sun. nights. **O** (See page 54.)

Dobbs House Luau. 3135 Poplar Ave., east of Memphis. Lunch, dinner. (See page 53.)

Frank's Cafe. U.S. 70E, 4 miles east of Camden. Lunch, dinner. **R** for large parties.

J & R Grill and Restaurant. Public Square, Franklin. Closed first week in June. (See page 52.)

Justine's. 919 Coward Place, Memphis. Dinner. Closed Mon. and Christmas Day. **R**

Montgomery Bell Inn. Montgomery Bell State Park (U.S. 70), Burns. **O—V—R**

Mountain View Hotel. Gatlinburg. **O—V** (See page 51.)

New Gatlinburg Inn. Parkway (U.S. 441), Gatlinburg. Dining room closed Nov. 1 to March 1. **O—V**

Newport Motor Court and Restaurant. West Broadway, Newport. Closed Christmas Day. **O—V** (See page 53.)

TEXAS

Albert Gee's Ding How. 6800 S. Main (U.S. 59), Houston. Lunch, dinner. (See page 97.)

The Barn Door. 8400 N. New Braunfels Ave., San Antonio. Dinner. Closed Mon., and from Aug. 9 to Aug. 31. (See page 98.)

Eagle Coffee Shop. Near U.S. 277, Eagle Pass. **O** (See page 98.)

Eddie's Covered Wagon. U.S. 83, between McAllen and Pharr. Closed Mon. **R** for groups and Sat. nights. (See page 99.)

Green Parrot. 2314 MacGregor Way, Houston. Dinner. Closed Mon., Tues., and Wed., and 2 weeks during Christmas and New Year's. **R** (See page 99.)

Grey Moss Inn. Scenic Loop Road, Resort Hills, northwest of San Antonio. Dinner. Closed Mon. **R**

Kelley's. 910 Texas, Houston. Lunch, dinner.

La Vieille Varsovie. 3914 Cedar Springs, Dallas. Dinner only. Closed Sun. **R**

Landrum's Restaurant. 838 E. Levee St., Brownsville. Lunch, dinner. (See page 101.)

Mayflower Hotel Restaurant. 1601 N. Shoreline Blvd., Corpus Christi. **O—V** (See page 100.)

Breakfast, lunch, and dinner served daily unless otherwise noted.
O—overnight accommodations   **V**—vacation facilities   **R**—reservations necessary or advisable

The Menger Hotel. Alamo Plaza (1 block south of U.S. 90), San Antonio. **O—V—R**

Mills' Wharf Cafe. North end of Capano Bay Causeway, Rockport. **O—V—R**

Shamrock Hilton Hotel. Main at Holcombe (U.S. 59 and 90A), Houston. **O—V**

Stage Coach Inn. Interstate Hwy 35, Salado (40 miles south of Waco). Lunch, dinner. **O—V** (See page 101.)

Tarpon Inn. Port Aransas, Mustang Island. Closed from the day after Labor Day to April 1. **O—V—R**

Trade Winds Restaurant. State Hwy 9 (Leopard and Lexington Sts.), Corpus Christi. **O—V** (See page 100.)

Western Hills Hotel. 6451 Camp Bowie Blvd., Fort Worth. Open 24 hours.

Ye Old College Inn. 6545 Main St., Houston. Open 5:30 p.m. to 11 p.m.; Sun., noon to 10 p.m. **R**

UTAH

Andy's Smorgasbord. 3350 Highland Dr., Salt Lake City. Dinner. **R** (See page 121.)

Beau Brummel. 3100 Highland Drive, Salt Lake City. Lunch, dinner; smorgasbord, Wed. through Sat. **R**

The Homestead. U.S. 40, Midway. Closed from Labor Day to Memorial Day. **O—V** (See page 121.)

The Lion House Cafeteria. 63 E. South Temple, Salt Lake City. Lunch only. Closed Sat. and Sun.

Maddox Ranch House. U.S. 30S, 91, 89, and 191, Brigham City. Lunch, dinner. Closed Mon. and from Jan. 2 to Jan. 21. (See page 122.)

Newhouse Hotel. S. Fourth and Main Sts., Salt Lake City. **O—V—R**

Parry Lodge. U.S. 89, Kanab. Closed Dec. 1 to April 1. **O—V**

VERMONT

Barrows House. State Hwy 30, Dorset. **O—V—R**

Blueberry Hill Farm. Off State Hwy 73E, East Goshen. Breakfast for houseguests only; dinner to non-houseguests by reservation; pot luck dinner during summer weeknights. **O—R**

The Clement's Tavern. 64 S. Main St., Waterbury. Closed Tues. evenings. **O—R** (See page 29.)

Colburn House. Junction of U.S. 7 and State Hwys 11 and 30, Manchester. **R** Sat. night and Sun. during the summer. (See page 29.)

The Dog Team. Off U.S. 7, 3 miles north of Middlebury. Closed Mon., except in summer, and the months of Dec. and Jan. **O—R** from Oct. 12 to June 1.

Four Chimneys. State Hwy 9, Old Bennington. Lunch, dinner. Open April 30 to Dec. 1.

Green Mountain Inn. State Hwy 100, Stowe. Closed April 15 to May 30 and Oct. 30 to Dec. 15. **O—V**

Green Mountain Restaurant. U.S. 7, Arlington.

The Little House and Pantry. 40 S. Main St., Northfield. Closed Dec. 20 to Jan. 2.

The Lodge. Rte 108, Smuggler's Notch. Closed April 15 to May 20 and Oct. 28 to Dec. 15. **O—V; R** for non-guests. (See page 30.)

Long Trail Lodge. U.S. 4 at Pico Peak, near Rutland. Closed April 5 to June 5 and Oct. 15 to Dec. 20. **R** on holidays.

The Paddock. State Hwy 11, Springfield. Lunch from June 1 to Nov. 1; dinner all year. Closed Mon. and the month of January.

Toll Gate Lodge. State Hwys 11 and 30, Manchester Depot. Dinner. Open May 25 to Oct. 22. **O—R**

The Waybury Inn. State Hwy 125, East Middlebury. Dinner and Sun. lunch to non-guests. Closed Tues. from Nov. 1 to June 1. **O—V—R** (See page 30.)

The White Cupboard Inn. #1 The Green (intersection of U.S. 4 and State Hwy 12), Woodstock. **O—V—R**

VIRGINIA

The Carriage House. 313 W. Bute St., Norfolk. Lunch, dinner. Closed Sun. and from July 1 to the day after Labor Day. **R**

The Cavalier. 42nd St. off U.S. 60, Virginia Beach. Closed Nov. 1 to April 1. **O—V—R**

Christiana Campbell's Tavern. Williamsburg Restoration. Lunch, dinner. **R** (See page 54.)

Collingwood-on-the-Potomac. 701 E. Boulevard Drive, Alexandria. Lunch, dinner. Closed Mon. and from Dec. 1 to March 1. **R** on weekends and holidays.

Dorothy's Inn. U.S. 11, south of Woodstock. **O** (See page 55.)

Evan's Farm Inn. 5743 Chain Bridge Rd., McLean. Buffet lunch, noon to 2:30 p.m.; dinner, 5 p.m. to 9 p.m. Closed Christmas Day. (See page 55.)

Homestead Hotel. U.S. 220, Hot Springs. **O—V—R**

Hotel Raleigh. Ninth and Bank Sts., Richmond. Closed Sun. **O—V**

Hotel Roanoke. Jefferson St. and Shenandoah Ave., Roanoke. **O—V**

Jack Trayer's Restaurant. 118 Moore St., Bristol. Open 6 a.m. to 1:30 a.m. daily. Closed Christmas Day.

Josiah Chowning's Tavern. The Market Square, Williamsburg Restoration, Williamsburg. Lunch, dinner. Closed Tues. and Wed. from Nov. to March. **O—V**

Seawell's Ordinary. U.S. 17, Gloucester. (See page 56.)

Skyline Terrace Restaurant. 708 S. Royal Ave. (U.S. 340), Front Royal.

Southern Restaurant. 415 W. Main St. (U.S. 250-340), Waynesboro. Closed Christmas Day.

Thomas Jefferson Inn. U.S. 29, north of Charlottesville. **O—R** (See page 56.)

Sykes Inn. U.S. 258, Smithfield. Closed Sun. **O**

Virginian Hotel. 8th and Church Sts. (intersection of U.S. 29 and 460), Lynchburg. **O—V**

Williamsburg Inn. Frances St., Williamsburg Restoration, Williamsburg. **O—V—R**

Williamsburg Lodge. S. England St., Williamsburg. Also has coffee shop. **O—V**

Breakfast, lunch, and dinner served daily unless otherwise noted.
O—overnight accommodations   **V**—vacation facilities   **R**—reservations necessary or advisable

WASHINGTON

Bush Garden. 614 Maynard Ave., Seattle. Dinner only. Closed Sun. **R**

Camlin Hotel. Ninth and Pine, Seattle. Lunch, dinner. **O—R**

The Crabapple. 326 Bellevue Square, Bellevue. Lunch, dinner. **R**

Desert Caravan Inn. Sunset Hill (U.S. 2, 10, and 395), Spokane. **O—V—R**

Dupuis Seafood. U.S. 101 (Rte 2), Port Angeles. Lunch, dinner.

Hotel Emerson. 701 Simpson (U.S. 101), Hoquiam. Closed Sun. **O—V** (See page 124.)

Illahee Ranch. U.S. 99 at 30602 Pacific Hwy S., Federal Way. Dinner. (See page 122.)

King Oscar's Smorgasbord. 4312 Aurora Ave., Seattle. Dinner only. Closed Mon.

Lake Crescent Lodge. U.S. 101, Port Angeles. Closed Labor Day to Memorial Day. **O—V—R**

Legend Room. Northgate Shopping Center, U.S. 99, Seattle. Lunch, dinner except Sun. and Mon. **R**

Log Cabin Inn. U.S. 101, 2 miles south of Quilcene. Breakfast, dinner. Closed Oct. 1 to May 1. **O—V—R**

Mary's Italian Dinners. East 4235 Hartson Ave., Spokane. Closed Thanksgiving Day and Christmas Day.

Ruby Chow's Chinese Dinner Club. Broadway and Jefferson Sts., Seattle. Dinner only. Closed Mon. **R**

Top o' the Town-Hotel Sorrento. At Terry and Madison Sts., Seattle. Dinner. Closed Sun. (See page 123.)

Trout Lodge. State Hwy 5, 17 miles from Naches. Closed during slow season. **O—V—R** (See page 123.)

The Village Cafe. 602 State St., Marysville. Closed Dec. 24 to Feb. 1.

The Wharf. 1735 W. Thurman, Fishermen's Terminal, Seattle. Closed Christmas Day. **R**

WEST VIRGINIA

Chancellor Hotel. Seventh and Market Sts., Parkersburg. Closed Sat. **R** (See page 57.)

El Rancho Restaurant and Motel. 2843 McCorkle Ave. (U.S. 60), St. Albans. Closed Dec. 24 and Dec. 25. **O** (See page 57.)

Frederick Hotel. Fourth Ave. and 10th St., Huntington. **O**

General Lewis Motor Inn. 301 E. Washington St. (intersection of U.S. 60 and 219), Lewisburg. **O**

Morgan Hotel. 127 High St., Morgantown. Closed Sat. except for special occasions. **O**

Park View Inn. S. Washington St., Berkeley Springs. **O—V**

Shenandoah Hotel. Queen and Martin Sts. (U.S. 11 and 9), Martinsburg. **O**

The West Virginian. U.S. 21 and 52, Bluefield.

WISCONSIN

Alpine Village. State Hwy 57, Mequon (12 miles north of Milwaukee). Dinner. **R** for private luncheon parties.

Arizona Inn. State Hwy 15, Delavan. Lunch, dinner. (See page 79.)

Brad Ryan's Lake Breeze Lodge. County Trunk X, Three Lakes. Closed from the day after Labor Day to the first weekend in June. **O—V—R**

Eagle's Nest. Junction of U.S. 18 and State Hwy 69, Verona. Closed Mon. (See page 81.)

The Fox and Hounds. State Hwy 167, Hubertus. Lunch, dinner. Closed Mon. during the winter. **V—R**

Garmisch, U.S.A. On Lake Namakagon (County Road D), 10½ miles east of Cable. Breakfast, dinner. **O—V—R** (See page 80.)

Hoffman House. 512-514 E. Wilson St., Madison. Lunch, dinner. Closed Mon. except during July and Aug. (See page 80.)

Hotel Manitowoc. 204 N. 8th St., Manitowoc. **O**

Karl Ratzsch's Old World Restaurant. 320 E. Mason St., Milwaukee. Lunch, dinner. Closed Tues.

Lake Lawn Lodge. State Hwy 50, Delavan. **O—V** (See page 79.)

Mader's Famous Restaurant. 1037 N. Third St., Milwaukee. Lunch, dinner.

The Simon House. E. Main and Butler Sts., Madison. Lunch, dinner. **R** (See page 81.)

Smith Brothers Fish Shanty. 100 N. Franklin St., Port Washington. Lunch, dinner. Closed Thanksgiving Day and Christmas Day. **R** in summer.

Tower House. Second St. (U.S. 63), Cumberland. Lunch, dinner. Closed Thurs.

Wally's Fountain Hotel. State Hwy 35, Fountain City. Dinner 5 p.m. til midnight. Closed Tues. and month of Jan.

WYOMING

Cassie's Supper Club. U.S. 20, 1½ miles west of Cody. Dinner. Closed Sun. (See page 124.)

The Chuck Wagon. U.S. 26, 187, and 89, Moose. Closed Labor Day to June 15. **O—V**

Hitching Post. 1600 W. Lincolnway, Cheyenne. Lunch, dinner. **O—R** (See page 125.)

Jack Moore's Open Range. U.S. 187 and 89, Jackson. Dinner. Closed Oct. 15 to May 15.

Lake Hotel. Main Loop, Yellowstone National Park. Closed Sept. 5 to June 15. **R**

Nobel Hotel. Third and Main Sts., Lander. **O—V**

Old Faithful Inn. Main Loop, Old Faithful, Yellowstone National Park. Closed Sept. 9 to June 8. **R**

Sheridan Inn Dining Room. At Fifth and Broadway, Sheridan. Breakfast, dinner. Closed Dec. 24 to Jan. 1. **O** (See page 125.)

Trail Coffee Shop. 216 W. 16th St., Cheyenne. Closed Christmas Day.

Recommendations of eating places in this book are based on reliable information available at the time of publication. If any establishment does not meet your expectations, please let us know. Address Nancy Kennedy, Publications Office, Ford Motor Company, The American Road, Dearborn, Michigan.

RECIPE INDEX

A

Almond: chicken, 116; cookies, 57; rum cream pie, 65

Almonds with Spanish onions en casserole, 94

Angel: pie, 44; puff (berry torte), 69

Apple: divinity, 62; pie, 7; pie, Swedish, 121; pudding, 114

Apples, stewed, 20

Apricot: cocoanut cream torte with, 6; strudel, 17

Apricots, in whipped cream topping, 62

Asparagus casserole, 57

B

Baked beans, Boston, 10

Banana: bread, 75; chantilly, 105

Barbecue sauce, 73, 101

Barbecued: chicken, 101; pheasant, 51; short ribs, 125; spareribs, 50, 67, 77

Beans: baked, Boston, 10; pork and, 108

Beef: and turkey tenderloin, 125; boiled, 90; Bourguignonne, 11; enchilada casserole, 117; estouffade, 35; filet Provençale, 107; filet tips sauté, 111; hamburg soup, 68; kibbie, 40; ribs, barbecued, 125; rolled roast with mushrooms, 52; sauerbraten, 64; sirloin steak wine merchant, 38; sirloin tips ragout au vin, 67; souflakia à la Turk, 91; sour cream noodle bake, 95; steak, broiling outdoors, 76; steak teriyaki, 60; steaks, charcoal-broiled, 88; stew, old fashioned, 117; Stroganoff, 110, 115; Swiss steak, 79; Swiss steak, potted, 72; tenderloin, tournedos of, 110; tenderloin pepper steak with wild rice, sautéed, 30; tenderloin tips en brochette, 73; Will Rogers special, 95; vegetable soup, 31

Berries (angel puff), 69

Biscuits, hot drop, 25

Bisque, chicken, 118

Black bottom pie, 53

Blitz torte, 71

Bordelaise sauce, 121

Boston baked beans, 10

Braccioline with sauce, 71

Bread: banana, 75; date and pineapple, 11; date nut, 115; egg, 43; homemade, individual loaves of, 122; hot, 17; Pell's, 53; spoon, Southern, 36

Bread pudding, Southern, 56

Broccoli and ham casserole, 112

Brook trout Polonaise, 37

Buffalo Swiss steak, 78

Butter rum sauce, 64, 112

Butterscotch: peanut chiffon pie, 9; sauce, 114

C

Cabbage, red, 68

Cake: chocolate, 65; chocolate applesauce, 107; chocolate fudge, 84; chocolate upside-down, 49; cupcakes, fruit, 14; Dutch cocoa, 80; fruit, 63; maple sponge, 19; pineapple icebox, 111; prune, 87. See also Cheese cake

Caramel dumplings, 87

Casserole: asparagus, 57; baked macaroni luncheon, 104; broccoli and ham, 112; chicken and ham, 21; crabmeat perfection, 38; enchilada, 117; pork chops à la Creole, 34; salmon and tomato pie, 26; shrimp jambalaya, 25; sour cream noodle bake, 95; Spanish onions en casserole with almonds, 94

Cheese cake: 89; ice box, 55; lemon, 94

Cheese spread, 63

Cherry cobbler, 48

Chicken: à la Polly, 69; almond, 116; and dumplings, 86; and ham (casserole), 21; baked, 12; barbecued, 101; bisque, 118; country captain, 36, 50; cream salad, 124; creamed, over stuffed ham rolls, 89; fried, with gravy, 54; giblet gravy, 77; in foil, 113; liver paste, 66; livers, 121; picnic, 40; pot pie, 74; soup, 111; stuffed in pancakes, 6; teriyaki, 60

Chili con queso, 92

Chocolate: angel delight, 86; applesauce cake, 107; cake, 65; fudge cake, 84; fudge pecan pie, 99; icing, 65, 80, 84; meringue pie, 34; pie, French silk, 72; pudding, German, 96; upside-down cake, 49

Chowder: clam, 13, 22, 49, 120; fish, one-pot, 8

Clam chowder, 13, 22, 49, 120

Clams: casino, 13; minced, steamed eggs with, 108

Clover leaf rolls, 86

Cobbler, cherry, 48

Cocoa cake, Dutch, 80

Cocoanut cream: torte with apricot, 6; pie, 51

Cole slaw, 46

Cookies, almond, 57

Corn: muffins, 14; pudding, 57

Cottage cheese spread, 15

Crab: gumbo, 35; soup, 47

Crabmeat perfection, 38

Cranberry: salad, jellied, 57; waldorf, 106

Crawfish patties, 90

Cream cheese molded salad, 39

Creamed chicken over stuffed ham rolls, 89

Crust: gingersnap, 53; graham cracker, 79, 81, 89; pie, 81, 84; strudel, 17; torte, 6; zwieback, 89, 94

Cupcakes, fruit, 14

Curry soup, 24

D

Date: and nut pudding, 44, 75; and pineapple bread, 11; nut bread, 115

Dressing: garlic, 98; pineapple cream, 106; Roquefort, 22, 85, 116, 121; salad, 18, 46, 123; Thousand Island, 74

Duck 'n' sauce, 19

Dumplings: and chicken, 86; caramel, 87

Dutch cocoa cake, 80

E

Egg: bread, hot, 43; custard pie, 85

Eggs: ranch-style, 98, 100; steamed, with minced clams, 108

Enchilada casserole, 117

F

Fish: broiled, 10; chowder, one-pot, 8. *See also* names of fish

Flounder: stuffed Southern, 48; stuffed with crabmeat dressing, 100

Fruit: cake, 63; compote, hot, 30; cupcakes, 14; muffins, 23; salad (heavenly hash), 88

Frosted lime walnut salad, 46

Frosting: *See* Icing

Frozen pineapple salad, 85

Fudge-bottom graham cracker pie, 81

G

Garlic: dressing, 98; toast, 105

Giblet gravy, 77

Ginger pie, 61

Gingersnap crust, 53

Goose: roast Watertown, with stewed apples, 20; stuffed with wild rice dressing, 73

Gravy: chicken, 54; giblet, 77

H

Haddock, one-pot fish chowder, 8

Ham: and broccoli casserole, 112; and chicken (casserole), 21; baked, country, 42; diced, fried rice, 78; loaf, 61; rolls, stuffed, with creamed chicken, 89

Hamburg soup, 68

Hasenpfeffer, 76

Hazelnut pie, 61

Heavenly hash (fruit salad), 88

Huckleberry pie, wild, 84, 124

Huevos rancheros, 98, 100

Huguenot torte, 55

Hush puppies, 38, 96

I

Ice box cheese cake, 55

Ice cream, lemon velvet, 69

Icing: chocolate, 65, 80; chocolate fudge, 84; maple, 19; orange, 87

J

Jefferson Davis pie, 52

Jelly, winter, 25

K

Kibbie, 40

Kidney bean relish, 30

L

Lamb. *See* Kibbie

Lemon: cheese cake, 94; filling, 81; pie, 9, 16, 113; velvet ice cream, 69

Lime walnut salad, frosted, 46

Lobster: à la Newburg, 91; Americano, 75; baked stuffed, 15; Fra Diavolo, 18

M

Macaroni, baked, 104

Maple: icing, 19; sponge cake, 19

Mexican rice, 92

Mince-pumpkin pie, 29

Molasses squares, 39

Muffins: corn, 14; fruit, 23; Scotch oatmeal, 70

Mushrooms, creamed, 27

Mustard sauce, 61

N

Noodle bake, sour cream, 95

Nut and date pudding, 44, 75

O

Oatmeal muffins, Scotch, 70

Obst kuchen (fruit cake), 63

Olive sauce, 93

Onion soup, 20

Onions, Spanish, en casserole with almonds, 94

Orange: chiffon pie, fresh, 79; topping, 87

Oyster: loaf, 119; pie, 26

Oysters à la Finellia, 93

P

Pancakes: old-fashioned German, 120; sour cream, 60; stuffed with chicken, 6

Pea soup, old-fashioned, 29

Pecan pie, 14, 42, 47, 99

Pell's bread, 53

Pepper relish, 29

Pepper steak, sautéed tenderloin, with wild rice, 30

Pheasant, 45; barbecued, 51

Pie: almond rum cream, 65; angel, 44; apple, 7; apple, Swedish, 121; black bottom, 53; butterscotch peanut chiffon, 9; chocolate, French silk, 72; chocolate fudge pecan, 99; chocolate meringue, 34; coconut cream, 51; egg custard, 85; fudge-bottom graham cracker, 81; ginger, 61; hazelnut, 61; huckleberry, wild, 84, 124; Jefferson Davis, 52; lemon, 9, 16, 81, 113; orange chiffon, fresh, 79; oyster, 26; pecan, 14, 42, 47; pumpkin-mince, 29; rum, 101; rum cream, 54; salmon and tomato, 26; strawberry, glazed, 56; walnut, 15

Pie crust. *See* Crust

Pineapple: and date bread, 11; cream dressing, 106; icebox cake, 111; pudding, 8; salad, frozen, 85

Plum pudding, 31

Popovers, 23

Pork: and beans, 108; Balinese, 43; ribs, barbecued, 67, 77, 125; souflakia à la Turk, 91

Pork chops: à la Creole, 34; baked, à la Bordeaux, 39; baked, Southern style, 114

Potato soup, Western, 122

Potatoes: fried (Steak House), 76; stuffed baked, 118

Potted swiss steak, 72

Prune cake, 87

Pudding: apple, 114; bread, Southern, 56; chocolate, German, 96; corn, 57; date and nut, 44, 75; pineapple, 8; plum, 31; rum, 28

Pumpkin-mince pie, 29

R

Rabbit: Hasenpfeffer, 76; sauté sec, 106

Red cabbage, 68

Redfish, 41

Request salad (carrot-raisin-pineapple), 68

Relish: kidney bean, 30; pepper, 29

Remoulade sauce, 99

Ribs, barbecued, 125. See also Barbecued spareribs

Rice: and turkey, 80; boiled, Chinese, 78; diced ham fried, 78; Mexican, 92; pilaf, 109; pilaf stuffing, 28. See also Wild rice

Rock Cornish game hens, 21, 28

Rolls: cloverleaf, 86; hot, 123

Roquefort dressing, 22, 85, 116, 121

Rum: cream pie, 54; cream pie, almond, 65; pie, 101; pudding, 28

S

Salad: carrot-raisin-pineapple (request), 68; chicken cream, 124; cole slaw, 46; cranberry, jellied, 57; cranberry waldorf, 106; cream cheese molded, 39; fruit (heavenly hash), 88; lime walnut, frosted, 46; pineapple, frozen, 85; request, 68; Thanksgiving mold, 64; tossed green, 123; tossed green Gorgonzola, 7

Salad dressing. See Dressing

Salmon and tomato pie, 26

Sauce: barbecue, 73, 101; Bordelaise, 121; butter rum, 64, 112; butterscotch, 114; caramel, 87; cherry, 21; duck, 19; mustard, 61; olive, 93; Philippet, 109; Remoulade, 99; seafood, 67; sour cream, 98; sparerib, 119; steak, 105; teriyaki, 60; tomato horse-radish, 90; wine, 51

Sauerbraten, 64

Scallops, fried, 24

Seafood sauce, special, 67

Shrimp: baked stuffed, 12; batter, 66; Cantonese, with lobster sauce, 97; jambalaya, 25; sauté Marsala, 109

Snapper soup, 27

Souflakia à la Turk, 91

Soup: beef vegetable, 31; chicken, Royal, 111; chicken bisque, 118; crab, 47; crab gumbo, 35; curry, 24; hamburg, 68; onion, 20; pea, old-fashioned, 29; potato, Western, 122; snapper, 27; Spanish bean, 41; tomato, crème of, with almonds, 37; vichyssoise, 74. See also Chowder

Sour cream: noodle bake, 95; pancakes, 60; sauce, 98

Spanish bean soup, 41

Spanish onions en casserole with almonds, 94

Spareribs: à la Hillvilla, 119; à la Sarabia, 104; barbecued, 50, 67, 77

Sponge cake, maple, 19

Spoon bread, Southern, 36

Spread: cheese, 60; cottage cheese, 15

Squash, baked, 42

Steak sauce, 105

Steaks. See Beef

Stew: beef, old-fashioned, 117; sirloin tips ragout au vin, 67

Strawberry pie, glazed, 56

Strudel, apricot, 17

Stuffed ham rolls with creamed chicken, 89

Swiss steak: 79; buffalo, 78; potted, 72

T

Teriyaki, chicken or steak, 60

Thanksgiving salad mold, 64

Thousand Island dressing, 74

Toast, garlic, 105

Tomato: and salmon pie, 26; horse-radish, 90; soup, crème of, with almonds, 37

Torte: angel puff, 69; blitz, 71; cocoanut cream, with apricot, 6; Huguenot, 55

Trout: broiled, 62; brook, Polonaise, 37; Marguery, 92

Turkey: and beef tenderloin, 125; and rice, 80; Creole, 24; curried, in pattie shells, 70; cutlet, with wild rice and olive sauce, 93

U

Upside-down cake, chocolate, 49

V

Veal: baked, savory, 16; braccioline with sauce, 71; scaloppine, 97

Vegetable beef soup, 31

Vichyssoise, 74

W

Walnut pie, 15

Whipped cream: filling, 80; topping, 62

Wild huckleberry pie, 84, 124

Wild rice: 51; dressing for goose, 73; with sautéed tenderloin pepper steak, 30; with turkey cutlet, 93

Wine sauce, 51

Winter jelly, 25

Y

Yams, Kentucky bourbon, 45